Utopia in the Factory

Rhiannon Firth • John Preston

Utopia in the Factory

Prefigurative Knowledge Against Cybernetics

palgrave
macmillan

Rhiannon Firth
IOE Faculty of Education and Society
University College London
London, UK

John Preston
Department of Sociology and Criminology
University of Essex
Colchester, UK

ISBN 978-3-031-87131-3   ISBN 978-3-031-87132-0 (eBook)
https://doi.org/10.1007/978-3-031-87132-0

Cover illustration: smartboy10/Getty Images

This Palgrave Macmillan imprint is published by the registered company Springer Nature Switzerland AG.
The registered company address is: Gewerbestrasse 11, 6330 Cham, Switzerland

If disposing of this product, please recycle the paper.

Preface

In 2018, after a successful funding bid to the EPSRC (Engineering and Physical Sciences Research Council) through its programme for New Industrial Systems in Manufacturing, we found ourselves working together on the large, multi-departmental *Chatty Factories* project, alongside four other teams from different universities and disciplines, including experts in robotics, data science and design engineering. The vision for the project drew on an imagined example of Industry 4.0 in action, which the project team envisioned would be a 'Chatty Factory' where the 'chattiness' signifies the constant, technologically enabled communication and analytics between products, production, machines and workers. In such a factory, production appears to be autopoietic as the product with sensors sends information about its use and situation back to the factory. Through advanced real-time design and research tools (such as digital twining and digital ethnography), the Chatty Factory would enable real-time real design in a fully digitised factory with conjoint human, robot and AI working and learning.

This project was not our typical sociological work and it is important to note at the outset our positionality as authors/researchers as well as our theoretical positions. John and Rhiannon are sociologists who have worked together for several years on various different research projects, and we have published together before (Preston and Firth 2020). We are both quite eclectic with the theory that we use, but Rhiannon is broadly coming from the perspective of someone who is sympathetic to anti-authoritarian, left-libertarian and anarchist thought and practice. Nevertheless, she thinks that a focus on class is important and is distinct (but not a priori) from other forms of oppression, such as race and gender. She believes that desire, imagination and mutual aid, rather than identity or labour, ought to form the basis for resistance, hence her interest in utopianism and utopias as expressions of desire for alternative socio-political and sociotechnical arrangements.

John is more situated in the Marxist tradition, although he prefers forms of Marxism, such as Open Marxism, that are anti-authoritarian, anti-vanguardist/statist and non-teleological. There is therefore much overlap between our positions, but there are also tensions which we hope are productive, but which might lead to conceptual contradictions in places. In particular, John favours the idea of unified working-class struggle as the primary mode of resistance and the creation of a future society, whereas Rhiannon sees the idea of desire as the basis for resistance—not desire in the Lacanian sense of lack but following Deleuze and Guattari in seeing desire as creative and productive, and as the basis for forming prefigurative communities and voluntary attachments. Rhiannon's perspective is more idealist (we can transform the world by first transforming our desires and values, which can inspire us to change our material conditions), whereas John's is materialist (we transform the world by first transforming material conditions, which helps shape our values). However, there is unity in theorisation through a shared view of grassroots autonomy, anti-capitalism, anti-statism and opposition to technicist solutions to problems (including cybernetics).

London, UK — Rhiannon Firth
Colchester, UK — John Preston

Reference

Preston, J. and Firth, R., 2020. *Coronavirus, class and mutual aid in the United Kingdom*. London: Palgrave.

Acknowledgements

This work was funded by the Engineering and Physical Sciences Research Council [grant number: EP/R021031/1]. The grant name was: *Chatty Factories: New Industrial Systems in Manufacturing*. Thanks to the Chatty Factories team, in particular Pete Burnap, Dave Murray-Rust, Kami Vaniea, Daniel Richards, David T. Branson III, Mojtaba Khanesar, Mike Lakoju, Katerina Gorkovenko, Dan Burnett, James Thorp and Nicola Edwards. We are also grateful to the Cybernetics Reading Group at the University of Essex, particularly to the organiser Tara Mahfoud, and to James Fox for ongoing discussions and productive disagreement on anarchist cybernetics, and also to external attendees including Christian Nold, Michael Reinsborough, Thomas Swann, Christine Aicardi and others. Thanks especially to all the organisations and interviewees who took part in the study.

Contents

Abbreviations

AGI	Artificial General Intelligence
ANT	Actor Network Theory
ASI	Artificial Superintelligence
BoD	Board of Directors
CME	Current Manufacturing Engineering
CMS	Critical Management Studies
CYBER4.0	Anonymous Industry 4.0 Manufacturer
DARPA	Defense Advanced Research Projects Agency
FLOSS	Free, Libre and Open-Source Software
HMI	Human-Machine Interface
HRI	Human-Robot Interaction
IEM	Isthmus Engineering and Manufacturing
ML	Machine Learning
OOO	Object-Oriented Ontology

List of Tables

CHAPTER 1

Introduction

Introduction

The idea that automation, artificial intelligence (AI) and robotics might lead to a utopian future for humanity is a powerful one both in mainstream and radical discourse. The paradigm of 'Industry 4.0' (Lasi et al. 2014) where digital manufacturing enables the seamless production of goods (and services) and 'lights out' factories where machines and robots effortlessly produce for our future needs and wants are seductive drivers of a capitalist, free market cybertopia (Schwab 2017). For some radicals, similar forms of technology and automation produce the conditions for a Fully Automated Luxury Communism (FALC) (Bastani 2019), drawing on a particular interpretation of Marx (1993), where human work would be replaced by a life of leisure and abundance for all. For others, an earlier discourse—cybernetics—and the use of AI and social media in communication and co-ordination enable forms of radical organisation through 'anarchist cybernetics' (Swann 2020). In Critical Management Studies (CMS), cybernetics is experiencing a renaissance, crossing the boundary from more conventional management and organisation paradigms where it still has a home.

This book questions technological optimism and technocracy—particularly that surrounding cybernetics, automation and AI—through an examination of these both as technologies and organisational forms. We argue that cybernetics and corresponding technologies and forms (particularly Industry 4.0) can never fully capture human forms of creativity

R. Firth, J. Preston, *Utopia in the Factory*,
https://doi.org/10.1007/978-3-031-87132-0_1

and emancipation or provide a liberatory model for a future society. Furthermore, there are problems with mobilising the 'cybernetic paradigm' as a radical form of organisation in social movements as it operates on the assumption that it is possible and desirable to capture human autonomy, creativity, desire and social prefiguration. In counterpoint we argue, drawing on qualitative evidence in a variety of organisational forms, that in the physical act of making and co-operating, tacit knowledge and autonomous and spontaneous human projects (which we define as 'hobbying') represent a fundamental break with 'blackboxing technologies'. We argue that return to the political, and ethical, rather than the organisational are critical for future emancipatory projects. Technological forms or amalgams (such as cybernetics) do not prefigure autonomous and spontaneous societies whereas forms of anarchist and autonomist-communist organisation, and emergent forms of prefigurative knowledge, against capital and the state, do.

In this introduction we consider some of the key concepts that will inform the discussion throughout the book—Industry 4.0 and cybernetics, factories as potential utopias, tacit knowledge and hobbying, critical pedagogy, and the prefigurative and utopian. We then present an overview of our methods and an outline of the book as a whole.

Industry 4.0 and Cybernetics

The historical position of our critique arises from the increasingly hegemonic backdrop of 'Industry 4.0', a term which is used as shorthand for the idea of a 'Fourth Industrial Revolution' (Schwab 2017). It refers to an historical narrative that segments the time since the industrial revolution into several distinct phases, each marked by the advent of disruptive technologies and processes. Previous industrial revolutions were seen to be produced through developments in steam (first), in electricity (second), and electronics and information technology (third). Similar to previous industrial disruptions, 'revolution' refers to a supposed paradigm shift caused by rapid changes in technologies for manufacturing and mass production, with implications for associated industries like logistics and services and also fundamental changes in the organisation of media, culture and society. The original idea that we are undergoing a fourth revolution was popularised by the World Economic Forum (WEF), particularly by forum Founder and Executive Chairman, Klaus Schwab (2017). The Fourth Industrial Revolution is understood to be driven by the fusion of biological and digital spheres through technologies like artificial intelligence, gene editing, digitisation, data analytics, sensors and advanced robotics. This presages the increasing automation of not only physical production but also cognitive and executive functions through technologies like artificial intelligence and algorithmic management.[1] Paradigmatically, this is not just a technological revolution but the integration of all entities into a cyber-physical technical system. It is not just a technological renaissance, but that these technologies merge in a confluence. This theorisation is in step with other 'confluent' theories and practices that predict an imminent merger of scientific disciplines and practices. One of these, beloved by billionaires and verging on the theological, is the concept of the 'singularity' whereby an ASI (Artificial Super Intelligence) advances science so fundamentally that it can achieve anything limited only by physical laws (such as creating what is known as a Dyson Sphere around a star to drain off its energy). Less fanciful is Mark Zuckerberg's company Meta (formally Facebook) based on a dream of the metaverse, a set of all possible universes (physical, virtual and cyber-physical) allowing inter-change (mostly in the form of commerce) between them. Industry 4.0 is another example of such a confluence, whereby technologies merge together to produce the digitisation of (what might be described previously as a largely 'analogue') manufacturing process. Manufacturing becomes a cyber-physical process, existing in both worlds simultaneously, because of a new, singular industrial discipline (Industry 4.0).

Advocates of Industry 4.0 (particularly Schwab 2017) argue that this paradigm shift leads to several benefits for industry and society. These include faster, more efficient and less wasteful production, an upgrading of worker skills and meaningful employment and enabling a societal shift to energy efficient technologies. The technologies included in this supposed paradigm include technologies that enable analytics, such as AI, machine learning (ML) and Big Data. The datafication of manufacturing through the continuous monitoring of production lines (through sensors on machinery, bio-sensors and constant measurement) produces many streams of data which are far too complex for human analysis in real time

[1] There is also an emerging discourse around the idea of Industry 5.0, which appears to seek to add a social justice and environmental sustainability element to Industry 4.0 discourse, although this has yet to enter mainstream currency, and it is not clear that it really represents yet another fundamental paradigm shift, so we tend to bracket it together with Industry 4.0.

or even retrospectively. ML and AI techniques enable continuous analysis of that data through statistical models that constantly improve themselves. Advances in computer processing (the speed and efficiency through which data can be analysed), data warehousing (the ability to store large quantities of data) and data engineering (the possibilities to merge data, triangulating on particular events or processes) mean that no information emitting from the production process needs to be discarded. This process depends on the ability to collect data, and we have also seen rapid advancements in sensors and identification, such as smart sensors which receive and process environmental data in order to identify objects and variables in their surroundings. These smart sensors not only replicate human senses and simple cognitive functions but can go beyond these in recording data on wavelengths (ultraviolet and infrared) and in modalities (mass spectrometry and radiation) beyond human senses. In turn, these technological advances intersect with advances in connectivity. For example, through the Internet of Things (IoT), which allows devices with sensors to connect and exchange data, or, in emerging colloquial discourse, to 'speak' to one another (hence, the idea of a 'chatty factory', which we discuss in more detail below). This then all fuses with developments in robotics, including 'co-bots': collaborative robots intended to 'work together' with humans rather than replicate human labour in isolation from them, and 'soft robotics' which is concerned with the production of robots from less rigid and more pliable materials (quite literally, softer robots), in order to enable them to work more safely with humans and mimic their biological functions. These technologies are considered to work together in a seamless way (Schwab 2017). Notably, Industry 4.0, Klaus Schwab and the World Economic Forum (WEF) have become key signalling words for 'conspiracy theorists'. Our argument, and critique of cybernetics, is not based on the idea of a global conspiracy. However, it is telling that a reified industrial concept (Industry 4.0) has ignited social media forums and rallies with folk theories about power and control. Our argument is an academic, not a conspiratorial one, but we note grassroots populist, as well as anarchist, Marxist and libertarian concerns with the idea of Industry 4.0.

As a techno-social paradigm shift, Industry 4.0 is also associated with changing organisational practices. These include 'quantified self' technologies whereby workers are able, if not willing, to quantify aspects of their experience at work using wearable devices with sensors, and thus to compare their efficiency and effectiveness with other humans and with machines (Moore and Robinson 2016). This can be combined with gamification techniques to motivate and engage workers. Gamification is the use of gaming techniques (from computer games or casinos) to reward and incentivise the worker for performing certain tasks. Technology also accelerates connection of industries through platform capitalism, which refers to the activities of companies like Google, Uber and Airbnb, which profit from offering a platform for other actors to conduct business (Srnicek 2017). Technologies like smart logistics and digital services act to streamline supply chains, allowing managers to visualise the location of goods, and 'manufacturing-as-a-service' allows companies to manufacture their products without investing in massive capital infrastructure (Schwab 2017). Through these technologies, industrial production becomes digital, fluid and ever more closely integrated with other areas of the economy. In Industry 4.0, industrial production becomes 'digital manufacturing' not only in terms of the application of technology to the manufacturing processes but also through the digitisation and analysis of all production data and its integration with other forms of data.

In terms of process, Industry 4.0 has led to greater use of data analytics and systems analysis in manufacturing and work, and the redesign of all aspects of the manufacturing process. Industry 4.0 is, in effect, a cybernetic system, where all entities are in relation with each other and embedded in nested systems. Cybernetics foreshadowed much of what is now called Industry 4.0. In Stafford Beer's book *The Brain of the Firm* (Beer 1981), he outlined a project (Cybersyn) as a model for the entire industrial economy regulated through cybernetic techniques—a cybernetic system for the management of the whole economy and society of Chile. Beer considered that the primary barrier to achieve the goal of project Cybersyn was technological rather than sociological. Beer wrote that:

> It is perfectly possible, these days, to capture data in real time, and to process them instantly. But we do not have the machinery for such instant data capture, nor do we have the sophisticated computer programs that would know what to do with such a plethora of information if we had it. Yet all of this is within the compass of current technology. (Beer 1981: 248)

Project Cybersyn was a confluence of various nascent technologies (or technological foresights) such as Cybernet (an all-encompassing communications technology that would link all industry signals) and Cyberstride (a system for industrial control) that would now seem very familiar to advocates of Industry 4.0. However, we can see elements of cybernetics in previous industrial revolutions. The First Industrial Revolution applied techniques of science and quantification to the production process, eventually producing its own theory of the management of organisations, called scientific management, or Taylorism. This revolution facilitated the transformation of craft production into mass production, through techniques including measurement and standardisation of practices to increase efficiency, and the transfer of knowledge between workers, and from workers into tools, processes and documentation. Knowledge, skill and talent were no longer seen to be properties of human workers, but of organisations, into which human beings could fit themselves, with the assumption that workers were interchangeable with each other and with machines. This had implications for skills and learning in the workplace, and it is widely accepted that processes like the decomposition of tasks into smaller components and the documentation of roles started with the division of labour in manufacturing, as discussed by Adam Smith. Taylorism led to a de-skilling of workers, lower wages and reduced job security. Breaking up tasks and systematising them through documentation also made the automation of processes easier, and is currently associated with the globalisation of labour since de-skilled tasks that are well documented can easily be outsourced elsewhere, to economically peripheral zones where labour is cheaper. Taylorism was associated with Fordism, another very similar set of techniques for mass production that relies on the standardisation of both products and labour. Despite many similarities, it appears that historically these arose independently from each other, and any influence is likely to have been indirect (Hounshell 1984). However, given their correspondences and similar integration into the current hegemony, we tend to use the terms interchangeably. Principles of control, data capture and overlapping systems were fundamental to previous industrial paradigms, and early factories displayed elements that may be considered to be cybernetic. These elements were also capitalist in that the measurement of the products of labour (commodity production) in a consistent period of time with a (socially) necessary labour time (which is also recorded) were all central elements of capitalist production.

We therefore situate Industry 4.0 management discourse within this longer historical narrative that starts with Taylorism and develops into cybernetics, which emerged around the time of the 'third industrial revolution', associated with information and communications technology. Cybernetics is (or claims to be) an exhaustive theory of all entities and relationships and could potentially be understood as the expansion of

Taylorism (or industrial capitalism) to the whole of social life (Beer 1981). Everything is a system with a signal that is optimised through cybernetics, homologous to a social factory. Cybernetics is a meta-theory of *everything* intended to be applied to electronics, mechanics, biology, animals, humans, social organisation and neuroscience. It looks at the ways in which the different elements in a system connect and communicate. The elements are viewed as discrete individual nodes rather than as wholly or partly constituted by their relationships as in more critical social theories, but the concept of complexity in cybernetics means that the elements and relationships are potentially ever-changing (this is perhaps the most significant departure from Taylorism, where mass production lines were somewhat more rigid, even though the elements were interchangeable). Historically, cybernetics had relationships not only with industrial control but also to military decision-making and rationality and the discipline seeped into other areas in the later twentieth century including sociology, anthropology and political science and theory, and of most relevance here, the management of organisations.

Factories as Utopias

Cybernetics was seen by Beer (1981) as a technological utopia but the earlier idea of the factory as a utopia is one that covers a spectrum of political and aesthetic philosophies. For the utopian socialists, as Marx and Engels referred to them in 1848, in *The Communist Manifesto* (1967)—Saint-Simon, Fourier and Robert Owen—the rational and equitable management of production and daily life was a pathway to communalism and socialism. As a factory owner in Manchester, Robert Owen introduced reforms to improve working conditions that were used as the template for his model community of 'New Lanark'. As an industrialist, Owen considered that the forces of production and the factory system were forces that could be both regulated and used for social reform—ultimately, seeing factories as the locus of co-operative production (Cole 2018). In practice, progress towards utopian socialism was limited and private property was never fully relinquished to workers who practically had limited democratic control of production (Harrison 2009). Although Marx and Engels valued nascent ideas of working-class control in utopian socialism, this outcome was, for them, more likely their conception of dialectic, scientific socialism. For Marx, the factory was a location of contradiction. On the one hand, it was where labour power was brutally, dangerously, and inhumanely extracted from the working class to produce commodities for the capitalist. However, although it was the primary site of alienation and immiseration factories were also where workers struggled and were concentrated, forming class consciousness amongst the working class. In factories, workers faced machines as their enemy as a materialised sublimation of their own labour power but also as a potential ally in a society where, collectively owned, they would remove the requirement to work (Marx 2024). In actually existing socialist states, through state socialism, the factory became an aesthetic and quasi-religious site and symbol of working-class emancipation and strength. As opposed to state-capitalism and capitalism, anarchist thinkers see the factory differently. Anarchists are opposed to hierarchy and power relations in factories. However, anarcho-syndicalism conceived of production in the control of the working class (Joll 1970).

In capitalism, neoliberalism, ordo-liberalism (capitalism with a strong and authoritarian state) and Fascism, the factory is also a site of social transformation. Henry Ford extrapolated the lessons of Fordist factory production to imagine a society built on factory principles. These were expected to produce a living, patriarchal wage, within factory-towns with Fordist social arrangements and a high standard of living. He extended this principle to include plans, and a prototype, for 'village industries' which would bring together agricultural and industrial workers around small-scale factories (Mullin 1982). Ford's factory vision also motivated fascists. Adolf Hitler was entranced by the Ford's vision for mass production of automobiles and Ford's antipathy towards Jewish people. He saw the production of a 'people's car' (Volkswagen) as a vehicle of pleasure—'Strength Through Joy'—enabling travel across Germany to explore its geography and history (König 2004). The Nazis saw the factory as the locus of neutralising class relations in favour of a plant system where the plant leader (factory owner) and their retinue would act in service of the state. The Nazi 'Labour Front' organised campaigns around factory workers—the 'Beauty of Labour' to improve the health and aesthetics of factory work and 'Strength through Joy', leisure activities intended to improve worker output (Welch 1993). In contemporary capitalism, the giga-factory acts as the material projection of the will of the capitalist, its apogee being the billionaire Elon Musk, champion of the populist Donald Trump, sleeping on the floor of Tesla's giant production plant to keep an eye on production. The Tesla factory is described as the most technologically advanced in the world, with Musk's production ambitions extending to a self-sufficient factory colony on Mars (Minchin 2021).

In this book we do not describe factories as utopias in and of themselves. As the above discussion has shown, the image of the factory as utopia is often put forward for purposes of propaganda or ideology, emptied of any actual prefigurative utopian possibility. Changing the ownership of factories, whether in the private, state form or collectivist, does not remove the exploitative and alienating nature of factory work and (only for the owning class or classes) the accumulation of power. This argument relates to our wider critique of cybernetics, as expounded in this book. However, we do recognise the contradictory nature of the factory. One side of this is in terms of how factories produce working-class consciousness and act as a locus for union and class struggle activity. Another is factories as the site of worker knowledges, and capabilities, which prefigure different forms of social organisation. It is the second form of prefiguration that is the focus in this book.

Key Components of Cybernetics

The history and theory of cybernetics will be outlined in more detail in Chap. 2, but at this point it is worthwhile to offer preliminary definitions of some key concepts associated with cybernetics that are used (and critiqued) throughout this book: control, feedback, blackboxing and complexity.

Control

Cybernetics assumes that the purpose of machines and living beings is to control their environment. The idea of control was developed in the work of British cybernetician, Stafford Beer, whose work in psychiatry and behavioural science represented both a continuation and departure from the origins of cybernetics in US military engineering. Beer sought to distance cybernetic understanding of control from definitions based on top-down domination, hierarchy, authoritarianism and loss of individual freedom. Rather, Beer emphasised that control could be exercised through the self-regulation of a system in terms of its ability to adapt to internal and external changes in a decentralised fashion (Beer 1981). This required studying complex systems and using probability to detect inconsistencies. For Beer, the purpose of cybernetics was to provide tools to do so. One of these tools was the idea of the black box.

Blackboxing

Cybernetics seeks to make systems more efficient and effective by focusing on generic, rather than particularistic, features of a system, for example through 'blackboxing'—a conceptual tool which reduces a device, system or object to its inputs and outputs without any need for knowledge of its internal workings unless, or until, the object malfunctions. Ross Ashby (1957), another cybernetician psychiatrist, saw imitating the behaviour of a black box as the first step in self-organisation. The metaphor of the black box came from electrical engineering, where the contents of the box are hidden, but the engineer can observe the output that results from an electrical input such that the engineer can infer the contents of the box by varying input, without ever seeing inside it. This metaphor was extended by cyberneticians to apply to all functioning parts of any complex system, whether human, animal or machine. This is highly evident in the language used by Norbert Wiener, commonly dubbed 'the Father of cybernetics'. Throughout his works, he tended to anthropomorphise machines by analogy—switches corresponded to synapses, wires to nerves, sensors to eyes and ears, etc. He also used machinic metaphors to describe human physiology (Wiener 2019). Cyberneticians assume a tight correspondence between humans and machines. While there is no resistance or feedback, the two had the potential to form a single entity or 'black box'. For both mechanic or organic devices, the principle is that it is more important to observe what things do, their outputs or behaviours, rather than to grasp their inner workings (Beer 1981).

Feedback

Feedback refers to the ideas that man/animal, and machines based on them, have kinaesthetic, sensory and conscious awareness of their environment that tends to oppose what a system is already doing if there is a lack of equilibrium. For Beer and Ashby, the problem with top-down control systems is that they are too simple to cope with the variety inherent within complex systems (Beer 1959: 50). As computer technology was being adopted in business and management through the 1950s and 1960s, Beer argued that it ought to be used to transform organisational structures into more networked forms of cybernetic management and decentralised decision-making (Beer 1959: 21). This involved restructuring organisations and systems towards a more stable state of homeostasis, by creating lateral horizontal links rather than vertical communication channels amongst sub-systems (Beer 1981: 156). Homeostasis is seen as a more flexible and adaptable form of control than domination or coercion, and it allowed for a degree of autonomy for parts of an organisation, without sacrificing the stability of the whole system. Beer (1981) created the 'Viable System Model' (VSM) to maximise the potential for homeostasis in a system, which in management and organisational scenarios recommend various forms of restructuring to attempt to balance and harmonise centralised/top-down and decentralised/bottom-up forms of control in order to regulate the behaviour of any of a range of organisations, including governments, factories and companies.

Cybernetics in Social Theory

One does not often hear the term 'cybernetics' in dominant discourse these days (as one would have in the 1960s and 1970s); however, like the 'black box' it may have been integrated into the hegemonic totality and rendered invisible by its pervasiveness. In a sense, as we will argue in Chaps. 2 and 3, it reflects and perpetuates the ethos, the mythos and the utopian vision of neoliberal capitalism. Within the social sciences beyond management and organisational theory, cybernetics was adopted by functionalist sociologists and integrated into theories of social behaviour. It has been used to understand crowd behaviour in disaster and sought to explain and intervene in spontaneous events like riots with the explicit aims of risk management and crowd control by sociologists including Talcott Parsons (Parsons and Smelser 2005). It has also been used in the field of Disaster Management and Disaster Risk Reduction by sociologists including Enrico Quarantelli and Arthur Sementelli (Quarantelli and Dynes 1977; Sementelli 2007). Cybernetics as a method for regulating mass population response is very much in keeping with cybernetics' militarised focus on social order and control. Cybernetics in this context tends to take a rational choice theory view of the subject: people are rational subjects and organisations are behavioural systems governed by authority-systems. To the extent that everyday social practices or individuals are considered, they are treated as bundles of aggregate behavioural outputs to be managed using incentives and nudges. This view of rationality seems to be the only category of agency available within this philosophy besides generic 'organisations' with hierarchies. Politically, the emphasis on decentralised and autonomous systems suggests that a non-authoritarian system, or even a utopian community of individual and grassroots autonomy, is entirely compatible with benign systems of technocratic governance and democratising technology. This kind of vision has been adopted by neoliberal governments, such as David Cameron's 'Big Society' or Barak Obama's 'Open Government' initiative (The Invisible Committee 2015: 103), whereby it is assumed that the withdrawal of state funds and welfare functions from communities can be ameliorated by encouraging autonomous action, which must still be integrated within a 'social capital' framework. We will later argue that this is often undergirded by authoritarian—even totalitarian—reasoning, which seeks to control, integrate or suppress dense systems of meaning, interaction and life which occur between people who are not part of an organisation. This critique of cybernetic government, and governance, will be considered in later chapters. A detailed history of cybernetics, with attention to its utopian promise, is offered in Chap. 2. A theoretical critique of cybernetics is given in Chap. 3.

Utopia and Prefiguration

Another key concept and methodological lens in our book is utopianism. The concept is important because cybernetics is a form of utopianism that disavows the normative claims underlying its vision through the anti-utopian strategy of scientism. The idea of utopianism is hard to grasp, and definitional debates have been ongoing since the inception of utopian studies in the early post-WWII period. Broadly, utopias are articulations of desire for radically different institutions, norms and relationships. It is the emphasis on socio-political relationships that distinguishes utopias from science fiction, where the difference may rest on biological or geological factors (Levitas 1990: 191; Suvin 2013: 181). Utopias encompass a variety of forms, which Lyman Tower Sargent dubs 'the three faces of utopianism': first, fictional accounts, which draw out detailed visions of societies intended to contrast favourably with the reader's; second, intentional communities where people choose to live and work together to enhance their shared values or prefigure a better world; and third, progressivist social theory or social programmes (Sargent 1994: 9). This latter point draws on the work of Ernst Bloch whose definition of utopia was expansive, including prefigurative epistemologies and promises of hope read through a very wide range of cultural artefacts and everyday experiences, including medicine, fairy tales, theatre, music, art and architecture (Bloch 1986). Utopias can also encompass a wide variety of ideological content.

Colloquial discourse usually associates the term with the radical Left (implicitly assumed to be hopelessly idealistic). However, other ideological positions such as conservatives, neoliberals and even fascists project visions of a desired society in their thought and programmes, but these visions are obscured or repressed through anti-utopian strategies such as *scientism* (asserting normative claims as scientific truth) or through *fatalism* (claiming there is no alternative) (Firth 2019).

Anti-utopianism arises from across the ideological spectrum. Marx and Engels were critical of utopianism, and their portrayal of historical materialism as 'scientific' was undertaken through a direct contrast with the utopian socialists, whereas for Liberal Karl Popper, Marxism itself was definitively totalitarian. He argued utopias portray a fixed vision of society and therefore necessitate a strategy to be executed 'all at once' by 'a strong centralised leadership' (Popper 2002: 173). For Popper the only possible form of government that could allow for institutional improvement without violence and bloodshed was liberal democracy.

Anarchists, autonomous and open Marxists and libertarian socialists tend to distinguish their relationship to utopia from the authoritarian and unequal utopias of both totalitarian forms of Communism and (neo)liberal capitalism with reference to the idea that utopia is a process rather than an end, so they have defined utopianism with reference to progressive, subversive, democratising or critical elements in a very wide range of social and cultural practices. There is a desire amongst anti-authoritarians to avoid the epistemological vanguardism associated with utopian blueprints to be imposed as a totality, as well as with ideas of progressivism and teleology (Firth 2013). Thus, anti-authoritarian utopias tend to centre the idea of prefiguration in their political strategy.

Prefiguration

The concept of prefiguration is an important one in anarchist theory and practice. Gradin and Raekstad trace the concept of prefiguration as it is currently understood to Carl Boggs' analyses of tensions between Marxism and the New Left in the 1970s, although they argue the practices that the term refers to have a longer history, for example in anti- and decolonial movements (Raekstad and Gradin 2020). Prefigurative politics is characterised by an antagonistic relationship with vanguard revolution or approaches advocating seizure of state power. This is accompanied by attention to informal as well as formal power relations, such as class relations, patriarchy, white supremacy and ableism. Boggs' definition focuses on prefigurative politics as the embodiment of the social relations, decision-making, culture and experience that are the 'ultimate goal' of a movement or organisation (Boggs 1977). There may be some rigidity and teleology implied in this idea of an 'ultimate goal' that belies some of the more self-reflexive and recursive aspects of anarchist movements, which face changing and unforeseen conditions as they attempt to transcend domination, and new values emerge (Raekstad and Gradin 2020: 15). We prefer definitions of prefiguration that emphasise experimentation and the experience of future-facing desire in the present, rather than a deferred goal, for example the definition offered by Raekstad and Gradin: 'the deliberate experimental implementation of desired future social relations and practices in the here-and-now' (Raekstad and Gradin 2020: 15).

However, in this book we expand the concept of prefiguration to encompass values and practices which are not always wholly deliberate or intentional, but which do enact something beyond neoliberal capitalism, that transgress cybernetic/technocratic categories. The idea that transgressive utopias need not always be wholly intentional has a precedent as mentioned above in the work of Ernst Bloch and can also be found in James Scott's idea of the 'hidden transcript' (Scott 1990) or Firth's 'disaster utopias' (Firth 2022). We believe that these kinds of emergent utopias have the potential to form embryonic social movements, or transformative utopias, so are worthy of interest. They also offer a novel standpoint from which to critique totalising systems.

Prefigurative Knowledges

We will argue throughout this book that human learning, creativity and freedom can never be captured by a cybernetic (or any hierarchical or formalised) system, and we articulate our argument through the concepts of 'tacit knowledge', and a concept which we introduce that we call 'hobbying'.

Cybernetics makes extravagant claims for learning that transcend Enlightenment ideals of the centrality of individual minds in learning (Rousseau 1990). Cybernetics claims that rather than beings or entities, it is systems that learn, and that organisation by cybernetic systems is the ideal for learning (Smith and Smith 1966). Learning occurs primarily at the system or sub-system level. Although most advocates of cybernetics would argue that individual entities in a system learn, this learning is not the primary value of cybernetic systems. In a cybernetic system, individual elements (including humans and human groups) are depicted as nodes (black boxes) in a cybernetic system. The incorporation of entities, through embedding them into a structure comprised of black boxes, produces forms of meta-learning that further optimise whatever is produced or circulates in a cybernetic system. Cybernetics foreshadows collective learning ideals such as learning communities or learning organisations. The learning that occurs is system learning, rather than individual learning.

In modelling learning in this form, there is neglect for human experience and agency. All entities are considered to be 'black boxes' (of concern only due to their inputs and outputs), and we lose all aspects of learning associated with individual experience and context. Individuals are reduced to the status of logic gates, with the mind and brain reduced in significance to an input-output mechanism. The only function of a mind or brain is in taking in an input or producing an output in a cybernetic system. Functionalist and behaviourist conceptions of the individual learner are an existential threat to human agency and humanity. As in CBET (Competence-Based Education and Training), any notion of individual craft, improvisation or mastery is unimportant (Preston 2017). Aside from privileging a narrow ontology of learning, it seems plausible that humans (brains, minds) are capable of learning that cannot be captured by the bounds of any existent (cybernetic or otherwise) physical system. We do not yet have technological AGI (Artificial General Intelligence) or ASI (Artificial Super Intelligence), and it may be that these things are not possible, at least in a human sense, as humans may have abilities that cannot be fully codified in a system and may never be. Tacit knowledge and hobbying are examples of non-codifiable knowledge.

Tacit Knowledge

One example of learning that humans (and animals) can uniquely demonstrate is tacit knowledges that are not possible to formalise. Polyani originally described this concept as tacit knowing. Humans can do more than they can express '*we know more than we can tell*' (2009: 4, our italics) or can be codified (Nonaka 1991). Ambrosini and Bowman (2001) consider tacit knowledge as being expressed primarily in practical domains, but there is no reason why it can't also be applied to other areas of knowledge work (Leonard and Insch 2005). Tacit knowledge is primarily individual (Ambrosini and Bowman 2001), but Collins (2007) expands the concept to include Collective Tacit Knowledge, which exists at the community or societal level. There are some forms of knowledge that we enact although we do not know the rules governing the activity. Collins (2007) gives the example of riding a bicycle. Many of us can do this although we do not know the laws of physics governing bicycle riding at every point in time that we are doing so. Cycling is somatic-limit tacit knowledge, where our knowledge seems to transcend our own personal powers to explain what we are doing. A robot equipped with an AI may eventually be able to ride a bicycle if they did have knowledge of the governing physics, but it may not necessarily be able to do this in novel domains (Collins gives the example of riding a bicycle on the moon where a human could adapt quickly, due to their tacit knowledge). In practice, tacit knowledge functions in social, collective environments that require reciprocal and shared social knowledge and Collins refers to this as Collective Tacit Knowledge (2007), which is a property of the human species (Collins 2007: 261) rather than of an individual.

In the context of the workplace, Winch (2017) claims that tacit knowledge is central to understanding autonomy and creativity in the work process and that tacit knowledge is an 'everyday' form of knowledge in jobs requiring expertise due to their complexity. Tacit knowledge is distinct from other ways of knowing as it is context-dependent (Winch 2017). In order for tacit knowledge to be demonstrated, it is dependent on interaction with some entity as it cannot be codified. The tacit knowledge to ride a bicycle can only be demonstrated with a bicycle. The limits of employee expertise are constrained by the capitalist labour process. De Angelis (2001) argues that the labour process itself is one in which human capacities are consistently in tension with the requirements of contemporary work. Work channels human capacities towards specific activities which are aimed at commodity production and profit. Although inevitable in a capitalist society, it is argued that these activities often limit human collective potential. Such potential is, in any case, hard to gauge. Sohn-Rethel (2020) discusses how processes of work optimisation, as used in Taylorism, are practically almost impossible to formalise. He gives the example of how recording simple work processes with full accuracy often takes time and motion experts months, or even years, and is always incomplete. Rather, Sohn-Rethel considers that work processes and timings are imposed in a top-down way, as a process of control, instead of emerging from work activity. Relatedly, Preston (2017) in a survey of the competency movement shows how competences are produced in terms of capitalist, binary, job requirements and not through an analysis of process. The reduction of human tasks to binaries is not compatible with the analogue nature of activities or human processes. Sohn-Rethel argues that this process means that time in factories is synthetic timing, determined through the necessity of the production line, rather than through time determined by human workers. These arguments suggest that Industry 4.0 and cybernetic systems are generated though 'top down' requirements external to knowledge of the capabilities of agents. Although that is inevitable in commercial workplaces, this is not in the 'utopian vision' of Industry 4.0 or cybernetics, which considers processes to emerge from the properties of agents that can be fully mapped. Indeed, there are forms of knowledge that are prefigurative but cannot be mapped.

Hobbying

Although cybernetic systems may (at the systems level) learn to adapt and change, these systems restrict human learning of the broad, creative type, of a form that we call *hobbying*. Hobbying describes the ways in which individuals play and experiment with artefacts in a creative and sometimes aimless sense. Collecting train numbers (trainspotting), outsider art and writing, or collecting and dancing to music might be considered forms of hobbying. There are two connected senses in which we employ 'hobbying' in this book. The first is in terms of the ways in which contemporary capitalism or statism can be subverted through acts of making. Franz (2005) uses the term 'tinkering' to describe the ways in which consumers of early automobiles would mechanically alter their characteristics and share information on how best to adapt their cars. This practice continues in the present day not only with reference to cars but in the context of manufactured objects where consumers or collectives attempt to improve or modify them in some sense. Although such activities can easily be recuperated by capitalism in terms of 'user experience' or 'gamification', we align hobbying with prefigurative activities such as the creation of convivial tools (Illich 1973), craft, hacking, culture hacking, radical craft (Myzelev 2009) and the creation of concrete utopias as will be explained below. We define hobbying as a consistent, playful improvisation in the process of making or using for the purposes of prefiguration. This somewhat distinguishes 'hobbying' from 'play' as hobbying has a prefigurative goal of some kind (following Heljakka 2018), but some of the ludic elements of play are contained within hobbying as we would define it. In more recent work Heljakka (2023) has argued that sharp distinctions between play, exercise and hobby are not clear in practice and that individuals engage with 'hobby' objects (in this case girls using an actual 'hobby horse') in diverse ways that reimagine the object in terms of various uses, values and activities. Hobbying can therefore meander between play and purpose.

The improvisational and seemingly purposeless nature of hobbying makes it anathema to cybernetic systems in which everything has a broader purpose in its linkage to each other. Cybernetics implies a functionalist grasp on human purpose that does not allow for hobbying activities. Advocates of cybernetics as a political form (Swann 2020) imply that exclusion from a cybernetic system is possible. Rather than individuals being expelled from this system, Swann argues that this would be negotiated in terms of the collective needs of the individuals who comprise the cybernetic system. A difficulty is what happens when people engage in non-system activities. Perhaps they make bread in the shape of ducks for fun, or because they are idiosyncratic, and float them on a pond. Either this creative person is ejected from the cybernetic system, persuaded to conform, or punished, or the system changes to an alternative system where bread can be produced in the shape of animals. Perhaps the next day the person refuses to make bread in the shape of animals but instead wants to paint with the flour. We can see how this sort of playful, purposeless, hobbying activity may be inconsistent with a functioning cybernetic society, yet it is prefigurative in its own terms. The idea that the hobbyist may freely 'exit' a cybernetic system (similarly to how Nozick (1974) expresses the idea of free exit from multiple utopias) is questionable as the cybernetic system may represent the only way to sustain life if it is predominant in a given territory.

Deschooling, Anti-school and Convivial Tools

Linked to our conceptions of tacit knowledge and hobbying are more radical conceptions of education. Ivan Illich is one of the most interesting precursors to our argument and offers useful conceptual tools. He also interestingly is one of the few radical authors who examines in depth the relationship between education and technology—advocating in his book *Deschooling Society* (1970) for a wholescale revolution in pedagogy via a technological infrastructure which appears remarkably prescient of the modern internet (minus its capitalistic features). Deschooling society looks like the internet but treats it as a tool not a technology; that is, it exists to enable learners to be matched to community skillshares and apprenticeships (similarly to the role played by Hackspaces in Chap. 6), rather than manipulating their consumer desires through advertising and platforms which monopolise the social. Illich developed these technological themes in another work, *Tools for Conviviality*, where he divides tools into convivial (aiding individual autonomy, social conviviality and ecology) and industrial (manipulative or dependency-forming) (Illich 1973: 12–14) areas. Industrial society subordinates humans to technological logics and may threaten human life (Illich 1973: 47). Convivial tools allow user autonomy, can be used or avoided at will, for different purposes by different users. Most low-technology tools are convivial (Illich: 22). Most high-tech tools (e.g. cars and hospitals) are industrial. However, some higher-tech tools, such as telephones and bicycles, pass Illich's test for conviviality (Illich 1973: 64, 79).

Referencing robotics, Illich depicts even simple machines as 'energy slaves' (Illich 1973: 14) dangerously substituting or supplementing human energy inputs and introducing unequal power (Illich 1973: 26). Machines stem from an earlier desire for a 'laboratory-made homunculus [that] could do our labor instead of slaves' (Illich 1973: 20). This fails to overcome the master-slave relation (Illich 1973: 20). Humans must then be educated to work alongside homunculi, and thus, subordinated to tools (Illich 1973: 30). Illich's followers provide criteria and typologies for convivial technology (Kostakis et al. 2015; Prieur 2011; Gordon 2009), generally focused on avoiding ecological harms, encouraging user autonomy and egalitarian and participatory societies, and providing 'meaningful' work. The work of Ran Prieur (2011) is particularly useful in this respect, as he offers a set of practical principles to distinguish convivial tools from enslaving technologies. These are: Freedom of Refusal (tools are part of a social system that does not coerce users into their use); Freedom of Reversal (tools that are 'non-addictive'—a counter-example is the car, which requires the building of massive road infrastructure, which then presupposes the continuing use of cars); Use Autonomy (tools can be used for more than one purpose—they fulfil the users' creative desires rather than embedding product assumptions); Make-Repair Autonomy (a user can make or repair the tool themselves); Systemic Participation (the technology fits with a system of democratic, widely distributed political power—solar panels are preferable to nuclear power plants); Manufacture Ecology and Use Ecology (making or using the tool does not destroy or poison environmental systems); Efficiency (Prieur makes a case for defining efficiency in terms of time rather than energy or capital); Human Contraction/Expansion (defined as the expansion of consciousness and communal experience); Skill Replacement/Creation (Prieur judges escalators as almost useless, because people in wheelchairs can't use them, and most other people could walk upstairs, whereas aeroplanes expand human ability because humans cannot grow wings and fly).

Choueiri et al. (2018) put a high-tech spin on the idea of conviviality, arguing that items such as prosthetic hands and voice-operated tilting tables are convivial because they enhance autonomy. Kostakis et al. (2015) take Illich's criteria more seriously, suggesting that 3D-printed prosthetic hands are more convivial than commercially produced equivalents. They are exponentially cheaper, user-repairable, customisable and more user-friendly. They also discuss 3D-printed wind turbines as convivial technology, and suggest a general overlap between conviviality, makerspaces and peer production. Serendipitously, the example of prosthetic limbs being produced in makerspaces appears in empirical Chap. 6.

The Arts & Crafts Movement

Another possible influence to draw on in constructing a theory of 'unalienated conditions of production and reception' (Petts 2008) is the tradition of embodied learning and craft on the Left exemplified by, for example, William Morris (in a squarely utopian tradition). The Arts & Crafts movement started in East London in the 1870s and spread through Europe and North America, and was motivated by three main principles: the 'unity' of art (artists and craftsmen working together); 'joy in labour' and design reform (making manufactured goods better) (Krugh 2014: 283). In this tradition, emphasis is placed on the need for workers to have creative autonomy and an artisanal relationship to their product. Labour should be seen as synonymous with art and antithetical to moral compulsion. The movements eschew mass production and division of labour both politically and aesthetically, yet they did codify their work through various societies and organisations, which produced lecture series, practical handbooks and political manifestos (Petts 2008: 31). The stance towards manufacturing technologies adopted by the movement is not straightforwardly luddite or primitivist as is often assumed, but rather there is a rejection of 'mechanised and narrow labor processes, which reduce the worker to a machine' (Petts 2008: 36). Machines are seen to have a legitimate role to play when they act as a 'servant' or tool, rather than the human worker becoming a tool to the machine, similarly to the stance adopted by other theorists advocating the tactical use of technology such as Gerald Raunig (2010) and Ivan Illich. Machines are not to be used to imitate or replace hand handiwork but rather to enhance it to create objects whose aesthetic value lies in their 'authenticity'. We find the concepts of craft, artisanship and creative autonomy useful for conceptualising the relationship to machines expressed by some of the workers at the co-operative in Chap. 5, and some of the hobbyists in the Hackspace in Chap. 6. The Arts & Crafts movement raises interesting questions useful to the book such as the embeddedness of thoughtful design in factory and automated environments or the emergence of 'slow' tech.

Methods

The research questions which motivated this work are twofold. Firstly, to consider the potential of cybernetics in terms of learning and organisation:

- Is cybernetics an appropriate and progressive model for future human societies and politics?

Secondly, to analyse real-world examples of cybernetic systems:

- To what extent do prefigurative forms of learning arise within them; and to what extent can we observe prefigurative knowledges within or despite cybernetics?
- Can prefigurative forms of learning be fully captured by cybernetic systems, do they disrupt cybernetics, and/or prefigure something else?

The first research question will be addressed conceptually and theoretically and the second and third through the conventional methods of qualitative sociology (observation and interview). In the conclusion, we answer all three of these research questions and bring them together to present our own, distinctly non-cybernetic, view of prefiguration employing concepts of 'tacit knowledge' and 'hobbying'.

Methodology

As part of the Engineering and Physical Sciences Research Council (EPSRC) project discussed in the preface, the work-package from which this project arose concentrated on critically interrogating the social and ethical aspects of an imagined (though based in emergent social tendencies) 'Chatty Factory'. This fictive entity was one in which all parts of the factory (products, machines, humans) were in consistent dialogue and communication. We also sought to identify other emergent trends in manufacturing and to think through the implications for skills and learning. This involved undertaking fieldwork and interviews in three different organisations that we will outline below. It is worth emphasising that we are not particularly knowledgeable on the technologies we examine, although other members of the research project team were. We hope that this does not undermine our argument too much as we seek to focus on the social role of automation in the broadest sense, rather than on any specific functions. There are researchers doing excellent work in this area which focus on more specific functions of actual and potential technologies, who critique and engage with the ethics on a much finer scale (e.g. Rose et al. 2023). Our methodology, as sociologists, was qualitative—we were more interested in human participants' subjective experiences of technology and social roles than in technical aspects. Therefore, we used interviews to explore the subjective experiences of people in a variety of different organisations working with automation technology. In terms of the technical aspects and details, we rely on the expertise of our interviewees.

Case Studies

We undertook research in three different organisations, which are the foci of Chaps. 4–6: first, a mainstream UK automotive factory (Chap. 4), whose identity remains anonymous at their request. Second (Chap. 5), a workers' co-operative in the United States that produces automation solutions for other organisations, and third, a Hackspace (Chap. 6), which is an informal, self-organised social space in which members share skills and tools. Our method of investigation was the case study. Case studies are bounded studies that make use of a variety of methods (Flyvbjerg 2011), in this case qualitative methods of interview and observation. A brief outline and justification of the case studies is given below.

CYBER4.0

Starting from a rather sceptical position on how far humans can be incorporated within the cyber-physical circuits in 'Industry 4.0', we wanted to consider the ways in which humans work within an advanced factory that employs digital systems and the latest manufacturing, computing and robotic technologies. The purpose of the investigation was to consider how people work within such a system, their integration within this system, and how novel and imaginative possibilities of activity (within the terms of the system) might emerge and how these capabilities are used within the factory. It is difficult to gain access to advanced manufacturing settings for research purposes due to issues of confidentiality. We were able to gain access to CYBER4.0 (a pseudonym), which was chosen as a case, and they kindly volunteered to take part providing data is anonymised, that the researchers were subject to a non-disclosure agreement (NDA) and that there was approval of the research findings prior to publication. Research in high-technology manufacturing environments, particularly of this scale, is unusual in sociological research. The research used a qualitative approach, including observations, documentary analysis, semi-structured interviews and discussion with visual prompts. Observations involved factory tours and note-taking. Seven interviews were conducted with eight CYBER4.0 workers who volunteered, and a programme and timetable was drawn up by our contact at CYBER4.0, who could be understood to be a 'gatekeeper'. The interviews were semi-structured, using broad questions (so as to apply the same questions across very different types of organisation), and the structure was left somewhat open in order to adapt the conversation to the particularities of the organisation. The questions included suggested prompts. A copy of the interview schedule can be found in *Appendix 1*. CYBER4.0 is a major multi-national manufacturer of premium automotive vehicles across several product lines with supply chains across Europe and distribution networks worldwide. It has a number of production facilities in the UK and worldwide. CYBER4.0 is a large employer and uses a range of advanced technologies typical of Industry 4.0.

We (the authors) undertook the visit to CYBER4.0 from 12th to 13th September 2019. As researchers, we were offered a tour of the factory, during which they were able to undertake observations at different departments including Tooling and Press, Body and White, Trim and Final, and Finishing. These are generic terms for factory processes, so they do not identify the CYBER4.0 company. Interviews were undertaken with representatives from each of these areas and others, including Human Factors and Current Manufacturing Engineering (CME). CYBER4.0 was a particularly interesting case because their factory uses robots and automation at nearly every stage of the manufacturing process, but some departments involve a much greater ratio of robots to humans than others. Interviews with workers were mainly undertaken by the researchers/authors Rhiannon Firth and John Preston; however, the logistics of workers' availability and location on the day meant that we were unable to follow our planned schedule. Two of the interviews had a somewhat unconventional format—one of which was undertaken with two workers at the same time by a CYBER4.0 manager who acted as our host on the day, and one of which had the two researchers (John and Rhiannon) present with one interviewee. This may be methodologically and ethically problematic because it means that not all of the interviews were undertaken using the same process, and also the interviewees may have modified their answers when being interviewed by a member of the management at their organisation. However, this was unavoidable on the day and the workers expressed they were happy being interviewed in this way—as stated in ethics the interview questions were about work processes and not individual or sensitive topics.

Isthmus Engineering and Manufacturing

Isthmus Engineering and Manufacturing Co-operative (IEM) (the real company name) is a US workers' co-operative that produces bespoke high-technology robotics that are used in manufacturing industries. Unlike the mainstream manufacturing corporation described in the previous section, the co-operative did not express any need for the organisation to remain anonymous in published outputs, and it is likely that it would be extremely difficult to write about the organisation at all if complete anonymity needed to be preserved, given the extremely small number of co-operatives doing any kind of work with automation and the unique nature of the organisation. Similarly to the previous organisational study, we selected IEM with the core purpose of thinking through how humans and machines work with advanced technology in different organisational settings. The purpose of the investigation was to consider how people work in such a system, their integration within this system, and how novel and imaginative possibilities of activity (within the terms of the system) might emerge and how these capabilities are used within the factory. Similarly to our work with the case study CYBER4.0, we began from a rather sceptical position as to how far humans can be incorporated within the cyber-physical circuits in 'Industry 4.0'. As IEM was a workers' co-operative working within a capitalist economy, we were particularly interested in the ways in which they would replicate but also transgress the dominant norms of cybernetic capitalism (indeed, the interviewees themselves had considered responses to these ideas and the role of co-operatives within capitalism was clearly an explicit topic of interest at the co-op). We sought to identify the explicit or implicit utopianism of the organisation, particularly in terms of human-technology relationships and learning, and the ways in which they might prefigure something against and beyond Industry 4.0. It is worth noting that the case studies differ in important ways aside from their organisational forms, particularly in terms of their core business. While the company in the previous section was an automotive manufacturing company that used automation to produce the product, the current case study created custom-build automation solutions—so it actually creates the automation which is then passed on to companies which use it to produce their products. This kind of work is arguably more creative, varied and bespoke, as each project will be different according to the specifications of the order. Later in the chapter on IEM, we consider whether this kind of work is particularly suited to the co-operative structure.

Rhiannon undertook the visit to IEM in Madison, Wisconsin, the United States, from 18th to 19th February 2019. The research involved one day of formal research with the co-op on the 18th February. She observed a MadWorC[2] city-wide co-operatives meeting on the evening of 18th, and on 19th visited the University of Wisconsin-Madison Centre for Co-operatives, which helped to provide context and background information on co-operatives in Madison. The research replicated the methods used in for CYBER4.0, involving a qualitative approach, involving observations, documentary analysis and semi-structured interviews. Observations involved a factory tour and note-taking. Six interviews were conducted with IEM workers who volunteered, which lasted around 30 minutes to an hour. The interviews were semi-structured, using broad questions (so

[2] Madison Worker Cooperatives—a member organisation of worker-owned and operated co-operatives in the Madison area with the mission of supporting and building the solidarity economy https://madworc.org/about-us/

as to apply the same questions across the very different types of organisation), and the structure was left somewhat open in order to adapt the conversation to the particularities of the organisation.

London Hackspace

London Hackspace (real name) is a space for both use of technology as consumption (within capitalism) and also pleasure and hobbying. The Hackspace did not express any need for the organisation to remain anonymous in published outputs; again, it is likely that it would be extremely difficult to write about the organisation at all if complete anonymity needed to be preserved, given the extremely small number of spaces of this type in any given city. Part of the interest in this space arises from attempting to unpick the recuperated, commodified aspects of the relation to technology from the prefigurative and utopian possibilities. We sought to identify the explicit or implicit utopianism of the organisation, particularly in terms of human-technology relationships and learning, and the ways in which they might prefigure something against and beyond Industry 4.0. Similarly to IEM, the Hackspace was not a space for mass production, but rather for creative and artisanal uses of automation. This kind of work is arguably more creative, varied and bespoke, as each project is chosen according to the individual desires of the Hackspace user or in voluntaristic collaboration with others. We consider whether this kind of work is particularly suited to the networked organisational form, enabling skillshares.

Rhiannon visited the London Hackspace on one of its regular Tuesday open days on 7 May 2019. The open day was very quiet—there were only three guests, and a similar number of members using the Hackspace. She was informed this was due to the Hackspace having recently moved from its previous location in Hackney, East London, to Wembley, due to increasing rents and gentrification. Nobody who was using the Hackspace during the time of the visit worked with automation, although the members present were all aware, they said, of several other members who worked with automation, and they also mentioned that there was a club that met regularly and worked on automation and robotics projects. An email was sent to the mailing list, and three different members responded who worked with automation and were willing to be interviewed. Rhiannon undertook one of these interviews in person, in a café in East London, and the others online using Skype. This was a novel use of technology for research interviews at the time, which was pre-COVID lockdowns (when use of videoconferencing software became widespread), and had been suggested by the interviewees.

Data Gathering

Interviews were undertaken with workers/members of the different organisations. The same interview schedule was followed in all three places, which can be found in Appendix 1. This was a semi-structured schedule with some fluidity as to topics, so alterations were made and topics of interest were followed up during the interviews, as required. Eight interviews were undertaken at the factory, six at the workers' co-operative, and only three were taken in the Hackspace due to the smaller number of people working with automation. Seventeen interviews were undertaken in total. The interviews varied from around 28 minutes to 1 hour 15 minutes, and there was 10 hours 14 minutes of interview material in total.

Ethics

In line with the ethical requirements of the project as approved by the University of Essex and the Engineering and Physical Sciences Research Council (EPSRC), all interviewees were provided with participant information sheets containing details of the research and contact details of the investigators. Participants were asked to sign consent forms. Individual workers' names have been pseudonymised in the text. All data from interviews and observations are stored securely on encrypted devices and institutional drives.

There are some specific ethical concerns relating to interviewing workers on their work processes, especially in the context of a project which is critical of capitalism and of factories. It is important to emphasise that the research, and particularly the theoretical critique, is focused on structures and on processes rather than individuals—we absolutely do not wish to single out any organisation or worker as being specifically complicit in a system (capitalism) in which we all seek to survive and thrive. Indeed, we found that our interviewees had their own critiques of their work process, of workplaces, and of the broader systems they are part of, which supplemented and sometimes exceeded our own and those drawn from academic debates. The assumption that interviewees' views are theoretically valuable is essential to our methodology: we do not seek to present empirically 'rigorous' scientistic social research; nor do we seek to 'give voice' to presumed marginalised participants in a condescending way. Rather, as theorists of 'the social' we seek to take the worldviews of workers and activists seriously as important sources of theoretical knowledge, alongside academic texts, which are useful in building our own theoretical critique and alternatives. The argument herein remains our own—we own any errors or omissions. Nevertheless, we often rely on rather long quotations from interviews, because we value the context our interviewees offer, rather than wishing to cherry-pick soundbites that support our argument.

An astute reader will undoubtedly pick up on the lack of gender, racial and ethnic diversity amongst our participants. Most of our participants are white men, with one woman, although we did not collect data on gender and ethnicity so cannot report on this accurately. The lack of diversity in our sample was reflective of the demographics of the organisations we interviewed within and therefore beyond our control. We acknowledge this as a lack, and a limit, yet in a sense it also affirms our argument: that even in some of the most utilitarian and homogenising environments that unsystematisable knowledges, experiences, and transgressive creative expressions will arise. We could expect environments with more human diversity to affirm a greater multiplicity of expression. At the same time, we acknowledge that racialised and gendered people are often working in more oppressive environments, especially on a global scale in the Global South, whose factories undoubtedly offer less leeway for creative expression, artisanal autonomy or hobbying knowledges in the workplace and beyond. We nevertheless expect that the exploitation and commodification of tacit and hobby knowledge remains a constant—this would be an important area for further study.

A broader ethical issue arises when we come to consider the usefulness of the knowledge produced by this research. A question arises as to whether the research might be useful to any of the participants or merely extractive (Bevington and Dixon 2005). In an attempt to offer something back to the organisations, we provided Research Reports to two of the organisations who expressed interest (CYBER4.0 and IEM). We frame the research—to our participants as well as to our readers—as an ethical intervention into how we see the future developing. We seek to understand the evolving relationship between humans and automative technologies within cybernetic systems, and we attempt to offer an ethical argument for collective emancipation. At the end of the day, all we can offer is yet another humble academic book, which exists alongside some incredibly powerful movements, platforms and discourses trying to shape society in a particular way—for example billionaires like Elon Musk, who mobilises cybernetic and transhumanist discourses; planned economies such as China making use of cybernetic technologies; global technocratic organisations such as the World Economic Forum; and an emerging discourse that positions developments in AI as both inevitable and as the only solution to flailing economics. Our book is a humble cautionary note to our undoubtedly small readership to be careful about the ideas you buy into.

Structure of the Book

In Chap. 2, we cover the history of cybernetics, with a focus on the utopian imaginaries and hope behind its historical vision. We also consider various strands of Left-utopian theorising that have grown out of the optimism of the cybernetic revolution, including Project Cybersyn, The New Left, Transhumanism and Extropianism, Fully Automated Luxury Communism, Actor Network Theory (ANT) and Anarchist Cybernetics. In Chap. 3, we critique all forms of cybernetic utopianism—including the mainstream, capitalist narrative as well as the seemingly more progressive Leftist uses of cybernetics and cyber-utopianism. We critique them in terms of their totalising tendencies, epistemological vanguardism, impoverished view of the human subject, and we conclude that cybernetics is a subordinating machine. In Chaps. 4–6, we centre the organisational studies in the order given above: CYBER4.0, IEM and London Hackspace. In order to answer our research questions, we structure the chapters using concepts we have identified in this introduction—covering concepts of prefigurative learning (tacit knowledge and hobbying) to consider how prefigurative forms of knowledge beyond cybernetics are present as emergent utopias within factories. We also consider a key concept from cybernetics—blackboxing and its common instantiation as the anthropomorphisation of machines—in order to consider the limitations of cybernetics and the way it is critiqued and transgressed by workers and their practices on the factory floor. To conclude each chapter, we consider the utopian possibilities and emergent, prefigurative utopian forms of knowledge within each type of organisation. In Chap. 7, the conclusion, we critique arguments concerning the naturalism of cybernetics as a model for economy, and for economic transformation, and examine utopian possibilities against and beyond cybernetics.

References

Ambrosini, V. and Bowman, C., 2001. Tacit Knowledge: Some Suggestions for Operationalization. *Journal of Management Studies*, 38(6), pp.811–829.

Ashby, W.R., 1957. An Introduction to Cybernetics. London: Chapman & Hall.

Bastani, A., 2019. Fully Automated Luxury Communism. London: Verso Books.

Beer, S., 1959. Cybernetics and Management. London: English Universities Press Ltd.

Beer, S., 1981. Brain of the Firm, 2nd edn. Chichester: John Wiley and Sons.

Bevington, D. and Dixon, C. 2005. Movement-relevant theory: Rethinking social movement scholarship and activism. *Social Movement Studies* 4(3), 2005, pp. 185–208.

Bloch, E., 1986 [1959]. The Principle of Hope [Vols 1–3], trans. Neville Plaice, Stephen Plaice & Paul Knight. Cambridge, MA: MIT Press.

Boggs, C., 1977. Marxism, prefigurative communism and the problem of workers' control. *Radical America*, 11(6), pp.99–122.

Choueiri, M., Duffy, S., Guria, S., McCarthy, C., Moure, P., Todalbagi, A., Wang, Y., Araujo de Aguiar, C.H. and Green, K.E., 2018. Can Interactive Systems Be Designed for Conviviality? A Case Study. In *Proceedings of the 2018 ACM Conference Companion Publication on Designing Interactive Systems* (pp.207–212).

Cole, D., 2018. The Life of Robert Owen. London: Routledge.

Collins, H., 2007. Bicycling on the Moon: Collective Tacit Knowledge and Somatic-Limit Tacit Knowledge. *Organization Studies*, 28(2), pp.257–262.

De Angelis, M. (2001). Marx and primitive accumulation: The continuous character of capital's 'enclosures'. The commoner, 2(1), 1–22.

Flyvbjerg, B. (2011). Case study. in Norman K. Denzin and Yvonna S. Lincoln, eds., The Sage Handbook of Qualitative Research, 4th Edition, 301–316. Sage. London.

Firth, R., 2013. Toward a Critical Utopian and Pedagogical Methodology. *Review of Education, Pedagogy, and Cultural Studies*, 35(4), pp.256–276.

Firth, R., 2019. Afterword. In Marie Louise Berneri, *Journey Through Utopia* (pp.331–392). Oakland: PM Press.

Firth, R., 2022. Disaster Anarchy: Mutual Aid and Radical Action. London: Pluto.

Franz, K., 2005. Tinkering: Consumers Reinvent the Early Automobile. Pennsylvania: University of Pennsylvania Press.

Gordon, U., 2009. Anarchism and the Politics of Technology. *WorkingUSA: Journal of Labor and Society*, 12(3), pp.489–503.

Harrison, J., 2009. Robert Owen and the Owenites in Britain and America (Routledge Revivals): The Quest for the New Moral World. Routledge.

Heljakka, K.I., 2018. More than collectors: Exploring theorists', hobbyists' and everyday players' rhetoric in adult play with character toys. *Games and Culture*, 13(3), pp.240–259.

Heljakka, K., 2023. Hobby Horses: A Hobby, Sport or Pure Play? A Contemporary Plaything as Part of Girlhood Leisure Activities in Finland. In: Mukherjee, U. (eds) Childhoods & Leisure . Leisure Studies in a Global Era. Cham: Palgrave Macmillan, https://doi.org/10.1007/978-3-031-33789-5_5

Hounshell, D., 1984. From the American System to Mass Production, 1800–1932: The Development of Manufacturing Technology in the United States. Baltimore: JHU Press.

Illich, I., 1973. Tools for Conviviality. New York: Harper and Row.

Joll, J., 1970. Anarchism—a Living Tradition. *Government and Opposition*, 5(4), pp.541–554.

König, W., 2004. Adolf Hitler vs. Henry Ford: The Volkswagen, the role of America as a model, and the failure of a Nazi consumer society. German Studies Review, pp.249–268.

Kostakis, V., Niaros, V. and Giotitsas, C., 2015. Production and Governance in Hackerspaces: A Manifestation of Commons-Based Peer Production in the Physical Realm? *International Journal of Cultural Studies*, 18(5), pp.555–573.

Krugh, M., 2014. Joy in Labour: The Politicization of Craft from the Arts and Crafts Movement to Etsy. *Canadian Review of American Studies*, 44(2), pp.281–301.

Lasi, H., Fettke, P., Kemper, H.G., Feld, T. and Hoffmann, M., 2014. Industry 4.0. *Business & Information Systems Engineering*, 6(4), pp.239–242.

Leonard, N. and Insch, G.S., 2005. Tacit Knowledge in Academia: A Proposed Model and Measurement Scale. *The Journal of Psychology*, 139(6), pp.495–512.

Levitas, R., 1990. The Concept of Utopia. New York: Syracuse University Press.

Marx, K., 1993. Grundrisse: Foundations of the Critique of Political Economy. London: Penguin.

Marx, K. (2024). *Capital: Critique of Political Economy, Volume 1*. Princeton: Princeton University Press.

Marx, K. and Engels, F., (1967). The Communist Manifesto London: Penguin

Minchin, T.J., 2021. The factory of the future. Historical Continuity and labor rights at Tesla. *Labor History, 62*(4), pp.434–453.

Moore, P. and Robinson, A., 2016. The quantified self: What counts in the neoliberal workplace. *New Media & Society*, 18(11), pp.2774–2792.

Mullin, J., (1982). Henry Ford and field and factory: an analysis of the Ford sponsored village industries experiment in Michigan, 1918–1941. *Journal of the American Planning Association*, 48(4), pp.419–431.

Myzelev, A., 2009. Whip your hobby into shape: Knitting, feminism and construction of gender. *Textile*, 7(2), pp.148–163.

Nonaka, I., 1991. The Knowledge-Creating Company. *Harvard Business Review*, 69(6), reprinted in *Harvard Business Review*, 85(7/8), pp.162–171.
Nozick, R., 1974. Anarchy, State, and Utopia. New York: Basic Books.
Parsons, T. and Smelser, N., 2005. Economy and Society: A Study in the Integration of Economic and Social Theory. Routledge.
Petts, J., 2008. Good Work and Aesthetic Education: William Morris, the Arts and Crafts Movement, and Beyond. *Journal of Aesthetic Education*, 42(1), pp.30–45.
Polanyi, M., 2009. The Tacit Dimension. Chicago: University of Chicago Press.
Popper, K., 2002 [1945]. The Open Society and Its Enemies, vol. 1. London: Routledge.
Preston, J., 2017. Competence Based Education and Training (CBET) and the End of Human Learning: The Existential Threat of Competency. London: Palgrave.
Prieur, R., 2011. TechJudge. Available at: http://www.ranprieur.com/tech.html [Accessed 6 August 2019].
Quarantelli, E.L. and Dynes, R.R., 1977. Response to Social Crisis and Disaster. *Annual Review of Sociology*, 3, pp.23–49.
Raekstad, P. and Gradin, S.S., 2020. Prefigurative Politics: Building Tomorrow Today. Cambridge: Polity.
Raunig, G., 2010. A Thousand Machines: A Concise Philosophy of the Machine as Social Movement. Los Angeles: Semiotext(e).
Rose, N., Aicardi, C., Mafoud, T., Reinsborough, M. and Burton, S., 2023. Looking Back on the Human Brain Project's Foresight Lab 2013–2020. In Bitsch, L. (ed.), *Ethics and Society in Brain Research: Implementing Responsible Research and Innovation (RRI) in the Human Brain Project (HBP)*. Human Brain Project, pp.16–19.
Rousseau, G.S. (ed.), 1990. The Languages of Psyche: Mind and Body in Enlightenment Thought. Univ of California Press.
Sargent, L.T., 1994. The Three Faces of Utopianism Revisited. *Utopian Studies*, 5(1), pp.1–37.
Schwab, K., 2017. The Fourth Industrial Revolution. New York: Currency Books.
Scott, J., 1990. Domination and the Arts of Resistance: Hidden Transcripts. New Haven and London: Yale University Press.
Sementelli, A., 2007. Toward a taxonomy of disaster and crisis theories. *Administrative Theory & Praxis*, 29(4), pp.497–512.
Smith, K.U. and Smith, M.F., 1966. Cybernetic Principles of Learning and Educational Design. New York: Holt, Rinehart and Winston.
Sohn-Rethel, A., (2020) Intellectual and Manual labour. A critique of epistemology (Vol. 224), Brill, Boston.
Srnicek, N., 2017. Platform Capitalism. New York: John Wiley & Sons.
Suvin, D., 2013. Theses on Dystopia 2001. In *Dark Horizons* (pp.199–214). London: Routledge.

Swann, T., 2020. Anarchist Cybernetics: Control and Communication in Radical Politics. Policy Press.
The Invisible Committee, 2015. *To Our Friends*, trans. Robert Hurley. Semiotext(e).
Wiener, N., 2019 [1948]. Cybernetics or Control and Communication in the Animal and the Machine. Cambridge, MA: MIT Press
Welch, D. (1993). Manufacturing a Consensus: Nazi Propaganda and the Building of a 'National Community'(Volksgemeinschaft). Contemporary European History, 2(1), pp.1–15.
Winch, C., 2017. Knowing 'Wh' and knowing how: Constructing professional curricula and integrating epistemic fields. *Journal of Philosophy of Education*, 51(2), pp.351–369.

CHAPTER 2

The Utopian Promise of Cybernetics

Cybernetics and Utopia

As we discussed in Chap. 1, cybernetics aims to be an exhaustive theory of every entity and relationship. It remains an influential theory, not only amongst technologists but in contemporary capitalist paradigms (Industry 4.0), and as a potential model for radical societies. The universal reach and utopianism of cybernetics can be surprising for those who consider it to be narrowly technocratic. Norbert Wiener, often referred to as the father of cybernetics, defined it as 'the scientific study of control and communication in the animal and machine' (Wiener 2019: 2). It is a trans-disciplinary approach applicable to mechanical, physical, cognitive, biological and social systems. Although cybernetics imposes a monadic structure on reality and ideas, expecting them to accord with cybernetic mapping, it is amenable to a utopian lens due to its holism and belief in a formalised model.

Cybernetics exhibits many surprising affinities and parallels with utopianism, and it is therefore unsurprising but not unproblematic that it has been taken up by a variety of progressive and radical thinkers. As a broad interdisciplinary approach, encompassing epistemological and normative strands, it articulates elements of a vision (of the seamless integration of humans and machines into self-managing systems) and a process (systemic, open-ended, allowing for adaptation through feedback mechanisms). Reading cybernetics alongside utopianism helps get to the heart of the relationship between the affective desiring-imaginary of non-alienated labour/subjectivity and the external integration of the human as a machinic

R. Firth, J. Preston, *Utopia in the Factory*,
https://doi.org/10.1007/978-3-031-87132-0_2

'node' into a system. This presents us with an unavoidable contradiction between non-alienated human liberation on the one hand and a mechanistic modality on the other which is at the crux of our critique of cybernetics.

There are many rhizomic and/or synchronic connections between cybernetics and utopianism. Cybernetics as a field of study for understanding systems arose around the same time as did utopian studies as a discipline for understanding utopias (not to be confused with the canon itself). Both arose during WWII and gained popularity in its aftermath. In its heyday, cybernetics was used to describe, understand and intervene in all kinds of phenomena, from experiments in children's playgrounds and a modular theme park (Pertigkiozoglou 2017; Sweeting 2016), experiments in planned socialist economies (Medina 2014), trends in management discourse (Boltanski and Chiapello 2007), eventually becoming a metaphor for the totality of capitalism itself (Ouellet 2010). Cybernetics is deeply imbricated in utopian discourse: its corpus creates detailed and specific visions of systems in equilibrium, that are empowered and better able to meet the goals of all their individual members. Despite this emphasis on improvement through a 'system-vision', cybernetic thought often claims not to express a blueprint or closed vision but rather imagines adaptive processes subject to feedback mechanisms. This is similar to visions of utopia as a process rather than a goal, expressed by antecedents of the Frankfurt School, including Ernst Bloch and Karl Mannheim, who imagined utopia as having critical, organising and potentially transformative functions in relation to social and material contradictions (Bloch 1986; Mannheim 2013).

The role of science and technology in utopia has been a long-running theme, and cybernetic-like utopias and dystopias which seek to integrate humans and machines as 'cogs in a machine', 'nodes in a system', 'workers in a planned economy' or (with a more positive, anarchistic tenor) 'grassroots organisers' in a system predate Norbert Wiener's use of the word cybernetics. Etymologically, the term 'cybernetics' can be traced back to that renowned utopian—Plato—whose dialogue *Alcibiades* portrays Socrates likening the art of governance to steering a ship, using the Ancient Greek word κυβερνήτης (Plato 1997 in Swann 2015: 15). In her book *Journey Through Utopia*, originally published in 1950, Marie Louise Berneri (2019) provides a comprehensive critical compendium of utopian writing since Plato. The integration of humans into hybrid techno-social machines is a recurring theme which finds its particular expression during the early Renaissance, Enlightenment and Industrial Revolution periods

(Berneri 2019)—arguably all periods of intensified technological development prefiguring the recomposition of capital into new forms (Wallerstein 2020). Utopias often express contradictions in society by articulating desires that are not realised within the prior social forms and therefore can contain an element of futurology, as they both express and mobilise new social forces that are taking shape. Francis Bacon's utopia *New Atlantis*, published posthumously in 1627, included the first description of an elite technocracy in a scientific college (Solomon's House) and the renovation of society through science, with scientists forming effectively a separate State within the State, where scientists wield immense power and monopoly over knowledge, seeking progress through the satisfaction of material needs, and the organisation of scientific research into a strict division of labour between explorers, collectors and field scientists with rigidly limited roles subordinated to the mechanical organisation of Solomon's House (Berneri 2019: 126–137). In the nineteenth century, Etienne Cabet's super-efficient factory machines for industrial production sought to establish a 'community of goods' and an 'equality of abundance', in the context of a society ruled by a representative democracy operating as a kind of machine, divided into 15 principle committees governing every aspect of life (Berneri 2019: 219–235). Dystopian satirists have also shown us that techno-social cyber-systems can be a force for evil, for example Zamyatin's 1921 novel involving integration of the timekeeping watch into the 'human mechanism' and his torture bell jar and electrical execution device, all of which were analogies for an over-arching authoritarian system which subjugated the human (Zamyatin 2020).

Cybernetic Capitalism, Consumption and Tech-Utopianism

A zealous faith underpins the transcendent potential of cybernetics. Norbert Wiener's obsession with the machine has been interpreted as a form of 'enchantment' that veered towards the spiritual and the cultish (Rid 2016: xii). In his narrative history of cybernetics, Thomas Rid argues that this religiosity acted as a basis for the direct translation and repackaging of military technology into industrial and consumerist contexts (Rid 2016: xii). Cybernetics transcendent meta-theoretical apparatus, and appeal to a formalist rigour, made it an ideal tool for management gurus, market researchers, advertising agencies and economic planners. Eventually

Wiener disowned his military past, rejecting funding from Boeing and invoking Nagasaki and Hiroshima to express his fears for technological futures. Nevertheless, he repackaged cybernetics for industry and consumer purposes, which Rid argues played a huge role in the post-war recomposition of capital, whereby 'engineers, military thinkers, politicians, scholars, artists, and activists started projecting their hopes and fears into the future of thinking machines' (Rid 2016: xii). After WWII, at the same time that it was playing important roles in Cold War mobilising and in capitalist recomposition, cybernetics as an emerging discipline also drew explicitly on the creative visions and energies of the utopian communard movement of the 1960s–1970s. Rid argues that the dual nature of cybernetics prefigured both dystopian and utopian visions: 'By the 1960s cybernetic inspired technologies gave rise to solutions diverging from exoskeletons to load nuclear bombers, as well as to deeper connections among wholesome hippies' (Rid 2016: xii–xiii). Cybernetics became a repository for a wide variety of both transformative and consumerist desires. Rid interprets cybernetics in a similar vein to conventional understandings of utopia: as 'a myth' that is ever projected into the future, which overcomes the limits of experience and possibility whilst adding 'emotional form to meaning' by appealing to hopes and fears about the future of technology and society (Rid 2016: xiv). Myths also embed claims about the future, positioning the cybernetician as a futurologist, and also as a hero, at the forefront of colonising cyberspace as a new frontier (Rid 2016: xiv). Boosterism, hyperbole and mythology have been a major part of the cybernetic story.

Throughout its development, Rid argues, two 'opposing' forces and their corresponding (implicit) utopian visions have shaped cybernetic visions of the future. One vision invests emerging technologies with utopian hope for a better world with less violence, more humane working conditions, and more democratic and liberating politics. The second invests emerging technologies with dystopian fears of 'robots pushing workers into unemployment, machines harming humans, systems breaking down, mass surveillance, mechanized regression' (Rid 2016: 4). These utopian and dystopian visions inflected oppositional movements and counterculture as much as mainstream society, although in somewhat different ways.

Fred Turner (2006) argues the rise of the internet was suffused by 'talk of revolution' and the potential of the internet to 'flatten society', to democratise politics, bring a global and cosmopolitan culture into being that would end wars, and to decentralise control and authority. The 'digital generation' would be 'playful, self-sufficient, psychologically whole' (Turner 2006: 1). Computers were associated with a 'countercultural dream of empowered individualism, collaborative community, and spiritual communion' (Turner 2006: 2). Turner problematises the 'utopian claims surrounding the emergence of the internet', including ideas that it would level hierarchies, drive the establishment of intimate decentralised communities, and render individuals more authentic and psychologically whole (Turner 2006: 3). He asks the vital questions: 'where did these visions come from? And who enlisted computing machines to represent them?' (Turner 2006: 3). He then traces the history and power relations behind the rise of extraordinarily influential San Francisco Bay area journalists and entrepreneurs in particular Stewart Brand, the author of the *Whole Earth Catalogue*. In the 1960s–1990s, Brand brokered a series of meetings and encounters between bohemians in San Francisco and the emerging technology hub of Silicon Valley. The Whole Earth Catalogue has been described as a precursor to the internet, and was many things at once—an American counter-cultural magazine, as well as a catalogue of tools, many with a focus on self-sufficiency and getting 'back to the land' that coincided with huge movement of hippies to rural intentional communities built on utopian ideas of ecotopia. It also featured essays, articles and opinion pieces with an optimistic and humorous tone. It did not sell products directly, but listed sellers details, and gave advice and tips for buying from international vendors and intentionally facilitated international trade, advocating for example the cost benefits of buying camera equipment from Asia, while blending consumer culture with hippy culture giving instructions on how to build a tipi or geodesic dome, or how to identify magic mushrooms (Whole Earth Catalog, 1968–1998).

In 1985, Brand gathered entrepreneurs via a conferencing system—the Whole Earth 'Lectronic Link, or WELL, including well-known leaders of the Californian Ideology and cyber-utopianism, including Kevin Kelly, Howard Rheingold, Esther Dyson and John Perry Barlow—all of whom also contributed to the formation of the ongoing magazine, *Wired*. Their vision was somewhere between an epistemology, a utopia and a religion: 'they began to imagine institutions as living organisms, social networks as webs of information, and the gathering and interpretation of information as keys to understanding not only the technical, but also the natural and social worlds' (Turner 2006: 4). Turner links the cybernetic view of the emerging Silicon Valley community with the tech-savvy, tool-desiring consumerist culture embodied in Stewart Brand's *Whole Earth Catalogue*, to the counter-cultural vision of the back-to-the-land intentional communities movement of the late 1960s to early 1970s, who gave up work in the cities 'to establish communes in the mountains and woods' because, Turner argues, they were disillusioned with 'traditional political mechanisms for creating social change' (Turner 2006: 4).

Intentional communities (in Turner's terminology, 'communes') have been interpreted in the utopian studies canon as grassroots utopias in practice, where people choose to live and work together for reasons other than kinship or profit, often in order to enhance their shared values and exemplify the future they want to see (Firth 2012). This turn towards more ethical and meaningful lifestyles in the 1960s–1970s coincided with the emerging abandonment of Fordism as the organising principle of the economy. For Turner, the intentional communities movement was inseparable from the capitalist consumer culture of the Whole Earth Catalogue that attempted to commodify it—the movement was already complicit and imbricated in capitalism and capitalist utopias. Initially, social movement radicals, along with many of the general public, saw computers as technologies of dehumanisation, centralised bureaucracy and the rationalisation of social life, and the strategic mobilisation of killing logics in the Vietnam War. Yet in 1990s the symbols of Cold War technocracy became the instruments of its transformation, as room-sized computers shrank to communication devices that could be used for creative purposes at home. Computers poised to bring to life the 'countercultural dream of empowered individualism, collaborative community, and spiritual communion' (Rid 2016: 2).

The most important event for technological utopianism after the Cold War was the birth and growth of the internet. The optimism and technological determinism of the early internet days (late 1990s to the early 2000s) led to a period where many saw the internet as a utopian force for democratisation and bottom-up cosmopolitanism. This gave birth to a swathe of pro-system utopias from the 1980s onwards, which sought to institute a rational form of governance by reconfiguring relations between humans and machines using new forms of technology, communications and networked organisation (The Invisible Committee 2015). Labelled 'The Californian Ideology', after its roots in Silicon Valley it blended libertarian attitudes prevalent in California since the 1960s, such as anti-authoritarian values, counterculture and drug-taking with techno-utopianism and free market economics. Barbrook and Cameron argue that the Californian Ideology appeared liberatory and empowering, yet it was elitist and racist, since it concealed the conditions of production of the technologies required to sustain it, as well as the exclusivity inherent in its fetishised commodities and processes of valorisation (Barbrook and Cameron 1996).

As the internet developed, a global orthodoxy emerged regarding the relationship between society, politics and technology that drew heavily on cybernetics. This had some rebellious and revolutionary aspects—for example crypto-anarchy movements against government attempts to regulate cyphers, and the idea that cryptocurrency could resist mass surveillance of cash spending. The utopian vision developed in a radical direction in the 1990s out of hacker culture, FLOSS (Free, Libre and Open-Source Software) and piracy, including people who thought self-organising systems would eclipse capitalism and the state and bring about a better world. This vision largely disappeared with the rise of social media and data mining in the 2000s, but it is in the background of media imaginaries when social movements in the Global South use new technologies (in terms of, for example, 'Twitter Revolutions' and in the adoption of Afrofuturist imagery in popular culture and advertising). It is notable that many of these utopias have been pro-capitalist but anti-state; for example, there is an ongoing belief amongst some libertarians that cryptocurrency, and technologies such as blockchain, might make the state obsolete (Rid 2016: 247–293).

The Californian Ideology was the target of critique from the beginning as being recuperated by neoliberal capitalist values (Barbrook and Cameron, 44). This critique will be covered in more detail below in the more general critique of cybernetics, but what is important to note at this point is that many authors portray the pro-tech movement as being ultimately embedded in the hippy movement and intentional communities movement, as though these radical movements were always-already recuperated and/or pro-capitalist. This viewpoint does not allow for a sense of utopian agency that is autonomous or looks/prefigures beyond capitalism.

Barbrook and Cameron tell a more complex story of a split movement. There was a shared utopia inspired by 'ecotopia': a future California where cars had disappeared, industrial production was ecologically viable, sexual relationships were egalitarian and daily life was lived in community groups, yet for some 'this vision could only be realised by rejecting scientific progress as a false God and returning to nature', whilst for others 'technological progress would inevitably turn their libertarian principles into social fact' (Barbrook and Cameron 1996: 48). This split can be further complexified by looking at how progressive strands in the Left have variously interpreted and developed the mutating relationships between humans and machines that have occurred in the late twentieth and early twenty-first centuries.

Cybernetics and the Progressive Left

Various strands of utopian theorising have grown out of the optimism of the cybernetic revolution that also drew heavily on earlier strands of twentieth-century utopian thought outlined previously in this chapter. Not all of these theories explicitly identify or embrace the definition as 'cybernetic' in principle, nor necessarily as 'utopian'; however, they do draw on some of the key concepts of cybernetics, and they are utopian in the sense that they invest their critiques and visions with hopes and fears based on desired futures. In this section, we focus mainly on the progressive Left, which is generally associated the with idea of linear historical progress towards the goal of a more equal and fairer society. This contrasts with the prefigurative Left, associated with anarchism, which will be covered after. The idea of linear progress is associated with single-vision, goal-oriented blueprint utopias which rely on statist epistemology rather than (our preferred model) prefigurative alternatives which derive their visions from grassroots creativity and democracy.

Project Cybersyn

One unique, and much-cited, example of how a cybernetic utopia was concretely manifested as a tool of socialism was its use in Chile between 1971 and 1973 during the presidency of Salvador Allende. This project, which was referred to in the previous chapter, is laid out in great detail in Eden Medina's ground-breaking work *Cybernetic Revolutionaries*, where she describes Project Cybersyn as the 'intersection of two utopian visions': the political vision of Chilean socialism, and the technological vision of cybernetics (Medina 2014: 3). Chilean socialism attempted to institute a socialist society peacefully through existing institutions, while the Cybersyn version of cybernetics 'attempted to build a computer system for real-time economic control more than twenty years before the Internet became a feature of everyday life' (Medina 2014: 3). The project was built in close collaboration with Stafford Beer based on his Viable Systems Model (VSM) and consisted of a network of telex machines that would monitor key production indicators on material supplies and worker absenteeism. This attempted to correct anomalies by alerting workers or in more drastic situations by sending information to the central government. Decisions on responses to emergencies would be made by managers in a centralised Control Room, with directives issued via the telex network. This illustrates how cybernetics, despite seeming to operate according to a decentralising logic, also embedded monitoring and top-down control functions: workers were expected to behave in ways that were modelled and planned, with deviation reported upwards and directives cascaded downwards. This was designed to 'help the state regulate the nationalized economy and raise production without unemployment' (Medina 2014: 211). The project was eventually abandoned after the military coup because its ethos of state planning and stability ran counter to neoliberal 'shock treatments' and disaster capitalism (although, as argued previously, not all versions of cybernetics are incompatible with neoliberal capitalism). The project was a top-down utopia in the sense that it was initiated by a government keen to use communications and computer technology to bring about structural change, and also illustrates how computer technologies embed political values in the design of technical systems (Medina 2014: 212). Beer and early members of the Cybersyn team tried to design a system that would enhance Chilean democratic socialism; for example, they limited the number of production indicators collected both to prevent unprocessable amounts of information and to guard against 'micromanagement and abuse', and they also designed the control room in a way that managers were seated in a circle and all had control of the display technology in order to encourage equal participation (Medina 2014: 213). Stafford Beer saw his project as contributing to 'experiments in social democracy' (Beer 1981: 384) and spreading 'industrial democracy' (Beer 1981: 346). In light of critiques of the project he proposed further interventions such as having representatives of different interest groups in the control room (Beer 1981: 370).

Nevertheless, opposition forces and international onlookers criticised the system as a tool for totalitarian control (Medina 2014: 213). Chile became an experiment for monetarist and neoliberal economics. The Austrian school of economics, particularly in the work of Hayek and Mises, as an epistemology underlying neoliberalism (and to some extent, monetarism), was fundamentally opposed to attempts to plan economies or societies. According to Hayek and Mises, it is not possible for a cybernetic (or any other) system to substitute for individual actions and intentions which are best met through emergent mechanisms such as markets. Although Hayek had an interest in concepts in cybernetics (Oliva 2015) to justify his principles of a spontaneous social order, Project Cybersyn can be seen as the antithesis of Austrian liberalism as it was motivated by socialist planning. Although apparently informed by decentralising impulses including the redistribution of control, involvement of workers in planning, and granting autonomy to workers and workplaces except in situations of extreme instability, Project Cybersyn is in many ways reminiscent of the modernist utopias of the nineteenth century. Similarly to the utopian socialists critiqued by Marx and Engels, the Chilean cybernetic project built a blueprint for a democratic society that could be engineered from the top-down through a blueprint for sociotechnical design. Cybernetics and related mathematical planning and programming techniques were also part of Soviet planning and utilised in Eastern European socialist societies, as well as in China, Cuba and North Korea. Despite the utopian vision of these societies, design-based solutions to human problems will always embed assumptions about value and about the scale and organisation of communities that crystalise the particular assumptions, beliefs and desires of a specific group of technocrats. Even if, for example, a human community were to be built completely from the bottom-up and by consensus then it would crystalise the values of the particular group involved in the decisions, and excluding, for example, future generations, nature, animals, and even the repressed desires of participants. Furthermore, it is quite possible to repurpose democratic technology in authoritarian ways, meaning that social solutions by technical design are always vulnerable to the eruption and shock of the 'other' when their ostensible purpose is stability.

Blueprint utopias derive from a view of the human subject as both an irrational Hobbesian beast who can only become civilised through discipline and control, as well as a rational-choice subject vulnerable to manipulation and nudges. These kinds of approaches sideline alternatives (such as psychoanalytic) that see humans as complex beings with conflicting desires and urges formed in part through their various situational and relational assemblages, and through unconscious psychoanalytic urges and authentic, embodied desires. On the contrary, they treat the inner emotional life of individuals as something to be quantified—as 'libidinal strip mines' (Beller 2018: 11 quoted in Ström 2022: 40). They also make assumptions about the autonomy of technological, formalist and statist solutions that have not developed independently of capitalism (to increase exploitation) and which are antithetical to human freedom. While this view of the human subject has continued to the present day, there have also been trends within the New Left that sought to critique this modernist view of humanity, yet continued to embrace aspects of cybernetic utopias.

The New Left, Postmodernism and Posthumanism

Around the same time as Chile tried to combine decentralising cybernetic utopias with a socialist humanism, theoretical and social movements in the Global North were producing ideologies that attempted to critique and ultimately supersede ontologies of the modernist human, with implications for utopianism/utopian studies, and for cybernetic utopias. The New Left social movements of the late 1960s and the 1970s were partly composed of feminist, black and gay radicals who broke with existing Marxist organisations, because they tended to be dominated by straight white men who claimed to represent interests of a homogeneous working class. Some of these groups created movements to decentralise power and resistance, such as feminist consciousness-raising groups, a movement which encompassed hundreds of thousands of women. These were small, voluntary, women-only discussion groups that met regularly to discuss the political aspects of personal relationships and everyday life (Shreve 1989). This was reflective of a broader historical concern to create movements that would allow diverse people to express their desires without vanguard or elite representation.

In the following decade in France and throughout Europe, a group of theories now called postmodernism or poststructuralism began to take shape in reaction to the critique of Marxism. At this time, many left-wing thinkers believed that utopianism died when the Berlin Wall fell in 1989. Enthusiasm for a rupture or insurrection was abandoned in favour of more modest, tactical gains in the present (Habermas 1986). While many post-structural theorists did not identify their work as utopian nor deal with utopianism explicitly, there are utopian themes in their work. In particular, they articulate desires for a less exploitative and alienating society, and they valorise grassroots creative processes (Deleuze and Guattari 1987).

Postmodernism and poststructuralism form the literature basis of posthuman theories outlined below. Postmodern thinkers like Lyotard focused on critiquing modernist universalism and grand narratives, and linear progress in science and epistemology (Lyotard 1984), which have influenced posthumanist ideas of decentring human knowledge and human moral and social goods as the foundation of history and progress. Foucault focused on the relationship between power and knowledge, and the way that these are used for social control through institutions. His work has influenced posthumanist critiques of the idea of 'man' as a universal category (Deleuze 1988: 65), situating the concept as a techno-social assemblage, tied to particular regimes of power/knowledge which entraps wider forms of life (Behrent 2013: 65). This has been developed into a critique of cybernetics (Deleuze 1988: 131), where humans and machines are sometimes treated as interchangeable units of labour (Deleuze 1988: 131; Deleuze and Guattari 1987: 510–512), although it will be argued later that it also influences some posthuman theories which embed technological determinism in cybernetic utopias. Another influence on posthuman cybernetic utopias is Derrida's deconstructive semiotic analysis, which provided a method of questioning and transgressing the dominant assumptions and subverting binary thinking of Western philosophy, culture and discourse (Derrida 1976). Derrida's work inspires posthumanists who celebrate the potential for technology to subvert dominant binaries and thereby undermine social oppression. Posthumanists reject ontological separation of humans from other kinds of objects and the anthropocentrism of modern thought (Zolkos 2018; Macris 2012; Lewis and Kahn 2010). In Derridean terms, it 'interrogates the relations among the terms in the cybernetic triangle of human/animal/machine' (Snaza et al. 2014: 40). Another key poststructural influence on posthumanism is Lacan, a psychoanalyst who focuses on the idea of desire, which is characterised by lack, as a means of relating to the Other/alterity. For Lacanians and Derridians, the Other is ultimately unknowable and unreachable. There is somewhat of a split between Lacanian theories and those inspired by Deleuze, who views desire as a productive force and therefore able to produce autonomous lifeworlds through authentic connections with the Other.

Postmodernists tend to be openly critical of modernist narratives of 'progress', and some thinkers, particularly those in the Deleuzian tradition, create theoretical conditions of possibility for understanding radical prefigurative alternatives. Nevertheless, there is still a paradoxical strand of technological determinism and temporal linearity running through many poststructural and posthumanist authors (encapsulated even in the prefix 'post' in names of these schools of thought). Posthumanism is a group of theories and social movements that are focused on subverting binaries between humans and non-human nature, animals and technology. It draws heavily on the postmodernist and poststructural theories outlined above, particularly the aspects that focus on critiquing and subverting essentialist categories such as 'man' and 'human nature', and there is a particular focus on critiquing Western humanism and its corresponding anthropocentric liberal subjectivity which relies upon dichotomous thinking that separates self from other. This is often valued *as such*, regardless of the extent to which technology might undermine other oppressive forces such as capitalism or the state. The underlying purpose of these theories is an ontological and an ethical imperative to more accurately and ethically understand our place in the world and relationship with non-human nature. Posthumanists therefore tend to value processes of becoming-other and decentring binaries understood to be immanent in technological/cybernetic assemblages. They tend to be enemies of *modernity*, within which 'humanism', 'the human', 'reason' and 'the subject' are necessarily enmeshed. Oppressions and violence (against women, humans, nature, animals) are seen to be rooted in linguistic binaries which operate pre-subjectively through interpellation. Modernity elevates 'Man' as subject of power and knowledge over its others, and this needs to be humbled or dispensed with. The utopianism (such as it is) of posthumanism is vaguer than many of the progressive Left, because of a basis in Derridean/Lacanian theories of 'lack'—utopia always appears as something unthinkable, unknowable, impossible, deferred. A trace of utopia appears in the form of perfect hospitality and care within self-other fusion in infinite responsibility for each other (which is also taken as unachievable but is a form of regulatory ideal). Coenen argues that although posthumanism is often deemed utopian, particularly insofar as there is a proclivity for engineering approaches to reality, particularly the idea of re-engineering human nature, 'the fulfilment of utopian longings appears to be at most a side effect of really important developments, even in left-wing posthumanist visions' (Coenen 2007: 151). Not all posthumanists are techno-futurists, with some tending to focus on relationships with nature and animals (Cudworth 2005, 2011), and rather than a focus on changing human nature the emphasis is on affirming the always-already animalistic aspects or exploring existing enmeshments with nature that cannot be systematised. Animal studies perspectives would hold that animal knowledges also cannot be codified in a cybernetic system (though their 'behaviours' can), and animals would be unlikely to desire to fulfil cybernetic roles, although some animals can certainly be trained or domesticated to do so. Critical animal studies literature looks at the transgressive and co-constructive nature of animal-human knowledges and relationships that alter both human and animal needs and desires in ways that create emergent systems with the potential to disrupt, resist and transform global power dynamics (Cudworth and Hobden 2011). These forms of posthumanism (often drawing on the Deleuzian rather than the Lacanian tradition) are compatible with our approach. After all, humans are animals too. The cybernetic framework assumes (like a State) that it can incorporate (and automate!) not only every existent entity but also all future entities and collectives. A cybernetics that is interested and colonising of every inorganic or organic entity is impossible.

Some theories of the posthuman seek to overcome binaries not merely as a means to undermine old modernist categories and oppressions but in pursuit of 'the perfection of mind, body and spirit' in an individualistic and narcissistic sense, associated with the capitalist strands of the Californian Ideology, which Barbrook and Cameron (1996) argue is divorced from a critique of capitalism and therefore merely a way of mediating the reality of dependence on forced labour. These theories are part of a large cluster of progressivist and teleological utopian thought under the cybernetic umbrella, sharing an underlying belief in historical teleology, evolution and improvement, articulated in various terminologies yet reflecting original cybernetic works in terms of themes of evolution, adaptation, learning, feedback and improvement—sometimes given almost religious connotations. Humanity in these theories is almost seen as conduit in nature's self-evolution towards ever greater perfection or efficiency; for example, Kevin Kelly, a leading editor of *Whole Earth Review* and *Wired Magazine*, expresses faith in a hivemind or technium, which is a holistic aggregate of humans, computers and nature (Kelly 1994: 174; cf. Kelly 2010). Complex systems (including markets and AIs) in these theories are alive, intelligent and smarter than humans. We need to surrender control to them (Kelly 1994: 233, 264, 289). This is less apparent in the related policy-relevant/evidence-based literature, but there seem to be similar fantasies at work there in a more muted form—such as the smart city as providing social integration through feedback and sensors (Gupta et al. 2019) and blockchain utopias (Schwab 2017). This strand of technological optimism in posthumanism blends into the transhumanist movement.

Transhumanism and Extropianism

Transhumanism is a political and philosophical movement that seeks to transform humanity through technological enhancement and modification. The transhumanist movement is politically complex with splits between right-wing, left-wing and centrist strands, as well as strands concerned with transcending different human limits. Examples include postgenderism (Dvorsky and Hughes 2008), which seeks to transcend biological limits and transgress binary gender categories, as a development from the work of Shulamith Firestone (1970), who advocated reproductive technologies to free women from childbirth, alongside some literary feminist utopias that portrayed cryogenic childbirth (e.g. Piercy 1976). Extropianism, particularly associated with the work of Max More, advocates overcoming the necessities of human labour and private property through the use of robots and artificial intelligence (More 2003). Techno-Gaianism develops eco-utopian themes while also advocating the development and use of new technologies, such as clean energy, climate engineering, and genetically engineered crops to meet the needs of the population while countering the effects of climate change and restoring the Earth's environment. Techno-Gaians believe in the eventual assimilation of humans and all bio-organisms into the collective consciousness of Gaia through electronic means (Howard 1998). Transhumanists and extropians promote overcoming biological limits and augmenting humans using new technologies. Like humanists, transhumanists favour 'reason, critical inquiry, intellectual independence, and honesty … rejecting blind faith'; however, they also see humanity as a 'transitional stage between our animal heritage and our posthuman future' (More 2003). New technologies can be used to become more-than-human, exceeding previously naturalised limits to the human condition. Examples include the idea of 'uploading' human consciousness into immortal robots or computers (Hanson 1994) or using Human Robot Interaction (HRI) to achieve immortality. One branch of this literature focuses on the 'Singularity', or a possible future point at which AI will surpass human intelligence. While this is recognised as posing existential dangers to humans, it is treated either as a means by which humanity transcends itself or a fulfilling of humanity's destiny on an evolutionary ladder. This is a teleological theory which invests existing technologies with utopian hopes for a better future and seems generally uncritical about the potentially dangerous and exploitative effects of technologies. In particular, AI itself, which is often considered by transhumanists as a source of the singularity, has been viewed as an existential threat by many technologists, including Nobel Prize winner, and inventor of artificial neural networks, Geoffrey Hinton. Some thinkers associated with cybernetics *stricto sensu* also have a foot in the transhumanist camp, such as aforementioned Kevin Kelly, who views cybernetic control as vital in harnessing complex systems: transhumanism might encourage individual diversity in hybrid forms, and complex systems preclude top-down control and state planning, but do not preclude cybernetic control through manipulating inputs and selecting outputs (Kelly 1994: 105–106, 281–282). Individuals are allowed to proliferate, but then are judged by performance, and selected-out through 'the destruction of the unfit' (Kelly 1994: 313–314) and the survival of a handful of 'chosen' beings from the 'random' field of noise (Kelly 1994: 236). This leads to utopias relating to perfect information flow and smooth systems, with eugenicist undertones. For example, Kelly's discussions of circular economies, in visions which reconcile ecology with capitalism and growth.

As an extreme example of a progressivist ideology, transhumanism is both cybernetic and utopian, but it is not a prefigurative grassroots utopia, it is a teleological and totalising utopia, where the embodied individual/subject is sacrificed to a perceived ideal future, as well as subjected to an idealised quasi-religious vision of the self-expansion of life, in which humans are simply a vector. Although control mechanisms are perceived as horizontal and networked, this approach has obvious authoritarian implications that are at odds with critical/prefigurative/grassroots utopias. Transhumanist/extropian positions are only utopian in a narrow and formal sense—they offer descriptive and detailed visions of a 'better world' involving the possibility and desirability of using advances in technology to improve human bodies and intelligence, ultimately transforming the human condition through elements such as bionic implants, cognitive enhancement and medical advances to prolong lifespan towards immortality, and have been heavily criticised for the nature of that utopia by primitivists and techno-pessimists (Kingsnorth 2015; Prieur 2005). Transhumanist utopias have been parodied by techno-pessimist authors as dystopias—for example in Baudrillard's Clone Story on the implications for the body (Baudrillard 2000).

FALC and Left-Accelerationism

Other left-futurist cybernetic visions include Fully Automated Luxury Communism (FALC) and left-accelerationism. These are subtly different theories, but they are grouped together because they have similar relationships to the utopian impulse, perceiving within present technologies the possibility of total automation and post-capitalism. FALC began as a jocular meme in London activist circles and was since developed by Aaron Bastani and other followers of the paradigm who make the explicitly 'utopian demand' for the automation of all labour processes in order to free humans from the need to work, alongside social ownership of all means of production (Bastani 2019). Similarly to transhumanism, FALC has an optimistic vision of the ability of technology to meet human desires without impacting negatively on the planet or exacerbating human inequality. Accelerating such technologies will apparently destroy capitalism and produce socialism through full automation and a universal basic income (UBI) (Srnicek and Williams 2015). With 'a taste for the thrill of the fast, the metallic and the new' (Pitts and Dinerstein 2017: 82), this theory embraces nearly all emerging technologies, including cyborg augmentations, artificial life, biotechnology, automation and econometric modelling (Reed 2014: 529). Accelerationism originated with the work of Nick Land (now associated with the dark enlightenment, neo-reaction and other 'right' leaning forms of accelerationism) and the Cybernetic Cultures Research Unit (CCRU) (Land 2014; CCRU 2017). Although it is similar to FALC, insofar as it seeks an intensification of capitalist sociotechnical infrastructure, accelerationism surpasses FALC in its abandonment of humanist and democratic residues, embracing the drive for 'a new posthuman state beyond any form of the subject, excepting the delirious processes of capital itself' (Noys 2014: 8). Some accelerationist philosophies critique cybernetics as being overtly obsessed with control (cybernegative processes) rather than with out-of-control feedback processes (the cyberpositive) (Plant and Land 1994), but even the cyber-positive uses the cybernetic notion of feedback in its formulation. Benjamin Noys argues that accelerationism is a cultural phenomenon that undergoes historical resurgences during particular conditions of capitalism and is indicative of intensified alienation in times of crisis (Noys 2014). The FALC/left-accelerationist cluster are unashamedly utopian but in a teleological and technologically determinist way. Although they seek social ownership of the means of production, they are uncritical about aspects of capitalist technology and the ways in which it embeds capitalist values. Within these discourses there is a somewhat simplistic, and populistic, assumption that it will be easier for people to take control of the means of production once everything is automated. With these assumptions, FALC is optimistic that the material substrate of capital (commodities and machinery) is separable from capital (as a form of value production based on the exploitation of labour by capital), which, in motion, is capitalism. Although the 'means of production' might be seized by the working class (although in FALC it is not clear how this should be done, other than by populist methods), this assumes that technology that evolved in the interests of capital can not only be repurposed but that the trajectory, and acceleration, of that technology is in the interests of the working class. This imagines that the tools of capital, created by the ruling class as forms of despotism the purpose of which was to exploit the working class, can be redeployed as tools of liberation.

FALC also attempts (somewhat unsuccessfully) to distance itself from Landian accelerationism. Land considers that a technological future will lead to capital itself becoming a technological monad which cannot be constrained by humanity. In contrast, FALC inserts a popularist working-class movement as seizing (at an undefined point of technological sophistication) scientific progress and the means of production. Both perspectives are equally uncritical of the path-dependency of technology in capitalism. Land is optimistic considering the independence of capital, perhaps through AI, from even the control of big-tech capitalists whereas FALC is optimistic considering the reappropriation of technologies designed to subjugate and oppress. Both are convinced that they have identified the key agent of historical technological determinism (respectively AI/capital and populist working-class movements) which will replace capitalism. As we discuss in the next chapter, there are problems with the technological and teleological assumptions associated with cybernetic accelerationism.

Actor Network Theory and Object-Oriented Ontology

Actor Network Theory (ANT) and Object-Oriented Ontology (OOO) are relatively new theories influenced by poststructuralism that are currently popular in critical Science and Technology Studies (STS). ANT is designed to explore relations in a network, foregoing explanation—knowledge is not a transcendental real but rather one practice amongst others (Law 2004: 175; Latour 1999). ANT sees knowledge-production and practice as forms of intervention which change the world, and rejects strong social constructivism, technological determinism and essentialism. ANT's flat ontology is compatible with decentralised cybernetic soft power because of the difficulty in motivating choices among assemblages, its embrace of manipulative power and the de-emphasising of human agency (Harman 2018: 136–139). ANT works with cybernetic ideas of 'blackboxing' but is critical of rendering the conditions of scientific/technological production invisible, and many works in ANT take on tasks of de-blackboxing technology consistent with practices of hacking and of tracing power within networks (Latour 1999: 314). Seminal ANT theorist Latour describes blackboxing as 'the way scientific and technical work is made invisible by its own success. When a machine runs efficiently, when a matter of fact is settled, one need focus only on its inputs and outputs and not on its internal complexity. Thus, paradoxically, the more science and technology succeed, the more opaque and obscure they become' (Latour 1999: 314). As a mode of study, ANT is satisfied to remain at the level of blackboxed nodes, so long as the model succeeds; however, if the model is insufficient then ANT must open up blackboxed nodes to create a swarm of new actors. Object-Oriented Otology (OOO) emphasises the humility of humans before objects, particularly 'hyperobjects' which are too big to know or control, yet are partially accessible through poetry or contemplation. This can have various political aspects, for example Graham Harman's politics is reformist or quietistic, whereas Bryant's discussion or eruptive rogue objects, including social movements and new technologies, allow for a more radical (and arguably grassroots/prefigurative utopian) stance (Bryant 2012).

What all of these theories have in common, in somewhat of a departure from their postmodern and poststructural roots, is a sense of technological determinism, teleology, and/or linear and progressive sense of development *within* the current sociotechnical framework. They enact a form of utopian replication—reproducing the utopias of the present in idealised or perfected forms, by extrapolating trends from the present and projecting them onto idealised future visions, often somewhat uncritically. While posthuman techno-futurism mobilises ideas from the tech-utopian tradition and exhibits traits of social utopianism, it is important to distinguish between technological and social utopianism (Coenen 2007). This is something that is often missed in both capitalist and left-futurist cybernetic utopias. The utopian tradition emphasises reforming educational and political systems to change culture and society—whether this be 'bottom-up' participatory democracy and pedagogy, or top-down authoritarian blueprint utopias. Cybernetic futurism, on the other hand, focuses on 'technological fixes' to social and individual problems. Furthermore, while both utopianism and techno-futurism seek solutions to age-old problems of 'society and the human condition' such as war, poverty and environmental degradation, the utopian tradition 'always includes an implicit or explicit critique of the economic and political structures of existing societies' whereas futurism 'is often nothing more than an extrapolation of trends' in science and technology—it offers a vision of a more high-tech version of the existing society, rather than one in which social relations are radically changed (Coenen 2007: 7).

Anarchist Cybernetics

In the cybernetic utopias that have been presented so far, there has been an underlying control fantasy. While capitalist cybernetic utopias *seem* decentralising, their authoritarianism resides in treating people as interchangeable and disposable cogs or nodes in a machine whose overarching motive is profit over any sense of human and ecological authenticity or good. Postmodern and Leftist cybernetic utopias may seek to democratise production, or childcare, or to subvert binaries that oppress some more than others, but where they do not question the values that are embedded in technologies, hierarchies or the sociotechnical frameworks that produced those particular technologies (e.g. state or capital), they maintain a top-down technocratic utopianism, defining the means of achieving social good in terms external to humans and their communities.

Some anarchists have drawn on second-order cybernetics, where the participants have a reflexive perspective on themselves as actors in a cybernetic system, to articulate a processual utopia that emphasises elements like 'autonomy', 'self-organization' and 'horizontality' in order to articulate a process in which there is neither transcendental epistemological insight nor any leaders or elites with privileged control. This is opposed to first-order cybernetics where participants are actors, or nodes, in such a system. There is no doubt that cybernetics was originally pro-system and blueprint utopian; it gets read as radical and potentially revolutionary after this by people like Paul Goodman (1970) and used against capitalist hierarchies, as a decentralising epistemology. Goodman's interpretation of cybernetics as essentially decentralising was challenged even by some of the more radical founders/advocates of cybernetics, including Gregory

Bateson, who believed some form of central power was still necessary using biological metaphors comparing centralisation in society to the organisation of the human brain (Duda 2013: 59–60, drawing on unpublished Bateson letter archives). Anarchists using cybernetics have tried to unpack the distributed, decentralising and self-organising aspects from the focus on control (Goodman 1970; Dolgoff 1989; Swann 2018, 2020; Fox 2023). The term *self organisation* is fundamental to contemporary anarchist parlance. John Duda traces this to the work of New York anarchist Sam Dolgoff in 1972, who introduced this term in his work on the influential Russian revolutionary anarchist Bakunin. Duda interprets this as a 'productive mistranslation' (because Bakunin used a slightly different term) which 'encapsulates an entire history of an encounter between, on the one hand, the tradition of anti-authoritarian political theory, and on the other, the *sciences* of self-organisation' (Duda 2013: 54).

Anarchists who explicitly use cybernetic theory tend to draw on the work of Stafford Beer, due to his emphasis on democracy and self-organisation (Swann 2018), although tellingly for our later arguments regarding the essentially anti-utopian character of cybernetics, Stafford Beer did not himself identify as an anarchist nor base his theories in any anarchist literatures or arguments, and his understandings of democracy were strictly limited to representative forms (cf. Project Cybersyn described above). The cybernetician Grey Walter had arguably more anarchist tendencies than Beer, and in 1963 Walter published in the British journal *Anarchy* under the editorship of Colin Ward. In this, he focuses predominantly on explaining cybernetics from the perspective of human physiology and early robotics and only briefly touches on political organisation (Walter 1963: 7). This provoked a reply in a later edition of the same journal from computer scientist John McEwan, whose essay 'The Relevance of Anarchism to Modern Society' (McEwan 1963) is interpreted by Duda as 'a kind of manifesto for cybernetic anarchism' which attempts to 'articulate a case for anarchy based in the scientific concept of self-organization' (Duda 2013: 63).

The idea of an entirely self-organising society facilitated by communication technology is appealing to anarchists and coincides with utopian imaginaries. A clear fictional example is the use of computers to substitute for state command functions in Ursula LeGuin's imaginary world Anarres in her novel *The Disposessed* (LeGuin 1974). Similarly in social theory, Ivan Illich advocates for the use of advanced computer technology that prefigures the internet to support 'learning webs' of self-directed education in his 1970 book *Deschooling Society* (Illich 1971). There are also many readings of self-organisation in anti-state social movements (Zibechi 2010; Chesters and Welsh 2006; Cleaver 1999). The prolific British Anarchist Colin Ward published the work of Walter and McEwan during his editorship of *Anarchy*, while his book *Anarchy in Action* presents a theory in which spontaneous, bottom-up organisation and decentralised decision-making are more effective and efficient in providing mutual aid and support systems in most practical circumstances, regardless of the values held by the participants (e.g. he contends that a conservative neighbourhood association can be self-organised in a way that is anarchy, even if the participants are far from anarchists) (Ward 1973).

Cybernetic theory and organisational models have also been adopted by practical anarchist projects. James Fox (2023) has undertaken excellent qualitative work on the use of cybernetics as both a tool for organising and for understanding participatory democratic organising. His case studies include a worker co-operative building digital tools for grassroots organising (114–115); a collective producing cola drinks that organises via an online forum (115–118); an organisation producing an online platform for real-world seed-sharing (118–119); the well-known SUMA wholefoods co-operative which explicitly uses cybernetics, Stafford Beer's VSM model, in its organisational structure (120); and an ecovillage which also consciously uses cybernetics (121). Although Fox persists in the use of cybernetics, and related terminologies, which we critique, his argument and ethos veer somewhat closer to ours than other authors examined here. Fox celebrates the messiness within cybernetics: 'the mess of patches, edits and ad hoc fixes' (342) that occur when cybernetics is practised as a form of participatory governance situationally, and his ethos advocates reappropriating cybernetics as a form of folk discourse or hobby knowledge to aid participatory governance, rather than a managerial model (346–347). While we find Fox's argument persuasive and his data is incredibly rich and interesting, speaking strongly to our own project, we maintain that cybernetics is irredeemable and wholly recuperated. We believe the 'messiness' and patches that Fox identifies as being part of cybernetics, are in fact external to and transgressive of cybernetics so need to be theorised as disruptive, prefigurative and potentially revolutionary forces.

Aside from Fox, anarchist cyberneticians often focus on self-organisation (as both an anarchist and cybernetic value) in terms of its 'effectiveness' or efficiency, and how this can be facilitated by communications technology and social media, or by mapping and modelling the functions of effective systems in order to understand or facilitate, enhance or replicate their existing self-organising capacities. Thomas Swann (2020) argues that in the context of radical Left and anarchist movements, the cybernetic concept of 'control' can be re-interpreted as self-organisation and as prefigurative forms of democratic and participatory decision-making. He argues that cybernetics provides a framework through which to ask questions about hierarchy—which he claims does not disappear in non-hierarchical movements but rather resides in 'functions that individuals can shift between depending on the particular roles that they are performing at a given moment' (Swann 2018: 211). Behind the anarchist valorisation of self-organisation and autonomy is sometimes a functionalist assumption that even radical organisations have fixed roles that people can slot into, even if they do so fluidly. This is an ontological and epistemological claim that radical organisations—and the utopian societies that they prefigure—can be understood through functional roles, rather than, for example, as expressions of inner authenticity or some creative immeasurable newness that emerges from social relationships. Duda argues in his discussion on Grey Walters that his 'refusal to engage with the politics of cybernetics, rather than the cybernetics of politics, is somewhat frustrating' (Duda 2013: 62–63), which is a criticism we would argue stands for most anarchist cyberneticians. Swann argues that the anarchist credentials of any cybernetic project may come down to 'whether ideas of complexity, self-organisation and autonomy are mobilised to empower individuals and groups or whether they are put to use in disempowering people and submitting to the control of the market as a mechanism for managing complexity' (Swann 2015: 38). However, we would argue, following Duda, that this is certainly at least part of the story, but also that any epistemology needs to be embedded in prefigurative social movements that also embrace a political ethic in which 'the revolutionary process is made to resemble, as much as possible, the desired post-revolutionary society in its essential ethical attributes', rather than valorising self-organisation as a form in its own right, devoid of political or ethical content (Duda 2013: 57).

The link between cybernetics and anarchist practice has been complex from the start. While the emerging Silicon Valley culture and the Whole Earth Catalogue played up the link to the anarchistic hippy and counter-cultural movement, in reality a lot of the 1960s/1970s radicals were hostile to what seemed to be a next step in existing managerial operationalism.

Fred Turner views the hippie movement as always-already complicit in capitalist cybernetics (Turner 2006), and Thomas Rid argues that leaderless movements like the 1980s and 1990s DiY punk and eco-activist subcultures, which engaged in direct action rather than organised protest, were more of an aesthetic movement or fashion statement than a political movement (Rid 2016: 436–437). Marxist thinkers are often critical of anarchism in terms that conflate it with cybernetics, and/or argue that anarchists and counter-cultural movements are complicit in the rise of neoliberalism. These thinkers often take an economic or technological determinist view to argue that the rebellious spirit and alternative/autonomous values of the communard movement were recuperated in and determined by material factors from the start.

Boltanski and Chiapello, following Max Weber, argue that the 'spirit of capitalism' refers to a set of desires and ethical motivations that are alien to capitalist logic, yet inspire entrepreneurs in activity conducive to capitalist accumulation (Boltanski and Chiapello 2007: 8–9). This view moves somewhat towards allowing for the idea of autonomous desires that are not (yet) recuperated in capitalism, even if their argument is that ultimately everything is recuperated. One might expand on this that just because capitalists *try* to commodify everything doesn't mean that thing was always merely reproducing capital. Theories that deny the possibility of autonomous ethics and desires are vanguardist as they assume that people need a specific Marxist analysis in order to achieve radical subjectivity. Anarchists and autonomous/open Marxists (the positions of us, as authors) converge on the idea that radical subjectivity begins from social recomposition, for example by forming autonomous or prefigurative communities. Our critique of the idea of the cybernetic utopia encourages us to broaden the scope of 'community' and subject formation to include the technologies and ecosystems we inhabit, and our relationships to tools, technologies, animals and nature.

Tactical Media

Another angle from which to approach the intersection of anarchism and cybernetics is by looking at prefigurative alternatives. Tactical media appeared in mid-1990s, with roots in art movements like surrealism, situationism and dada, which used détournement to subvert and transform existing works of art and advertising. It draws on the work of de Certeau (1984), in particular his concept of 'bricolage', which draws a distinction between elements of a society and the system in which they're used (or between a machinic assemblage and its parts). Elements, once rearranged in a creative manner, can fall outside of the system, to 'reestablish a means of expression and a space of temporary autonomy within the realm of the social' (Critical Art Ensemble 2001: 115). Tactical media differs from earlier forms of détournement in that it subverts the media themselves rather than their products. The movements' conditions of possibility arose with the availability of cheaper technology and more open forms of circulation, 'made possible by the revolution in consumer electronics and expanded forms of distribution' (Garcia and Lovink 1997), such as camcorders, cable television, the internet. Tactical media activists and hackers do not necessarily self-define as either anarchists (although they sometimes do) or cyberneticians (though again there is some crossover), yet meet the key characteristics in terms of firstly organising without hierarchy, secondly embracing a 'do it yourself' ethos and thirdly being organised by individuals who are 'aggrieved by, or excluded from, the wider culture' (Garcia and Lovink 1997). In the tactical media cluster, alongside self-organised groups and social movements there are also writings and utopian visions related to experiences of new technologies as flow, empowerment and liberation from older blockages. For example, the Hacker Manifesto depicts mainstream society as a dystopic realm of meaningless competition, alienation, authoritarianism and sadism. In contrast, the coolness of computers frees the hacker from this world: 'And then it happened … a door opened to a world … rushing through the phone line like heroin through an addict's veins, an electronic pulse is sent out, a refuge from the day-to-day incompetencies is sought … a board is found. "This is it … this is where I belong"' (The Mentor 1986). Hacker culture is portrayed as a subversive counterculture involving the gift economy and an ethos of sharing, non-instrumentality and information freedom (Levy 1984; Stallman 2015; Coleman 2003; Raymond 1999). Albert compares meshnets and earlier tactical media, suggesting that both create 'a sense of belonging and mutual generosity' beyond traditional communities (Albert 2003). Other works point towards a specific hacker assemblage, 'closer to the creative artist and the ivory-tower professor than to the risk-taker or the possessive individualist' (Boutang 2011: 90). Examples of technology-related activism that might fit into this model include pirate radio, meshnets, FLOSS, anonymity software, hacklabs and hacktivism.

While not explicitly tactical media nor anarchist, the work of Manuel DeLanda (1991) is useful for understanding the theory of grassroots cybernetic utopias that mobilise technologies in decentralising ways. For DeLanda, it is not technology in and of itself that is harmful, but the sociotechnical assemblages and systems that pre-exist it, which it is inserted into. DeLanda's thesis is that evolution of technology is intrinsically neither good nor bad; however, it can be centralising or decentralising, and there does seem to be a value judgement attached to these terms, with DeLanda expressing preference for decentralisation. In capitalism, both centralising and decentralising technologies are used for purposes of exploitation, profit and primitive accumulation, and the lines between them are blurred. To imagine a contemporary example, a decentralising technology that enables individuals to call taxis from anywhere and for taxi drivers to run their own accounts is a method of control used by a co-ordinating capitalist monopoly (Uber). The centralising tendencies of assemblages can be self-perpetuating; for example, artificial intelligence removes transparency and shifts moral culpability, blurring the distinction between advisory and executive capabilities. Centralisation removes humans from the decision-making loop whilst decentralisation prioritises co-operative behaviour. The evolution of technology can be reappropriated for decentralising, co-operative purposes, qua tactical media. Expert systems can become replacements for human knowledge, or they can aid in the diffusion of expertise, and which path is taken often depends more on the design of the interface than on users' intentions, which provides grounds for tactical intervention. In the context of the early internet, a group of hackers arose in an 'interactivity movement' who had an unwritten ethical code committed to the cause of interactivity and the free flow of information unrestricted by bureaucratic control. This commitment was embodied in practices which involved keeping software in open access locations, viewing programmes not as private property but as tools to be distributed as widely as possible (DeLanda 1991: 225). Similarly to the counter-cultural movements of the 1960s, Turner suggests that Tactical Media is already recuperated in neoliberal cyberculture (Turner 2006); however, we would argue it offers useful tactics for resistance, which resonate with some of the knowledges we encountered in our fieldwork.

Conclusion

Subversion is a form of grassroots resistance associated with tactical media which both resists cybernetic capitalism and contains prefigurative elements. The Invisible Committee argue that 'it's possible, in some places, to use Facebook against itself, against its essential function, which is policing' (The Invisible Committee 2015: 104). Examples of social movements using technology in subversive ways include Occupy Sandy!, who used social media like Twitter and Facebook to organise radical disaster relief and used the Amazon wedding gift list function to enable people worldwide to donate goods (Firth 2022). Social media have for decades been used to organise protests (Juris 2020). Richard Hall argues that the fight against cybernetic control is not about destroying or refusing high technology but rather 'focuses upon using technology and technique to reveal the internal, totalising dynamics of capitalism. From this position, alternatives rooted in self-organisation and a societal complexity based on variety, improbability, and adaptability emerge' (Hall 2017). Later in this book (Chaps. 4–6) we will examine the subversive potential of human creative labour, even in relation to capitalist technologies.

In this chapter, we covered the utopian promise of cybernetics, which we associated with vanguardist, blueprint utopias which disguise the accelerationist fantasies underlying their visions behind anti-utopian scientistic and technocratic discourses (whether these be capitalist or socialist). Cybernetics is an inexhaustible theory of every entity, perhaps a transdisciplinary theory, that has connections with both mainstream, pro-capitalist and pro-statist movements, as well as radical authoritarian and anti-authoritarian ones. The seemingly ambiguous nature of terms such as control, regulation, feedback and embeddedness means that it has found itself applied to both technological and societal progressive movements. The fluidity of cybernetic theory and language means that it can act as a framing for blueprint utopian movements and can be used post hoc to justify social formations (including decentralised mutual aid) as cybernetic. This does not mean that cybernetics is empty of meaning; on the contrary, it is not as benign as its advocates would like to present it. Cybernetics in reality comprised assumptions about how human societies should be best organised, which we aim to expose in the next chapter, where we continue our critique of cybernetics by concentrating on the dystopian effects of vanguardist forms of cybernetics when they are put into practice in state-capitalist assemblages. Given its fluid nature, we should be unsurprised that cybernetics both contributes and draws concepts from critical social and political theory, including ANT, transhumanism, posthumanism, accelerationism, Marxism and even anarchism. Many critical theorists have tried to claim cybernetics as part of their radical repertoire. In doing so, they are perhaps trying to represent social theory as something that can be 'engineered' or 'formalised', but we are sceptical of attempts to do this, as we shall see in the next chapter, which is a more general critique of cybernetics.

References

Albert, S., 2003, 'Free as in Air: An Interview with Vortex', in Sarai Collective (eds.), *Sarai Reader 03: Shaping Technologies*, Delhi, CSDS/Sarai, pp. 337–345.

Barbrook, R., and Cameron, A. 1996, 'The Californian Ideology', *Science as Culture*, 6(1), pp. 44–72.

Bastani, A., 2019, *Fully Automated Luxury Communism*, London: Verso Books.

Baudrillard, J., 2000, *The Vital Illusion*, Columbia University Press.

Beer, S. 1981, *Brain of the Firm*, 2nd edn, Chichester: John Wiley and Sons.

Behrent, M.C., 2013, 'Foucault and Technology', *History and Technology*, 29(1), pp. 54–104.

Beller, J., 2018, *The Message is Murder: Substrates of Computational Capital*, London: Pluto.

Bloch, E., 1986, *The Principle of Hope [Vols 1–3]*, trans. N. Plaice, S. Plaice & P. Knight, Cambridge, MA: MIT Press.

Boltanski, L. and Chiapello, È., 2007, *The New Spirit of Capitalism*, London: Verso.

Berneri, M.L., 2019 [1948], *Journey Through Utopia: A Critical Assessment of Imagined Worlds in Western Literature*, Oakland, CA: PM Press.

Boutang, Y.M., 2011, *Cognitive Capitalism*, Cambridge: Polity.

Bryant, L., 2012, 'Five Types of Objects: Gravity and Onto-Cartography', *Larval Subjects*, available at: https://larvalsubjects.wordpress.com/2012/06/17/five-types-of-objects-gravity-and-ontocartography/ (Accessed 6 September 2019).

Chesters, G., and Welsh, I. 2006, *Complexity and Social Movements: Multitudes at the Edge of Chaos*, London: Routledge.

Cleaver, H., 1999, 'Computer-Linked Social Movements and the Global Threat to Capitalism', available at: https://la.utexas.edu/users/hcleaver/polnet.html (Accessed 6 August 2010).

Coenen, C. 2007, 'Utopian Aspects of the Debate on Converging Technologies', in Banse, G., Grunwald, A., Hronszky, I. and Nelson, G. (eds.) *Assessing Societal Implications of Converging Technological Development*, Berlin: edition sigma, pp. 141–172.

Coleman, B., 2003, 'The (Copylefted) Source Code for the Ethical Production of Information Freedom', in Sarai Collective (eds.), *Sarai Reader 03: Shaping Technologies*, Delhi: CSDS/Sarai, pp. 297–302.

Critical Art Ensemble and Institute for Applied Autonomy, 2001, 'Contestational Robotics', in Critical Art Ensemble (eds.), *Digital Resistance: Explorations in Tactical Media*, New York: Autonomedia, pp. 115–134.

Cudworth, E., 2005, *Developing Ecofeminist Theory: The Complexity of Difference*, London: Palgrave.

Cudworth, E., 2011, *Social Lives with Other Animals: Tales of Sex, Death and Love*, London: Palgrave.

Cudworth, E. and Hobden, S., 2011. *Posthuman international relations: Complexity, ecologism and global politics.* London: Zed Books.

Cybernetic Cultures Research Unit 2017, *CCRU Writings 1997–2003*, Falmouth: Urbanomic.

de Certeau, M., 1984, *The Practice of Everyday Life*, Berkeley, CA: University of California Press.

DeLanda, M., 1991, *War in the Age of Intelligent Machines*, New York: Swerve.

Deleuze, G., 1988, *Foucault*, London: Continuum.

Deleuze, G. and Guattari, F. 1987, *A Thousand Plateaus*, London: Continuum.

Derrida, J., 1976, *Of Grammatology*, trans G. C. Spivak (Baltimore: John Hopkins University Press).

Dolgoff, S., 1989, *The Relevance of Anarchism to Modern Society*, Chicago: Charles H. Kerr.

Duda, J. 2013, 'Cybernetics, Anarchism and Self-Organisation', *Anarchist Studies*, 21(1), pp. 52–72.

Dvorsky, G., and Hughes, J. 2008, 'Postgenderism: Beyond the Gender Binary', *Institute for Ethics and Emerging Technologies*, 20, pp. 44–57.

Firestone, S., 1970, *The Dialectic of Sex: The Case for Feminist Revolution*, London: Verso Books.

Firth, R., 2012, *Utopian Politics: Citizenship and Practice.* London: Routledge.

Firth, R., 2022, *Disaster Anarchy: Mutual Aid and Radical Action.* London: Pluto.

Fox, J., 2023, 'Dis/agreement in Participatory Organisations: Low Theory and Democratic Governance in Cybernetics', [PhD Thesis] Department of Management Studies, University of Essex. Date of submission: January 15th, 2023.

Garcia, D. and Lovink, G. 1997, 'The ABC of Tactical Media', *Nettime*, available at: http://www.nettime.org/Lists-Archives/nettime-l-9705/msg00096.html (Accessed 6 August 2024).

Goodman, P. (1970) New Reformation: Notes of a Neolithic Conservative. New York: Random House.

Gupta, P., Chauhan, S. and Jaiswal, M.P., 2019, 'Classification of Smart City Research: A Descriptive Literature Review and Future Research Agenda', *Information Systems Frontiers*, 21(3), pp. 661–685.

Habermas, J., 1986, 'The New Obscurity: The Crisis of the Welfare State and the Exhaustion of Utopian Energies', *Philosophy and Social Criticism*, 11.

Hall, R., 2017, 'Notes on Reading the Cybernetic Hypothesis', available at: http://www.richard-hall.org/2017/07/07/notes-on-the-cybernetic-hypothesis/ (Accessed 6 August 2023).

Hanson, R., 1994, 'If Uploads Come First: The Crack of a Future Dawn', *Extropy*, 13, pp. 10–15.
Harman, G., 2018, *Object-Oriented Ontology: A New Theory of Everything*, Harmondsworth: Pelican.
Howard, R.G., 1998, 'Researching Folk Rhetoric: The Case of Apocalyptic Techno-Gaianism on the World Wide Web', *Folklore Forum*, 29(2), pp. 53–73.
Illich, I., 1971, *Deschooling Society*, Harmondsworth: Penguin.
Juris, J.S., 2020, *Networking Futures: The Movements Against Corporate Globalization*, Duke University Press.
Kelly, K., 1994, *Out of Control: The New Biology of Machines, Social Systems and the Economic World*, Self-published, available at: https://kk.org/mt-files/books-mt/ooc-mf.pdf (Accessed 6 October 2019).
Kelly, K., 2010, *What Technology Wants*, New York: Viking.
Kingsnorth, P. 2015, 'Planting Trees in the Anthropocene: A Conspiracy Theory', *Dark Mountain*, 8, pp. 30–42.
Land, N., 2014, *Fanged Noumena: Collected Writings 1987–2007*, ed. R. Brassier and R. MacKay, Falmouth: Urbanomic.
Latour, B., 1999, *Pandora's Hope: Essays on the Reality of Science Studies*, Cambridge, MA: Harvard University Press.
Law, J., 2004, *After Method: Mess in Social Science Research*, London: Routledge.
LeGuin, U. 1974, *The Dispossessed: An Ambiguous Utopia*, New York: Harper and Row.
Levy, S., 1984, *Hackers: Heroes of the Computer Revolution*, New York: Doubleday.
Lewis, T. and Kahn, R., 2010. *Education out of bounds: Reimagining cultural studies for a posthuman age*. London: Palgrave.
Lyotard, J-F., 1984, *The Postmodern Condition: A Report on Knowledge*, trans. G. Bennington and B. Massumi, Minneapolis: University of Minnesota Press.
Macris, V., 2012, 'A Review of "Education Out of Bounds: Reimagining Cultural Studies for a Posthuman Age (Education, Politics, and Public Life)"', *Educational Studies: A Journal of the American Educational Studies Association*, 48(6), pp. 576–580.
Mannheim, K., 2013 [1929]) *Ideology and Utopia*. London: Routledge.
More, M., 2003. *Principles of Extropy*, Version 3.11. [online] Available at: https://web.archive.org/web/20110806105153/http://www.extropy.org/principles.htm [Accessed 17 February 2019].
McEwan, J. 1963. 'Anarchism and the Cybernetics of Self-Organizing Systems'. *Anarchy*, 31, pp. 270–283.
Medina, E., 2014. *Cybernetic Revolutionaries: Technology and Politics in Allende's Chile*. Cambridge, MA: The MIT Press.
The Mentor, 1986. 'Hacker's Manifesto: The Conscience of a Hacker'. *Phrack*, 1(7).
Noys, B., 2014. *Malign Velocities: Accelerationism and Capitalism*. Alresford: Zero Books.

Oliva, G., 2015. The Road to Servomechanisms: The Influence of Cybernetics on Hayek from *The Sensory Order* to *The Social Order*. Centre for the History of Political Economy Working Paper, No. 2015-11. [online] Available at: https://hope.econ.duke.edu/sites/hope.econ.duke.edu/files/The%20Road%20to%20Servomechanisms.pdf [Accessed 6 August 2024].

Ouellet, M., 2010. 'Cybernetic capitalism and the global information society'. *Cultural Political Economy*, pp. 177–196.

Pertigkiozoglou, E. 2017. '1969: Gordon Pask'. *Medium*, 19 February. [online] Available at: https://medium.com/designscience/1969-ab2783c47cbf [Accessed 6 August 2024].

Piercy, M. 1976. *Woman on the Edge of Time*. New York: Alfred A. Knopf.

Pitts, H. and Dinerstein, A., 2017. 'Corbynism's conveyor belt of ideas: Postcapitalism and the politics of social reproduction'. *Capital and Class*, 41, pp. 423–434.

Plant, S. and Land, N., 1994. *Cyberpositive*. Available at: https://www.sterneck.net/cyber/plant-land-cyber/index.php. Accessed 19 June 2025.

Plato, 1997, 'Alcibiades'. In: Cooper, J.M. and Hutchinson, D.S. (eds) *Plato. Complete Works*. Cambridge, MA: Hackett, pp. 557–595.

Prieur, R., 2005. 'The Age of Batshit Crazy Machines'. [online] Available at: http://www.ranprieur.com/essays/machines.html [Accessed 6 August 2019].

Raymond, E.S., 1999. *The Cathedral and the Bazaar: Musings on Linux and Open Source by an Accidental Revolutionary*. Sebastopol, CA: O'Reilly.

Reed, P., 2014. 'Seven Prescriptions for Accelerationism'. In: Mackay, R. and Avanessian, A. (eds.) *#Accelerate: The Accelerationist Reader*. Falmouth: Urbanomic, pp. 521–536.

Rid, T. 2016. *Rise of the Machines: The Lost History of Cybernetics*. Melbourne and London: Scribe.

Schwab, K., 2017. *The Fourth Industrial Revolution*. New York: Currency Books.

Shreve, A. 1989. *Women Together, Women Alone: The Legacy of the Consciousness-Raising Movement*. New York: Ballantine.

Snaza, N., Appelbaum, P., Bayne, S., Carlson, D., Morris, M., Rotas, N., Sandlin, J., Wallin, J. and Weaver, J. 2014. 'Toward a Posthumanist Education'. *Journal of Curriculum Theorizing*, 30(2), pp. 39–55.

Srniček, N., and Williams, A. 2015. *Inventing the Future: Postcapitalism and a World Without Work*. London: Verso.

Stallman, R.M. 2015. *Free Software, Free Society: Selected Essays of Richard M. Stallman*. Boston, MA: GNU Press.

Ström, T., 2022. 'Capital and Cybernetics'. *New Left Review*, 135, pp. 23–41.

Swann, T., 2018. 'Towards an Anarchist Cybernetics: Stafford Beer, Self-Organisation and Radical Social Movements'. *Ephemera*, 18(3), pp. 427–456.

Swann, T., 2020. *Anarchist Cybernetics: Control and Communication in Radical Politics*. Policy Press.

Swann, T., 2015. *Anarchist Cybernetics: Control and Communication in Radical Left Movements.* PhD Thesis, University of Leicester.

Sweeting, B., 2016. 'The role of Gordon Pask in the Fun Palace Project'. *An Afternoon with Cedric Price* [Conference Paper]. [online] Available at: https://research.brighton.ac.uk/en/activities/the-role-of-gordon-pask-in-the-fun-palace-project [Accessed 6 August 2024].

The Invisible Committee, 2015. *To Our Friends.* London: Semiotext(e).

Turner, F., 2006. *From Counterculture to Cyberculture: Stewart Brand, the Whole Earth Network, and the Rise of Digital Utopianism.* Chicago, IL: University of Chicago Press.

Wallerstein, I., 2020. *World-systems analysis: An introduction.* Durham: Duke University Press.

Walter, W.G., 1963. 'The Development and Significance of Cybernetics'. *Anarchy*, 25, March, pp. 75–89. [online] Available at: https://www.thesparrowsnest.org.uk/collections/public_archive/8723.pdf [Accessed 6 August 2024].

Ward, C., 1973. *Anarchy in Action.* London: Freedom Press.

Wiener, N., 2019 [1948]. *Cybernetics or Control and Communication in the Animal and the Machine.* Cambridge, MA: MIT Press.

Zamyatin, Y., 2020 [1924]. *We.* London: Penguin.

Zibechi, R., 2010. *Dispersing Power: Social Movements as Anti-State Forces.* Edinburgh: AK Press.

Zolkos, M., 2018. 'Life as a Political Problem: The Post-Human Turn in Political Theory'. *Political Studies Review*, 16(3), pp. 192–204.

CHAPTER 3

The Dystopian Realities of Cybernetics

Introduction

There is no doubt that cybernetics was originally pro-system and implicated in the war machine.[1] In the preceding outline history of cybernetic utopias, we argued that cybernetics arose primarily from blueprint utopias oriented to command and control during the Cold War, underpinning the conception of a technological capitalist consumer utopia, yet running parallel to these authoritarian and commodified visions, there has been a relationship between cybernetics and the grassroots. Theorist-historians covered in the foregoing chapter including Rid, Turner, and Barbrook and Cameron, have all written long and seminal works on the history of cybernetics and the Californian Ideology, which co-conspire that hippy culture, back-to-the-land intentional communities movement, Do-It-Yourself hacktivism and anarchist self-organising have always been essential to, complicit in and essentially commodified by neoliberal capitalist

[1] The US army set up the forerunners of the internet (ARPANET) as a method of distributed (i.e. centreless) command and control in the event of nuclear war. The internet is designed rhizomatically, partly because the US army designed it on a model meant to stop other armies logistically disrupting it. It is a military project, but a project with a deterritorialising function, directed *against* the logic of logistical control. This is something that armies are arguably always doing, trying to preserve or extend their own power, stop others from logistically controlling them, while trying to logistically control others. These arguments are elaborated using the terminology of the 'war machine' in Virilio (1990, 2005) and Deleuze and Guattari (1987: 387–467).

R. Firth, J. Preston, *Utopia in the Factory*,
https://doi.org/10.1007/978-3-031-87132-0_3

cybernetics utopias. On the other hand, many cyberneticians *proper*, especially second-order and quasi-libertarian ones including Stafford Beer, Grey Walter and John McEwan, tend to view their techniques as oriented towards increasing the freedom and empowerment of the whole of society, whilst some anarchists attempt to mobilise cybernetic ideas like self-organisation to argue that an anti-authoritarian, non-commodified cybernetic thought and practice is possible. There is also a strand of left-accelerationism related to socialist and communist conceptions of the automation of production. Despite its varied meanings across political philosophies, including liberatory ones, it is our contention here that there is something essential to cybernetics, particularly the view of the subject and its totalising, functionalist tendencies at system-level, that prevents it from being a critical utopian alternative to capitalism or statism. These prefigurative, utopian alternatives can and do exist, but they are beyond the limits of cybernetic categories. Although proto-states could emerge from the application of cybernetics as a prefigurative (and anti-state) alternative, these reinstate capitalist and statist tendencies.

Our critique is based upon elements common to theories of cybernetics: its totalising tendencies, epistemological vanguardism, inherent functionalism, impoverished view of the subject, rejection of alternative perspectives and ultimately the positioning of cybernetics as a machinic form of social domination.

Totalising Tendencies

The capitalist cybernetic model, based on a rational choice, behaviourist and blackboxed view of the subject, is totalitarian. Totalitarians pursue the total mobilisation of society and thus seek to incorporate and mobilise the population as emotionally committed participants—meaning they must accept and apply the regime ideology to themselves and their close ones—this moves beyond top-down authoritarianism to a form of crowdsourcing of policing. Cybernetics as originally conceived during the Cold War corresponds to a military disaster model. While it appears decentralising, it does not seek to abolish hierarchies but rather to make them invisible or internalised. As an organisational model on a broad social level, despite the rhetoric (which often emphasises a role for 'autonomous groups'), it can involve central decisions which are coercively implemented by a layer of obedient conformists (army, police, bureaucrats, managers) ignoring the needs and wishes of other groups, who are cast as the passive victims or beneficiaries of the policy (Firth 2022: 21–45). The Hobbesian model of politics (Hobbes 2006), which is authoritarian and is in essence a top-down vertical command-and-control model, assumes that people are either evil or atomised, and therefore war-like; they need to be controlled for their own good. Cybernetics arose partially as a reaction to this. *Tiqqun*, following Deleuze and Guattari, argue that cybernetics, which as we already saw arose in the aftermath of WWII, is the *automation* of the 'war machine', whereby 'politics becomes the continuation of war, *it is peace that will release, technically, the unlimited material process of total war*. War ceases to be the materialization of *the war machine*; the war machine itself becomes materialized warfare' (Tiqqun 2020: 24, italics in the original). Paulo Virilio and Sylvere Lotringer (1998) make similar arguments regarding the way in which military doctrines come to capture social planning. Cybernetics seeks to extend and tighten the chains of social interdependence and increases the division of labour of population management through surveillance and delegation of political power, so that the 'production of singular subjectivities and production of collective totalities mesh together' (Tiqqun 2020: 31)

This claim of totalitarianism might seem extreme when applied to neoliberal cybernetics, and particularly radical cybernetics, especially when considering the foregoing history (Chap. 2) imbricated with both the fulfilment of individualistic consumerist desires as well as communal utopian imaginaries. However, one might consider that as an early emergent discourse, cybernetics was more visible and less influential, but it has arguably become more pervasive throughout society, and more invisible, as neoliberalism has gained hold. Recent government policies around the COVID-19 pandemic, for example, rely more on social policing from neighbours than on direct policing (Preston and Firth 2020) while governments formulate explicit policies to mobilise radical movements to fill gaps and stand in for their failures as the Fordist welfare state recedes (Firth 2022). Cybernetics might be best associated with ordo-liberalism, rather than neoliberalism, with cybernetics providing the organisational, totalising framework, a state-form required to maintain liberal capitalism.

Cyberneticians might argue that cybernetics is not a utopian model, blueprint or a normative vision to be imposed from the top-down but rather a metaphor or conceptualisation. Stafford Beer described it as a 'diagnostic tool' (Beer 1981: 155) and Roger Harnden called it a 'hermeneutic enabler' (1989; cited in Swann 2018: 437). So it is arguably more of an epistemological device than a planning framework. Thomas Swann, following Stafford Beer, argues that:

> The point of the VSM is, therefore, not to prescribe organisational structures or practices but to provide the tools those involved in organising can use to better understand the processes in which they are participating. The VSM, rather than outlining the exact structure of a viable organisation is intended to highlight the necessary functions and lines of communication that any organisation, however it is in fact structured, will need to have. In this sense, it is intended as a heuristic of sorts that can assist people in thinking through and responding to questions of organisational structure rather than as a blueprint they ought to follow. (Swann 2018: 437)

However, even this form of heuristic still relies on an assumption of the generic nature of people and the way that they organise—it rests on the assumption that everyone is an individual node fulfilling a function as part of an organisation. We concede that there is a difference between what might be called the 'heuristic' VSM as presented by Swann (2020) and the original VSM of Beer which is far more functionalist in presenting a circuit diagram of inputs and outputs where the status of humans as mere nodes is apparent. The 'heuristic' form of cybernetics, particularly when it is expressed diagrammatically (cyberneticians such as Beer are particularly fond of not only diagrams but also cartoons and squiggles which blunt the formalism of cybernetic models) masks the sequential and logical circuit maps that are the components of cybernetic organisation. In practice, we would argue that through its use of heuristics, metaphors and pictures, cybernetics is masking a more co-ordinated, circuit-based cyber-state.

Between the heuristic and functional, cybernetics is two things at once: it is a blueprint utopia in which a range of normative demands are optimised, for example: efficiency, transparency, lack of conflict and consensus, which are euphemised as 'control' and 'co-ordination'. It is also an epistemological exercise in 'legibility' which seeks to make self-organised systems legible and understandable, and commensurable with other self-organised systems. Following James Scott, we would argue that legibility is naturally a part of an urge for oversight and control, which is part of the logic of the state (Scott 1990). Since cybernetics seeks to apply a generic model (e.g. Stafford Beer's VSM) to any form of social group or organisation, it assumes that all entities that exist can be slotted or mapped into this—there is an implicit operationalism which defines things by how they function, and it relies on the idea that the only things that exist are 'individuals' and 'organisations'.

This form of cybernetics is ultimately a form of planning—the specific blueprint and goals may vary, and they may be subject to varying levels of input and transformation from their participants/stakeholders/users, but they are usually oriented towards efficiency and/or stability, and the fact that there is a plan remains. This will also affect specific agents, emergent tendencies, groups and movements to the extent that they are 'coordinated' into the overall plan, i.e. they will tend to be nudged towards performing recognised generic functions rather than other functions. One might argue this is a problem of politics rather than cybernetics—but even anarchist cybernetics embodies normative claims that orderliness, organisation and consensus are primary, since this is the problem-field that cybernetics arises from. Controversially, we argue anarchist versions of cybernetics maintain vestiges of a control fantasy, since they rely either on an outright blueprint utopia (i.e. a technocratic solution intended to solve social ills); or encourage participation (yet are instituted through designs which crystallise the desires of the architect); or because they rely on a transcendental God's-eye view of knowledge, reminiscent of modernist faith in the ability to operate society in accordance with scientific laws by making society 'legible' through standardised measures and languages. In this sense, cybernetics might be seen as a standardising device, of the type described by James Scott in *Seeing Like a State* (Scott 1990). Similarly, cybernetics also imposes a legibility, and a quantification, of outputs or flows in a system. A cybernetic mode of organisation imposes a model of political economy on a group of people, or entities, with a measurable output. Autonomist Marxists have been sceptical of attempts to impose models of political economy with new forms of measurable 'value' and instead focus on prefigurative alternatives that abolish the law of value in favour of a society that meets the collective interests of the working class. Cybernetics reinstates a form of political economy based on a measurable value or signal. Qualitative, indeterminate and prefigurative entities are not the 'flows' of a cybernetic circuit, rather quantitative signals or binaries (inputs and outputs) are. Cybernetics can be seen to run contrary to future working-class self-determination in a communist society as it quantifies the outputs of individuals in a form that does not rise from the consciousness or praxis of the individuals themselves but through a cybernetic practice that is supra-ordinate to those individuals.

Cybernetics is ultimately based on the desire to protect from shocks, change and the disintegration of order and organisation, which reifies the social. All cybernetics requires this; i.e. a complex system that is stable, categorisable and mappable. Entities must be single or connected in understandable relations; they cannot be multiple and involved in fluid, multiple or conflicting relations. Even where this is acknowledged or accounted for, for example in second-order cybernetics, it is limited. Where self-organisation is seen merely as a technical problem, the root metaphor of cybernetics conflates technological development with utopian progress, when, in fact, technological progress reifies the desires of the society that created the technology, so blocks the expression of new political agency.

Epistemological Vanguardism

The top-down control elements of first-order cybernetics are obvious, yet there are also elements of vanguardism in second-order cybernetics. As discussed earlier, differentiating between vanguardist and non-vanguardist, or prefigurative/revolutionary and reformist utopias cannot be considered as a simple binary. It is almost certain that cybernetics had authoritarian origins, and many subaltern groups invested aspects of cybernetics with utopian hopes, desires and fears, many of which were recuperated into consumerist ideology. But is there anything essentially vanguardist about the *desires* underlying cybernetics? Rid points out that machines are about control—they give humans more control over their environment, over their own lives and over others. However 'gaining control through machines means also delegating it to machines. Using the tool means trusting the tool' (Rid 2016: 2). There is a cybernetic assumption that 'nature' has a tendency to increase entropy and disorder, and that it is in the nature of man, animals and machines to interact and shape the environment. This replicates and furthers modernist claims that pit humans against nature and civilisation against wildness. Cybernetics as an epistemology and as a planning/management technique tries to incorporate everything into a system in order to protect that system from instability and shocks. Alexander Galloway argues that the assumptions and techniques of cybernetics include 'an epistemology rooted in arrays or systems containing discrete entities', the organisation of entities into systems and 'the regularization of difference or asymmetry within the system overall' (Galloway 2014: 124–125). This epistemology is to be applied to society at large and everything incorporated into it. While early cyberneticians touted interdisciplinarity as a strength, critics claimed that the 'interpretative flexibility and broad applicability of cybernetic ideas' rendered the field little more than a pseudoscience proceeding through analogy and metaphor (Medina 2014: 21, 11). There are several anarchist theorists of cybernetics who try to overcome vanguardism, as outlined in Chap. 2, and as authors we are very much sympathetic and invested in anarchist critiques and social movements. However, the question remains as to how cybernetics is useful to anarchism, which already has decent critiques of capitalism, hierarchy and vanguardist knowledge in its armoury.

We consider that cybernetics obscures as much as it reveals, even when used as a heuristic and that it is not possible to break cybernetics with its formation within capitalism. As previously stated, cybernetic heuristics obscure their origins in what are, to all extents, circuit diagrams. In these cybernetic systems there is a 'signal' or 'input/output' that, in essence, is the legitimisation of the cybernetic system. In capitalist political economy, the cybernetic system is orientated towards maximisation (of profit). Although cybernetics might be used for alternative political economies (such as socialised planning), this is still orientated towards the optimisation or maximisation of this 'signal' or 'output'. It is difficult to see how a prefigurative cybernetics could arise without making the entities who comprise the cybernetic system subordinate to the production of a prescribed value. Cybernetics is therefore a form of statism where individuals who comprise it are subordinate to a system and a prescribed value. It has a definitive social epistemology which is not compatible with the maximalist forms of human freedom in anarchist, or autonomist Marxist, perspectives which reject, rather than attempt to reinstate, political economies (see Pitts 2018). According to Ström cybernetics, from its origins, instituted a form of abstraction peculiar to capitalism. Capitalism is a 'mode of practice' (Ström 2022: 27) that brings communication and information into the realm of quantification and commodification. Speech between people becomes abstracted—first quantified and then commodified—as a potential commodity that can be produced through capitalist means (such as the speech acts of social media influencers on Instagram which are essentially a form of labour). Cybernetics represents a break with the analogue natural world for the 0/1 digital binary a colonial project, flattening reality and creating new opportunities for abstraction and profit on an *ontological level* (Ström 2022: 40–41). As technologies develop, the epistemological vanguardism of cybernetics becomes an ontology, describing the ways in which worlds are not only mapped but created. For example, the current conception of the Meta corporation's Metaverse is not just a virtual world (virtual reality) but the set of all possible virtual worlds that intersect with real worlds (augmented reality) and will eventually be the set of all possible virtual, augmented and real worlds (the literal metaversal). What Meta has described using terms founded in cybernetics (systems/worlds/meta) becomes their corporate utopian project through the application of new technologies (Lucia et al. 2023).

Despite disavowing functionalism as a philosophy, cybernetics relies on certain concepts that seem irredeemably vanguardist or blueprint utopian—for example the instrumental rationality inherent in treating people, interchangeably with machinic nodes, as 'black boxes'. This presupposes people as instruments of the system—even if that system is decentralised—as it is interested in behavioural feedback rather than internal life, which is impossibly complex. For cyberneticians, what goes on inside a 'black box' only matters if the system is out of equilibrium. A radical cybernetician might argue that one can draw the lines of the system wherever one likes, but it is impossible and/or pointless try to understand the internal complexity of every part of the system. In this system living labour becomes subordinate to the cybernetic machine in a State form which is a correlate of that predicted in the Gundrisse:

> Labour appears, rather, merely as a conscious organ scattered among the individual living workers at numerous points of the mechanical system; subsumed under the total process of the machinery itself, whose unity exists not in the living workers, but rather in the living (active) machinery which confronts his individual, insignificant doings as a mighty organism. (Marx 1993: 693)

The ability of 'living labour' (working class or autonomous agency) to influence a cybernetic system is questionable given that, once instituted, the active machinery of cybernetics subsumes the human as discussed above. Related to cybernetics, Actor Network Theory (ANT), which draws on the core concepts of cybernetics, and particularly blackboxing, has been criticised for its political assumptions, as both a theory of power and a research methodology that can sometimes have a Hobbesian or Machiavellian character (Harman 2018: 136–139). For example, by advocating building and maintaining collective relations or a community solely for a research project, or by naturalising power relations that gather interests through 'acts of manipulation that realign the will of those that are enrolled', whilst also displacing competing actors (Nold 2017: 28, 46). It is because of this instrumental rationality and functionalism in cybernetics that automation of labour is made possible—because cybernetics treats both people and machines as functional nodes subservient to an overall system.

Cybernetics is not only a tool for organising workplaces or for understanding social organisations but infiltrates broader culture as public pedagogy. Karen Ferneding, in her work on the artist Roy Ascott, offers a broader critique of cybernetics as a cultural pedagogy. She describes the work of Ascott as 're-conceptualization of art and pedagogy' involving the 'application of cybernetics and telematics' (Ferneding 2005: 1). Ascott uses computers and telecommunications systems in his installations to create collaborative works 'manifesting a utopian vision of a unified, global consciousness'. Ferneding argues that 'as a cybernetic artist, his way of seeing the world arises from the experience of modelling reality in reified formations based upon the application of information and systems theory' (Ferneding 2005: 1). She argues that in this context, the equation of control with freedom is not a contradiction, since the virtual 'place' of the internet offers an idealised virtual 'freedom'. Ferneding draws on critical pedagogues such as Neil Postman to argue that contrary to this technologically determinist utopian outlook, the present condition of our society is more like a dystopian technocracy, 'the total surrender of culture to efficient, technological outcomes', which phenomenologically signifies alienation from nature and a deepening mind-body split (Ferneding 2005: 2). Cybernetics is ultimately about organising effects in order to institute systems for the automatic control of these effects, using communication and data processing as a 'control technology' in an information society where 'information is produced as a commodity' (Ferneding 2005: 4). Technological apparatus can alter perceptions, engendering profound changes in consciousness—while Ascott portrays this as a new and utopian way of 'experiencing' that is 'unencumbered by embodied or physical encounters with others' and expresses the 'utopian aspiration of realizing collaboration and overcoming difference via global connectivity', Ferneding argues there is ultimately a paradox at the heart of Ascott's art and the cybernetic utopias it mirrors: while it celebrates postmodern flux, it also 'holds on to the modernist telos' of 'transcendence via techno science' (Ferneding 2005: 7). Ultimately, she argues, Ascott's techno-utopian position does not offer the artist/audience space to negotiate their own visions of the future, portraying the message that 'the future is only techno-utopian and you will like it' (Ferneding 2005: 8). This is a recurring theme in cybernetic utopias—it offers a utopian vision which extracts idealised aspects and trends from the present, and portrays them as utopia, but really they are just amplifications and representations of an idealised version of the status quo which affirm the present and are thus ultimately anti-utopian in character. Cybernetics locks people into systems that are fixed and prioritise the quantitative, rather than qualitative, features of life. Craft, improvisation and idiosyncrasy (which we theorise as tacit knowledge and hobbying) are not made visible in cybernetic systems.

Impoverished View of the Subject

Cybernetics assumes a human subject similar to that of behaviourism, viewing people like machines, as 'black boxes', that are replaceable and serve particular functions within the system, but whose inner lives, subjectivities and relationships that do not serve the needs of the system are to be discarded or repressed. They are seen as vulnerable to manipulation by nudges and incentives, rather than as creatures with complex inner lives or engaged in complicated relations other than those that can be described cybernetically. The French autonomist collective *Tiqqun* have written one of the few extended critiques of cybernetics and also highlight its impoverished view of the subject:

> In fact, the cybernetic hypothesis calls for a radically new structuring of the individual or collective subject, in the direction of a *hollowing out*. It dismisses interiority as a myth along with the entire psychology of the 19th century, including psychoanalysis. It's no longer a matter of separating the subject from their traditional external ties as the liberal hypothesis has demanded, but of reconstituting the social bond by stripping the subject of any substance. (Tiqqun 2020: 52)

McLaverty-Robinson argues that the cybernetic model of rationality resonates with those found in pop psychology and cognitive behavioural therapy, in contemporary managerialism, and in Third-Way politics. In all these psycho-political approaches, people are urged to avoid, or at least to repress, anger and authentic desires, to accept uncertainty in the future and develop resilience to shocks, and to embrace uncomfortable feelings like anxiety as learning opportunities. This creates a kind of subject who is vulnerable and compliant to a cybernetic system which relies on feedback and 'nudging' for social control. He contrasts these with alternative models like psychoanalysis which indicate that people do not have control over their feelings, which 'arise "irrationally" from unconscious fantasies, desires, repressed memories, and other structures which are beyond conscious control' (McLaverty-Robinson 2020: 382) and hence feelings and desires cannot be shaped mechanically in the way that the dominant behaviourist and cybernetic paradigm presumes.

Claus Pias argues that cybernetics is about capitalising knowledge and experience by making it commensurable: 'I think the utopian impact of cybernetics was its dream of various modes of reconciliation. ... The experiment lies in the re-ordering of knowledge in a way that psychological and sociological, political and economical, aesthetical and biological phenomena can all together be rooted in the same fundamental terms of information and feedback' (Pias 2005). This is reflected in the idea of the quantified self, whereby systems use cybernetic self-tracking technologies to 'monitor, measure, and desperately optimize every one of its gestures and each of its affects' (The Invisible Committee 2015: 110). Empirical work on the quantified self shows how workers are increasingly being asked to measure our own productivity, health and wellbeing using self-tracking apps and devices, in the context of increasingly precarious work and competition, leading to a process of self-objectification, and losing one's sense of subjective feeling and authentic desire, as well as the ability to relate to others as authentic, desiring subjects (Moore 2017).

This process is echoed on the political Left, as people replicate and/or are forced into the cybernetic models of subjectivity that they are used to, and it can be found in elements of poststructural and posthuman political theories in universities, as well as rule-bound 'safe spaces' in activist circles and Left discourse in social media, where there is considerable anxiety about being judged, ostracised and disposable. *Tiqqun* argue that one of the problems of the traditional left including socialists and many communists is that they 'struggle against a single effect of capitalism: in all its forms socialism struggles against separation by creating social ties between subjects, between subjects and objects, without contesting the totalization by which THEY can assimilate the social to a body and the individual to a closed entity' (Tiqqun 2020: 108–109).

The argument of *Tiqqun* for social change is based on ideas of communisation, which eschews utopianism, making it difficult to imagine what an 'outside' to capitalism and the state might look like. There are alternative epistemologies, for example those of indigenous people, which do not make such distinctions, and it is worth drawing on anthropological literatures here. For example, Nurit Bird-David offers an anthropological worldview of merged, fluid and changing subjectivities and transpersonal relationships that cannot be mapped or blackboxed in her study of the Nayaka hunter-gatherers in South India. Unlike cybernetic assemblages which enslave their constituent parts into subservient roles and fixed identities, she offers a way into thinking about distinctions between empowering and disempowering experiences of insertion into assemblages. Bird-David's concept of a 'band society' is one where families are not dominated by larger organisational structures (such as state, capitalism, institutions, corporations) but are themselves the locus of socio-political and economic practices (Bird-David 1994). Bird-David argues that technology 'works its way through human relationships', and webs of social and economic relationships which constitute their own level of causality, which belies simple technological determinism. Bird-David critiques English society and sociology, where individuals are understood to be rational, unique and autonomous individuals, yet in a sense are incomplete; they are '"socialized" into their parts within society, which is in itself a whole' (Bird-David 1994: 597). This 'whole' is akin to the cybernetic machines critiqued by Foucault, Deleuze, Raunig and others, into which humans are inserted like replaceable parts, expected to mould their desires to the functioning of the overall machine. To this, Bird-David contrasts what she calls the 'oil in water' sociology of the Nayaka forest-dwelling group of South India. The 'oil in water' metaphor comes from a Nayaka mourning ritual, in which oil is poured in a hollow filled with water near the last living place of the deceased. 'As the oil reaches the surface of the water, it forms floating drops. As the drops get nearer, and then touch each other, they add and amalgamate into a greater drop' (Bird-David 1994: 596). The metaphor encapsulates a 'sharing perspective' found in the society where, for example, spouses might have an object that 'belongs to one, belongs to the other, and to both of them, all at once' whilst a hut could be 'mine, Kungs's, Bomi's and ours' (Bird-David 1994: 596). The kinds of immediacy and 'we relationships' experienced by the Nayaka are eroded by distance, which is created by 'time, space or objectification', meaning that 'the other is no longer experienced as a "vivid", "biographic" person' (Bird-David 1994: 598). Mediating structures such as 'typificatory schemes' and 'role relationships' ensure a person comes to be defined and understood by their position in the machine, rather than their intrinsic or inner value and desires (Bird-David 1994: 598). Even the practice of theorising or talking about relationships is seen to impose a distance that erodes the immediacy of 'we relationships' (Bird-David 1994: 599).

While the contrast to cybernetic capitalist blackboxing is obvious, one might also argue that some anarchist and communist theories which emphasise organisation over interiority and relationships replicate the functionalist viewpoint which objectifies people. For example, some of the anarchists influenced by cybernetics cited above, such as (some aspects of the work of) Colin Ward, place emphasis on parallels with various physical sciences to emphasise non-hierarchical organisation or self-organisation as the basis of the 'social principle'. These can be contrasted with those who emphasise the need for an authentic ethical relation between subjects, such as Max Stirner's union of egoists (Stirner 1995), Martin Buber's I-Thou relation (2004), and the existentialist Emmanuel Levinas' ideas around ethics as first philosophy and the ontological primacy of the Other (Levinas 1969).[2] The former is an outer relation at a purely microsocial scale, so a group is enacting the 'social principle' if it is structurally horizontal and undertaking mutual aid, even if it is exclusive to a specific group, or the participants are neither anarchists nor committed to any particular ethical relation (so, for example, mutual aid could arguably occur amongst a group of billionaires). The latter is wider, including an ethical element (all relations ought to be social principle) and also interior (social principle means relating unique-one to unique-one, rather than performing a role for others).

Cybernetics silences and represses forms of knowledge that cannot be subsumed as replaceable nodes in a system. For example, anthropologists studying indigenous societies and social movements have argued for the importance of gossip and 'backstage activity' in both sustaining societies and in questioning and undermining domination and emerging hierarchies (Lagalisse 2013; see also Clastres 1977 and Scott 1990). The cybernetic ideal of a transparent system with unhindered transfer of information between pre-defined/reified 'autonomous' nodes and groups devalues

[2] Levinas' argument is much different to Stirner and Buber, insofar as Levinas moves towards the Derridean and Lacanian view that no authentic subjectivity/desire is possible without the other. However, he allows for the possibility of an authentic relationship with the Other, whereas the later Derridean theorists seem to see it as a psychoanalytic projection. Andrew Robinson traces the 'transition from psychoanalysis as a clinical theory to psychoanalysis as a set of discursive tools to silence opponents' to 'the denial of psychological depth in certain strands of the Lacanian/Althusserian heritage' (Robinson 2018: 268).

and reppresses the possibility for people and relationships beyond that system to form their own autonomous groups in order to create secret and potentially resistant and disruptive knowledge that might ultimately undermine the vested interests of the system. Erica Lagalisse argues for 'enchantment' as a radical form of knowledge and locates the emergence of many anti-authoritarian social movements, including anarchism, in forms of 'enchantment' provoked by popular religion, occult knowledge and magic. These are often dismissed by secular scientism, which attempts to apply the logic of property to spirituality and culture (Lagalisse 2018: 70–78).

We argue that other forms of knowledge—which cannot be planned in advance or mapped as part of a system—include tacit knowledge, as well as artisanal and crafts-based knowledge and relationships to technology. Other forms of knowledge might involve breaking black boxes in order to tinker and experiment with the components, to find out how they work, rather than breaking down production into pre-defined Taylorist components. These kinds of knowledge, which will be discussed further in Chaps. 4–6, might be seen as prefigurative forms of transgressive knowledge that by their very natures cannot be easily recuperated into any state-capital formation nor mapped as rigid functions that can be filled by replaceable or automated labour. Of course, profit-seekers and authoritarians might try to find ways to do so if they stood to benefit (Walker et al. 2018), but the ultimately transgressive forms of these knowledges are inherently disruptive of even emergent forms of state and capitalism.

The important role of conflict in knowledge-production is also ignored in cybernetic systems, which tend to seek stability through the repression of disagreement and discords, by assuming that subjectivity is infinitely malleable to objective functions and does not rely on any authentic inner experience or essence (Hibernicus 2023: 18). This precludes an authentic consensus being reached as consensus is imposed by diktat. In particular, recognition of class struggle and the limits to capitalism becomes impossible. Cybernetics ultimately is an exercise in bureaucratic empire building—the approaches usually emphasise the transfer of knowledge into agencies which can then claim oversight, or alternatively they presume consensus on particular values as true in advance. For example, authors in texts invested in cybernetic discourse frequently talk of what is 'generally accepted' or 'generally impossible' and attempt to formulate 'general principles' (Quarantelli 1998: 1). There is also a presumed hierarchy of forms of knowledge, with the author positioning themselves as the creator of higher-level general knowledge which trumps specific, situational knowledge, with the latter framed as basically unknowable—but also of secondary importance.

Subordination to Capital: Cybernetics as a Subordinating Machine

Cybernetic discourse imposes consensus by diktat and makes itself unquestionable through a rhetoric that appears to harmonise contradictory and opposing forces. For example, the texts emphasise both 'vertical and hierarchical integration', or 'autonomous groups' with 'management systems' and reconciling 'freedom' with 'control' (Beer 1994; Quarantelli 1998; Ambinder et al. 2013). Stafford Beer's books attempted to reconcile management discourse with art, poetry and science. Cyberneticians propose a kind of utopia where the autonomous dream of anarchism is reconciled with the authoritarian social control of Hobbesianism and the competitive individualism of capitalism. The only way to critique these theorists is to track the contradictions and to show how they are handled in practice, where they are forced to break their own rules, and where contradictions reveal themselves in the disjuncture between academic/policy rhetoric and practice (see, for example, Firth 2022; and Chap. 4 of this book). A frequent issue is that cybernetic approaches tend to rely on 'generic' or 'general' responses, and specific individual and community needs are largely invisible in standardised 'efficient' responses; people's attempts to meet their own needs are then seen as threatening to the integrity of the organised response. The emphasis on generic responses also encourages authoritarianism and securitisation—for example with COVID-19, a focus on 'public health' instead of 'health as human right' and in a disproportionate reliance on police instead of health services, and reiteration of measures designed for short-term disasters (such as lockdowns) being used in a long-duration situation, alongside the neglect of COVID- or virus-specific responses such as PPE, antivirals, etc. (Preston and Firth 2020).

We would go further to argue that even anarchist cybernetics is vulnerable to becoming subordinate to capital, and cybernetic utopias are particularly prone to recuperation in totalitarian formations. An important criticism, which we also made earlier in this chapter, of radical cybernetics is that it is utopian in a totalising sense because it starts from theory (cybernetics and anarchism) and sketches out a utopian design (Duda 2013: 65); however, it might be argued in response that the emphasis on self-organisation and flexibility partially answer this (Swann 2018; Fox 2023). A stronger argument is that cybernetic anarchism tends to ignore or underplay the potential for recuperation of networks. Whilst cybernetics praises self-organisation as an effective and efficient form of governance, which may have seemed a radical idea under the more hierarchical and massified structures of the earlier Fordist regime, it is still often extolled for its efficiency, stability and productiveness, which are values that are of use to, and not contradictory with, capitalism, therefore ripe for recuperation, since 'the political question of reaching this goal and fending off institutional ossification is hardly posed at all, and many questions remain unaddressed' (Duda 2013: 65). This can be seen in neoliberal forms of cybernetic capitalism which valorise networks and flexible production but still rest on exploitation of labour. Furthermore, anarchist cyberneticians can sometimes ground the basis of self-organised social change as arising from self-organised technological change, which can give somewhat of a tautological, determinist or accelerationist account: 'by framing the idea of self-organisation in technological terms, the content of anarchism becomes something given in advance' (Duda 2013: 68). This is not to say that existing, new and experimental technologies cannot be useful for anarchists and other anti-authoritarians and anti-capitalists; however, this would usually be through hacking and other forms of tactical, tacit, artisanal and craft knowledge. These are forms of knowledge and relationship that it is difficult to map, automate, replicate or reify, as argued above. Richard Hall and Bernd Stahl show how cybernetic commodification through technological innovation in manufacturing and material labour is mirrored in the university through immaterial labour. Capital utilises emergent technologies to incorporate labour into its self-valorisation, for example virtual and augmented reality, cloud computing, human-machine symbiosis and affective computing artefacts which perceive, express and model human emotions. Each of these is a frontier and a way for capital to commodify relations and to 'enclose how and where and why people assemble, associate and organise' (Hall and Stahl 2015: 197–198).

Cybernetics portrays itself as a separate sphere of production of information and communication but has become 'an autonomous world of apparatuses merged with the capitalist project insofar as the latter is a political project, a gigantic "abstract machine" made up of binary machines deployed by Empire, a new form of political sovereignty … an abstract machine that has turned into a global war machine' (Tiqqun 2020: 24). Cybernetic capitalism refers to the emerging social formation since the 1970s that has replaced Fordist capitalism and 'results from the application of the cybernetic hypothesis to political economy' (Tiqqun 2020: 63). It is the recomposition of the social body devastated by capital into a new formation to allow for 'a further cycle to the process of accumulation'. As a new frontier of capitalism, it implies destruction, yet 'it must reconstruct a semblance of the "human community" which implies a circulation' (Tiqqun 2020: 63).

Cybernetics as Vanguardist

Cybernetics appears to have non-vanguardist potential, because, like anarchism, it proposes decentralised, non-hierarchical systems. However, it is also possible to identify vanguardist elements, and ultimately, cybernetics can be understood as the epistemological and sociotechnical correlate (or root metaphor) of a particular state-capital formation. This is most evident in first-order cybernetics, where understanding of self-organised systems is to be used as a means of manipulation and control. While previously discussed historians of cybernetics, like Rid, Turner and Barbrook and Cameron, tend to see the rise of the internet, as well as the rise of networked social and cultural movements, as always complicit in cybernetics, our contention is that these arose autonomously whilst cybernetics acts as a means of capture for neoliberal capitalism. The early twentieth century saw the rise of Fordism as a centralised and organised form of capitalism, based on mass production and consumption, where the state acts as an organiser and stabiliser for capital. In the late twentieth century and early twenty-first, the development of post-Fordist neoliberal capitalism led the state to significantly relinquish this role, while at the same time, in developed countries, manufacturing has given way to the service economy and more precarious forms of work (Lash and Urry 1987). In the 1980s, the discourse of cybernetics underpinned Third-Way politics and the rise of a discourse of New Public Management from the 1980s onwards. The professional strata (e.g. doctors and lecturers) in both public and private institutions largely relinquished their autonomy and authority to managerialists, who embodied a state-capitalist logic with decentralised cybernetic components. Rather than acting as rigid Fordist bureaucrats and taking a top-down approach to managing organisations, they were trained to plan and manage predicted risks in terms of behavioural nudges, proactive measures, quantification and flexibility, all requiring huge amounts of surveillance and data, e.g. via metrics. Despite outwardly appearing to resemble decentralised organisation and endowing social actors with a sense of autonomy cybernetics lends itself to applications in platform algorithmic capitalism that privilege precarious labour, and precarious public services, as seen in the rise of platform capitalism and the 'quantified self' in industries such as Uber and now in 'Industry 4.0' manufacturing, as shall be discussed in Chap. 4.

The position of the cybernetic analyst is 'how do we control behaviour in these systems?' Andrew Robinson argues that the aim is to turn capitalism into a self-sustaining, self-regulating system, to try to stop it breaking down because it never recovered from the 1973 financial crisis, when the dollar was unpegged from gold leading to the collapse of the Bretton Woods system and the financialisation of the economy. Cybernetics is trying to freeze it at this point so as to prevent social change and to repress or recuperate any movements which threaten it quickly (Robinson 2018). In this sense, anything external to capitalism (even social movements) can be internalised. *Tiqqun* similarly argue that this is part of a much longer tendency of financialisation that Fordism and Taylorism were part of, and that cybernetics is the development of control and manipulation of values and desires through marketing and advertising, after the end of the nineteenth century, when 'it was noted that *predictability was becoming a source of profit seeing that it was a source of confidence*' (Tiqqun 2020: 67). Capitalists make use of information and data in order to map, profile, view patterns, catch resistance quickly before it happens, and this happens through processes of increasing surveillance, monitoring and control backed up by an ethos of '*total transparency … a will to know to such a degree of accumulation that it becomes a will to power*' in the information society (Tiqqun 2020: 70).

Conclusion: The Impossibility of Cybernetic Anarchism

It is one thing to argue that cybernetics is recuperated in capitalism or, as we hope to have argued, that it acts as a kind of recuperating-machine for capitalism. However, many of the thinkers outlined in this chapter, including Rid, Turner, and Barbrook and Cameron, all take the position that the counter-cultural movements, DiY politics and horizontalist social movements that arose simultaneously with the ascendency of cybernetics were always-already co-opted and complicit in capitalist forms of cybernetics. This view was echoed in the series 'All Watched Over By Machines of Loving Grace' by popular documentary film-maker Adam Curtis (BBC/Curtis 2011), which offers an excellent correlate to these histories. The implication in all these narratives is that the anarchist, autonomist and ecological movements of that time used networked forms of non-hierarchical organisation, which mirrored the decentralisation of capital, meaning they were ultimately recuperated from the beginning—either because their organisational forms meant that they were 'not political' enough to really challenge capitalism; or they argue that there is 'no outside' to capitalism (even subjective or experiential) so therefore movement activists were naïve to think so. There is a strong tendency in Liberal thought as well (some) Marxist analyses to conflate anarchism/anarchist movements/decentralised organising with cybernetic capitalism, and to imply that the possibility of a utopian community, or even an authentic interiority/subjectivity is impossible. Decentralising tendencies are often conflated with capitalist deterritorialisation, because they do not propose a centralised entity to redistribute resources, and concepts such as self-organisation, complexity, autonomy and horizontality are seen as always-already complicit in capitalism, or at least the concepts themselves are seen to embody authoritarian tendencies as well as liberating ones (e.g. Fisher 2009; Freeman 2005). The problem with these approaches is that they leave no space for agency, expressions of autonomous desire and solidarity, or prefiguring non-capitalist, anti-authoritarian lifeworlds. They are structuralist theories, in which every person or action is complicit in the reproduction of oppression.

From a radical utopian standpoint, this Leftist discourse of 'no outside' is incredibly debilitating. We would assert that, rather than this position, we need to be putting positive utopian ideas forward. People have had enough of neoliberalism, but it is so pervasive they are unable to think outside it, especially for those who in an increasingly securitised culture have never had experience of autonomous zones or places outside capitalism. Without utopian visions, thought and practice, it is very hard to envision anything else (while our own approach in this book is more critical than utopian, we attempt to articulate our utopian standpoint in the conclusion). Despite the paralysis of the contemporary (elite/academic) Left, there is certainly a desire for something more radical, and to take it beyond capitalism, but there does not seem to be any feeling or description of what this might look like. From the 1970s onwards cultural products such as utopian literature begin to blend into dystopian literature (Moylan 1986; Firth 2019), while at the present juncture, utopian literature seems to have entirely given way to the dystopian (Suvin 2013). This is the case not only in the utopian literary genre but in the worldviews of both cybernetics and the Leftist correlates: they seem to critique an out-dated version of capitalism and decry the lack of alternatives without realising the radical utopianism of previous autonomous countercultures and social movements, such as communes, drugs, back-to-the-land tools, New Age spirituality and geodesic domes which got de-radicalised into capitalism. There is a sense they are trying to reinvent the wheel around hippy culture from the 1960s and 1970s, or imagining that it has already been realised, so launching critiques or attacks retrospectively on the original vision, for example, that it was always and everywhere hierarchical, or exclusive, or always recuperated in capitalism. Their critiques then seem to invest hopes in current technologies as a form of utopian replication which acts as a pedagogy to normalise a posthuman era of technologically connected future as inevitable and positive and elitist, because it does little to offer autonomous alternatives. There is also a tendency to play down the radicalism of working-class mutual aid movements (Preston and Firth 2020), as well as the utopian potential in many everyday forms of (subaltern/ non-capitalist) knowledge, subjectivity and relationships (examined in more detail in the later chapters of this book).

In the upcoming Chaps. 4–6 we will focus on some spaces and practices that we believe offer utopian potential, even though they are in no way to be understood as fully 'autonomous spaces' (and many would see one of these as the antithesis of autonomous). While we believe that there is even more utopian potential in autonomous spaces (Firth 2012, 2022), the purpose is to show that there are also forms of grassroots knowledge and everyday experience that transgress or evade the capture of capital, and which it would be impossible to understand using cybernetic management techniques or to automate using a machine, robot or AI. We have chosen specifically to focus on a range of organisations that use automating technology in either mainstream (Chap. 4) or in unconventional organisations (Chaps. 5 and 6). Our selection is not necessarily about whether they call themselves 'cybernetic'-inspired or not, as we have already theorised cybernetics as pervasive throughout capitalist society, yet concealed in a culture of silence. Neither do we want to criticise any the organisations for complicity—rather, we are focused on what they are prefiguring. The most radical forms of prefiguration would escape the key tenets of cybernetic rationality because they would embody forms of subjectivity beyond measure; that cannot be broken down into nodes or blackboxed, nor moulded into functional nodes in a technocratic design.

The prefigurative cases we draw on in Chaps. 5 and 6 are a workers' co-operative that makes custom automation solutions in the United States and a non-hierarchical Hackspace in the UK, which is a community-run non-profit workshop for people to share tools and knowledge. We have chosen these two cases, because whilst they are both very different, they exhibit common features that speak to the idea of cybernetic utopias. They are both organised with a non-hierarchical ethos and are owned and run democratically by the workers or members that use them. They both exist with the aim of empowering their workers/members to develop skills to use technology and automation in non-capitalist ways, or for creating some forms of common wealth for their member-owners. Our rationale for using these organisations is that they offer critique and inspire alternatives to the forms of skills and learning assumed by capitalist cybernetics. In the following Chap. 4, however, we focus on a mainstream organisation, to argue that even in an organisation that is fundamentally driven by capitalist values, emergent utopias in the form of prefigurative knowledges that cannot be captured by cybernetics do still exist.

References

Ambinder, E., Jennings, D. M., Blachman-Biatch, I., Edgemon, K., Hull, P. and Taylor, A., 2013. *The Resilient Social Network*. Department of Homeland Security Science and Technology Directorate (DHS), Publication Number: RP12-01.04.11-01. pp. 24–5.

Beer, S., 1981. *Brain of the Firm*. 2nd ed. Chichester: John Wiley and Sons.

Beer, S., 1994. *How Many Grapes went Into the Wine: Stafford Beer on the Art and Science of Holistic Management*. R. Harndon and A. Leonard, eds. Chichester: John Wiley and Sons.

Bird-David, N., 1994. Sociality and Immediacy: Or, Past and Present Conversations on Bands. *Man*. New Series, 29(3), pp. 583–603.

Lucia, B., Vetter, M. A., & Adubofour, I. K. (2023). Behold the metaverse: Facebook's Meta imaginary and the circulation of elite discourse. New Media & Society, 0(0). https://doi.org/10.1177/14614448231184249

Buber, M., 2004. *I and Thou*. London: Continuum.

Clastres, P., 1977. *Society Against the State*. Oxford: Blackwell.

Curtis, A., 2011. *All Watched Over by Machines of Loving Grace.* [TV documentary], episodes 1–3. BBC 2. 23 May – 6 June 2011.
Deleuze, G. and Guattari, F., 1987. *A Thousand Plateaus.* London: Continuum.
Duda, J., 2013. Cybernetics, Anarchism and Self-organisation. *Anarchist Studies*, 21(1), pp. 52–72.
Ferneding, K., 2005. Embracing the telematic: A techno-utopian vision of art and pedagogy for the post-human age of control. *Journal of the American Association for the Advancement of Curriculum Studies (JAAACS)*, 1. Available at: http://www.uwstout.edu/soe/jaaacs/vol1/ferneding.html [Accessed 7 August 2024].
Firth, R., 2012. *Utopian Politics: Citizenship and Practice.* London: Routledge.
Firth, R., 2022. *Disaster Anarchy.* London: Pluto.
Firth, R., 2019. Afterword. In: M.L. Berneri, ed. *Journey Through Utopia.* Oakland: PM Press. pp. 331–392.
Fisher, M., 2009. *Capitalist Realism: Is There No Alternative?.* Winchester: Zero Books.
Fox, J., 2023. *Dis/agreement in participatory organisations: low theory and democratic governance in cybernetics* (Doctoral Dissertation, University of Essex).
Freeman, J., 2005 [1972]. The Tyranny of Structurelessness. In: *Untying the Knot.* London: Anarchist Federation. pp. 1–5.
Galloway, A.R., 2014. The Cybernetic Hypothesis. *differences*, 25(1), pp. 107–131.
Hall, R. and Stahl, B., 2015. Against commodification: The university, cognitive capitalism and emergent technologies. In: C. Fuchs and V. Mosco, eds. *Marx and the Political Economy of the Media.* Leiden: Brill. pp. 65–97.
Harman, G., 2018. *Object-Oriented Ontology: A New Theory of Everything.* Harmondsworth: Pelican. pp. 136–9.
Hibernicus, D., 2023. *Node Theory: An Anarchist Analysis of Cybernetic Control Society and Proposals to Resist it.* Berkley, CA: LBC Books.
Hobbes, T., 2006 [1651]. *Leviathan.* Mineola, NY: Dover Publications.
Lagalisse, E., 2013. Gossip as Direct Action. In: S. Cole and L. Phillips, eds. *Contesting Publics: Feminism, Activism Ethnography.* London: Pluto Press.
Lagalisse, E., 2018. *Occult Features of Anarchism.* London: PM Press.
Lash, S. and Urry, J., 1987. *The End of Organized Capitalism.* Madison: University of Wisconsin Press.
Levinas, E., 1969. *Totality and Infinity: An Essay on Exteriority.* Pittsburgh, PA: Duquesne University Press.
Marx, K., 1993. *Grundrisse: Foundations of the Critique of Political Economy.* London: Penguin.
McLaverty-Robinson, A., 2020. *Homi Bhabha: An Introduction and Critique (Volume 2: Colonialism and Inbetweenness).* Morrisville, NC: Lulu Press.

Medina, E., 2014. *Cybernetic Revolutionaries: Technology and Politics in Allende's Chile*. Cambridge, MA: MIT Press.

Moore, P.V., 2017. *The Quantified Self in Precarity: Work, Technology and What Counts*. London: Routledge.

Moylan, T., 1986. *Demand the Impossible: Science Fiction and the Utopian Imagination*. New York: Methuen.

Nold, C., 2017. *Device Studies of Participatory Sensing: Ontological Politics and Design Interventions*. Doctoral thesis, UCL (University College London). pp. 28 & 46.

Pias, C., 2005. Analog, digital, and the cybernetic illusion. *Kybernetes*, 34(3/4), pp. 543–550.

Pitts, F.H. 2018. Critiquing Capitalism Today: New Ways to Read Marx. London: Palgrave.

Preston, J. and Firth, R., 2020. *Coronavirus, Class and Mutual Aid in the UK*. London: Palgrave.

Quarantelli, E.L., 1998. Major Criteria for Judging Disaster Planning and Managing Their Applicability in Developing Countries. *University of Delaware Disaster Research Center, Preliminary Paper #268*. Available at: http://udspace.udel.edu/bitstream/handle/19716/286/PP268.pdf?sequence=1&isAllowed=y [Accessed 9 July 2020].

Rid, T., 2016. *Rise of the Machines: The Lost History of Cybernetics*. Melbourne and London: Scribe.

Robinson, A., 2018. Episode 89: What is Anarchism in 2018 with Andy [podcast]. *The Brilliant*, 28 December 2018. Available at: https://thebrilliant.org/podcast/episode-89-what-is-anarchism-in-2018-with-andy/ [Accessed 7 August 2024].

Scott, J., 1990. *Domination and the Arts of Resistance: Hidden Transcripts*. New Haven and London: Yale University Press.

Stirner, M., 1995. *The Ego and Its Own*. Cambridge: Cambridge University Press.

Ström, T., 2022. Capital and Cybernetics. *New Left Review*, 135, pp. 23–41.

Suvin, D., 2013. Theses on Dystopia 2001. In: *Dark Horizons*. London: Routledge. pp. 199–214.

Swann, T., 2018. Towards an Anarchist Cybernetics: Stafford Beer, Self-Organisation and Radical Social Movements. *Ephemera*, 18(3), pp. 427–456.

Swann, T., 2020. *Anarchist Cybernetics: Control and Communication In Radical Politics*. Bristol: Policy Press.

The Invisible Committee, 2015. *To Our Friends*. Trans. R. Hurley. Los Angeles: Semiotext(e).

TiqB44qun, 2020 [2001]. *The Cybernetic Hypothesis*. Trans. R. Hurley. Los Angeles: Semiotext(e).

Virilio, P., 1990. *Popular Defense & Ecological Struggles*. Los Angeles: Semiotext(e).

Virilio, P., 2005. *The Information Bomb.* London: Verso.

Virilio, P. and Lotringer, S., 1998. *Pure War.* Los Angeles: Semiotext(e).

Walker, D., et al. (2018) 'Feasibility of capturing crafts-based knowledge in an AI system for future autonomous precision surface manufacturing'. [Project report] Available at: https://connectedeverythingmedia.files.wordpress.com/2019/05/capturing-craft-expertise-project.pdf [Accessed: 7 August 2024]

CHAPTER 4

Industry 4.0 Utopias? Human Potential and Prefiguration in Advanced Cybernetic Manufacturing

Description of the Interviews

In this chapter, eight interviewees were interviewed in seven sessions. Two were in management roles and the remainder were engineers in diverse roles and departments. Somewhat out of step with our planned methodology, two of the interviews were undertaken by a manager who was our host in the factory, and one of these interviews was undertaken with two workers simultaneously. We realise this raises various ethical and methodological issues. In particular, the workers may have felt under pressure to participate since their manager was present, although in a sense this was the case for all the interviews as the manager acted as a gatekeeper. It is also worth consideration that workers may also have withheld information due to being interviewed by a manager; however, the questions were not of a personal or politically sensitive nature. We consulted with the workers to check they were happy with this arrangement, and all interviewees signed consent forms. Pseudonyms are used throughout. (Table 4.1).

Introduction

In the previous chapter we outlined our critique of cybernetics in terms of its functionalist nature, disavowal of politics and subjectivity, the 'black-boxing' of individuals and entities, and its neglect of other forms of human knowledge and subjectivity. In this chapter we examine how, in practice, cybernetic relationships can never capture human potential and agency

R. Firth, J. Preston, *Utopia in the Factory*,
https://doi.org/10.1007/978-3-031-87132-0_4

Table 4.1 Details of interviews

Interviewee alias	*Interviewed by*	*Date*	*Job/department*
Thomas	John Preston	12 September 2019	Production leader in Body & white
Lydia	John Preston	12 September 2019	Technology manager—leading human centric manufacture
Jamie	John Preston and Rhiannon Firth	12 September 2019	Maintenance engineer, working with robots in paint shop
Riley and Lewis	CYBER4.0 manager	12 September 2019	Two interviewees: CME—paint application engineer (Riley) and new process engineer (Lewis)
Evan	CYBER4.0 manager	12 September 2019	CME—manufacturing/engineering
Adam	Rhiannon Firth	12 September 2019	Shift manager—maintenance
Jacob	Rhiannon Firth	12 September 2019	Tooling quality and CME manager

even within a capitalist organisation which attempts to capture the skills and knowledge of those individuals. Although this is not (necessarily) a 'prefiguration', it provides empirical evidence of the limits to cybernetic logics. In the introduction to this book, we considered the development of 'Industry 4.0' as a contemporary manifestation of cybernetics. This system applies cybernetic elements to link the 'cyber' elements of manufacturing (datafication, quantification, AI and machine learning) with the 'physical' elements (production of commodities) and the 'human' elements of labour. 'Industry 4.0' aims to create a closed system where all inputs and outputs can be monitored, explored and controlled across various manufacturing ecologies (including supply chains and production). It is a complete cybernetic 'ecology' going beyond the boundaries of the firm to include external forces such as suppliers and competition. Industry 4.0 has obvious correlates with a cybernetic system that aims to meet the goals of an organisation, normally profit and revenue.

In a book that aims to develop a critique of cybernetics from a largely anarchist and autonomist perspective, it may seem strange to start with an obviously capitalist organisation that uses 'Industry 4.0' methods. There is an obvious line of critique in terms of worker autonomy, exploitation and commodification. In this chapter we provide a different line of critique in terms of examining the limitations of cybernetic/Industry 4.0

organisations in their own terms because of the implausibility of such systems as containing human agency, skill, and knowledge. We are also interested in the prefigurative and utopian aspects of human agency, skill and knowledge that transgress and resist cybernetic capture. One identified problem with fulfilling the potential of any cybernetic system (including Industry 4.0) is the status and integration of humans in the system, including human labourers and workers. In a complete cybernetic system, every component should be mapped and integrated or at least 'blackboxed' in terms of inputs and outputs. This has been a critical point of difficulty for progress (from the perspective of capital) towards 'Industry 4.0'. One approach to this has been to attempt to quantify and digitise aspects of worker behaviour. The 'quantified self at work' (Moore 2017; Moore and Robinson 2016), including the use of smart watches, body sensors and video tracking, has been one approach, although workers often change their behaviour to account for these devices and there are many aspects of work that cannot be monitored. Moreover, workers often resist attempts to monitor their work in this way, either informally or through organised trade union activity. Another approach has been to 're-engineer' workers to behave in ways that are compatible with Industry 4.0 systems. This may include working conjointly with robots, or other machines, in a structured way that is responsive to new digital information (that could also be gamified). It may also include new methods of training and competency that stress measurability and performance. In making humans 'machine readable', 'robot compatible' or 'digitised', there are inevitably losses in terms of human performance that is far beyond the capability of machines (Preston 2017).

In order to incorporate the 'human in the loop', it has been suggested that the paradigm of Industry 4.0 should be extended to Industry 5.0, which incorporates human skills, abilities and resilience in a new paradigm. The difficulty is compounded as Industry 4.0 fully adopts cybernetics and systems analysis in terms of the acceptability of 'blackboxing'. In cybernetic systems (typical of Industry 2.0 and 3.0) industrial production accepted 'blackboxing' of component systems (Leng et al. 2022). If a supplier, worker or consumer could not be fully mapped, then they could be at least 'blackboxed' and their inputs and outputs modelled as a statistical model. Industry 4.0 is 'hungry' for data and knowledge about entities as a useable 'set' within (and outside of) a factory that it can use to meet their goals (Leng et al. 2022). Hence, Industry 4.0 aims for (but never achieves) a fully specified cybernetic system and a system-of-systems.

The question of how humans could be included in Industry 4.0, or in a new paradigm, is a political, theoretical and empirical one. In this chapter we will not look at the political consequences of Industry 4.0 (or 5.0) as a model, other than to ask to what extent it is possible within its own terms. In particular, if Industry 4.0 offers a concrete, cybernetic-type industrial utopia, to what extent is that possible within its own logics? We will first consider the theoretical arguments of why humans might not be similar to the other 'data' in such a model and examine, through an empirical case study, of a major, advanced, digital manufacturer in the UK, the validity of these arguments. The data in this chapter is based on an extensive case study of a real-world, high-technology, leading multi-national corporate manufacturing company (with the pseudonym CYBER4.0), the details of which are provided in the introduction.

Background: Human Workers in Industry 4.0 and the Limits of Cybernetic Logic

There are various arguments that suggest it might be difficult to incorporate humans into a system of Industry 4.0 and a cybernetic system more generally. In the previous chapter we have considered arguments from anarchist thinkers and critical theorists on the politics of constraining humans in mechanical systems. Human workers were, and are, treated as a 'black box' in industrial systems, and it was only their outputs that were of interest. Taylorism, and competence-based qualifications, 're-engineered' human workers to meet the requirements of the task at hand. Statistical modelling and simulation allowed for an analysis of work rates and variances which could be modelled, and interventions could be used to manipulate these, but this still concentrates on outcomes. Industry 4.0 disrupts this paradigm due to its cybernetic approach to entities that are contained within what might be called the 'set' of the manufacturing process. In an agile production system, entities may be combined in different ways to attain production goals, but to do so these entities need to be opened up to an analysis of their possibilities and potentials. Of course, this task has previously been attempted by Human Resources departments. Sometimes even researchers have been embedded in factories. Sociologists have had a long-standing interest in factory studies. The Ford

Motor Company created their Sociological Department in 1914 with a pragmatic interest in improving work efficiency, family life and language skills (Loizides 2004). The 1970s was a time of considerable interest in factory studies in sociology with studies of the affluent worker and industrialisation. There are many reasons why human capacities might not be captured by cybernetic systems, and we discussed these in the previous chapter. In terms of parallels between humans and machinery, Dreyfus (1992) has argued that there are ontological and epistemological arguments which set limits to how far it is possible for computers, or any cybernetic system, to emulate human capabilities. Ontologically, and drawing on Heidegger, tools (such as computers or cybernetic grids) only have meaning in terms of the meaning in their relation to other tools, which are in turn meaningful only in terms of human social arrangements. A hammer has meaning only in terms of nails and wood, and in terms of the human activity of building, for example. Epistemologically, knowledge cannot be abstracted from social arrangements. These arguments can be pivoted to consider why it would not be possible to incorporate human knowledge and capabilities within Industry 4.0 and indeed in cybernetic systems more generally. The biological argument is that the human brain is not a digital device and cannot be simulated by cybernetic or computational processes. Rather, the brain is a complex analogue device whose neurophysiological processes are not open to digitisation. For human workers, mental processes or 'states' are not open to digitisation and, it is argued, might never be open to machine capabilities. Humans are biologically and psychologically unpredictable (and possess agency), and although statistical regularities in behaviour might occur these cannot be depended upon and there is no digital, cybernetic or statistical model that can replace the 'human brain' in an Industry 4.0 system.

Dreyfus argues that although components of human behaviour might be reproduced they operate only in very limited domains. Human capacities involve selectivity of information from a wide range of contexts, and sensing (through physical sense organs that operate on an analogue basis) means that there are limits to the capacity of an expert system (in Industry 4.0) to mirror human knowledge. The epistemological argument is that human performance cannot be fully formalised (as a set of rules) as this is always dependent on context. Dreyfus identifies several forms of human performance that cannot be formalised, such as fringe consciousness (where information on the fringes of conscious thought is taken into account), ambiguity tolerance (allowance for idiosyncrasies that appear to be out of context), essential-inessential discrimination (to determine parameters for action rather than allowing the parameters to be imposed) and perspicuous grouping (to recognise similarity and difference based on emergent modes of grouping) (Dreyfus 1992: 155–206). Finally, the ontological argument is that humans have bodies and histories, and exist in socio-physical settings where entities have meanings and relations to each other. These cannot be incorporated into a cybernetic system, including Industry 4.0.

As will be discussed, the results our investigation show that there are many human forms of work that cannot be integrated into a cybernetic system or into an Industry 4.0 model. We identified several themes which we call tacit knowledge and hobbying that break blackboxing where human work activity is captured within the factory process but cannot be classified as part of a cybernetic or Industry 4.0 system. We also identified areas where the attitude of workers and managers was more in line with the forms of subsumption suggested by Industry 4.0 in terms of anthropomorphism, attitudes favourable to 'Industry 4.0' techniques and in terms of human enhancement by machines. This has implications for both cybernetic mapping and Industry 4.0, or further iterations of it, as well as utopianism and speculative futures. We will explore these ideas through the themes that emerged from the interviews with the CYBER4.0 workers.

Tacit Knowledge

One theme that came out in the interviews was that of what has been called 'tacit knowledge' (Polanyi 2021; Collins 2010). Tacit knowledge refers to a creative or artisanal relationship to the work and technology, and to types of knowledge held by individuals or collectives that are not being captured by the organisation. This includes people doing their own projects (a process that we refer to as hobbying, see below) or inputting their own knowledge into the processes, in ways that cannot necessarily be recorded or systematised by management for future training materials or for automating processes. There may be conflicting imperatives or priorities here; for example, it may be in the workers' interests to keep knowledge local whereas the company may want to systematise the knowledge so that it can be modularised or automated. Tacit knowledge, craft and artisanal (qualitative) relationships, cannot be modelled in cybernetic systems.

One stark way in which tacit knowledge presented itself was in the relationship between human senses and mechanical processes, such as pressing and stamping. Mechanical processes were, of course, monitored in terms of rates and efficiencies in a form that could be entered easily into cybernetic-type systems for data analytics. We observed a wide variety of mechanical processes in CYBER4.0, from production lines to pressing and stamping facilities where a batch of materials or components could be processed. In one particular area of the factory, which featured an enormous pressing machine which was the size of a row of large houses, it was possible to feel the process of pressing with one's entire body. Even in the nearby offices, the noise and vibration were palpable and became familiar even in a short time period. Whether through individual or shared experience, workers we interviewed stated that they had an ability to 'read' materials and processes in ways that cannot be put into words and could only be expressed as matters of experience that were bound up with senses and the body. For example, hearing when a machine is going wrong, or reading a metal plate for imperfections. One worker reflected on this:

> The noise the press generates obviously requires ear protection, but can also be heard and felt when you're in the offices as well. And I've lived and breathed stamping all of my working life and I've grown up and lived in press shops all my working life, and when you work with the press machine day in day out, when it's running, you kind of synchronise yourself with the press, so when the press is running, for example, 7.5 strokes a minute, I can hear it's 7.5 strokes a minute. When it's running a different part at say 12 strokes a minute, you definitely notice the difference in speed through the sound that the press produces. … When the press stops, depending on what noise it makes when it stops, sort of depending on whether it's sending alarm bells to me. For example, if the press stops and dumps a load of air, then we know there's a potential problem. If the press stops and we hear a whirring noise as it stops, then I know that the servo drives are shutting down which also could lead to a potential problem. So before we've even gone down to the shop floor to clarify the problem, you get a gut feeling on some of the symptoms that were being presented during the press stopping or starting. (Jacob)

This interview extract shows that there is a connection between the worker's experience, their body and the industrial process. They have 'lived and breathed' stamping and 'grown up and lived in' press shops. This enables a tacit knowledge and a 'synchronisation' with the process which enables faults to be detected as a 'feeling'. This involves experience, embodiment and a feeling, qualitative notions which cannot be included into a cybernetic system.

Tacit knowledge was also involved later in the production process in the upholstery fitting of the CYBER4.0 production, which involved ascriptions of taste and aesthetics:

> The robots will never be able to open the door, the interior smells nice inside, everything's clean and tidy, it is that intuition and appreciation for things ... I just believe that that quality aspect, but I won't even say that, it is just that human element, keeping the human race in touch with what is going on. I think it would be difficult to go for fully automation from end to end. (Thomas)

> You can teach somebody to write the programme, put dots in a sequence so the robot will follow them, that's relatively straightforward. The art, if you like, of getting the product in the most optimised condition it can come with experience, it's very difficult to teach that, and it takes a bit of time to understand what adjustment with the robot can affect that particular part of the appearance that's either good or bad. (Lewis)

Tacit knowledge can also include fine perceptions or measurements, such as fitting a door with repeated attempts and re-positionings, that robots, or a cybernetic system, would be unable to judge:

> After the actual measurement process we have door finesse ... the robot cannot know that. I am applying this to where we are currently working. (Thomas)

Tacit knowledge can include knowledge that cannot be automated, for example because there is a high level of variability, which one worker imputed to management tasks in particular, in response to the question of whether robots could replace managers:

> No. I'm looking at this from a maintenance perspective. You do get the same repetitive breakdowns, but there's anyways a situation where you have to think out the box, it's not the norm, so how are you going to deal with

> this? You have to overcome certain difficulties. I can't see how that would be replaced, that comes down to experience. (Adam)

Tacit knowledge tends to be learnt through experience on-the-job rather than through formal/theoretical training or qualifications and involves aspects of lifelong learning:

> I had my GCSEs from school which allowed me to get on the apprenticeship and I got a craft apprenticeship, and it's really since then that my qualifications have started to excel. (Jacob)
>
> I don't think I'll ever stop learning. I'm learning every single day. I think we're all learning every day. Even colleagues in their 50s are still learning. (Jacob)

Automation was sometimes cited as a threat to the accumulated tacit knowledge in the company:

> It's all about reducing that head count, because the biggest cost to any company is people, but it's a balance, because there's a lot of experience within those people as well. So it is a real fine balance and a real critical business decision if you are going to start reducing heads of associates, or your head count, by introducing technology. (Jacob)

It should be noted, though, that some workers saw tacit knowledge as different from other forms of judgement which could act as an obstacle to quality, due to the variation in knowledge between workers:

> There are some processes which are quite easy to manipulate, so some operators will do it differently to others, so you can see quite a bit of variation in the part quality depending on who's been on the job, so this is an issue that we're always trying to address and trying to reduce variability. (Evan)
>
> Where we are now, your basic trackline of movements … in my opinion it will *never be an end to end system*, particularly not with luxury products. I doubt if everything will be automated, we do have a lot of human interaction as well … AI is exciting, the future is exciting. (Thomas, italics for emphasis)
>
> At no point would I think – like the Terminator – with robots *the human is always the initiator. Nothing happens without us.* If we didn't tell them they were robots they wouldn't know what they were … they are a very good

> tool because they are repeatable … any learning behaviour we can step in and teach … we would use a series of cameras to *check data points … when we would go in and teach we would show pictures … if machine learning was implemented we wouldn't have to do this.* (Jamie, italics for emphasis)

These points suggest that there is variety in human knowledge that can never wholly be reduced to mechanic processes and that humans possess an aesthetic sense that cannot be automated. These are features of tacit knowledge.

Hobbying

Connected to tacit knowledge was an element of playing and experimenting with technologies and going beyond the limitations set on them by the cybernetic system of production. For a number of the people we interviewed, this was almost of the order of a (useful) hobby within the factory, becoming a practical interest that involved elements of creativity of play. We call this 'hobbying'. For one of our respondents, playing with the pendants that taught the robots, and with robotic technology more generally, solidified into an interest which went beyond tacit knowledge and became almost like a 'hobby':

> Before I joined CYBER4.0 I had very little robot experience, I hadn't really been exposed to robotics at all. I did a couple of courses while I was here, but I would say that a lot of the knowledge I gained was from actually picking up a pendant and having a go. I was given a bit of confidence to do that by watching other people doing it, watching the contractors when they were installing the equipment, they were quite helpful at explaining how certain things worked, but other than that, ultimately the main learning was done by having a go and making mistakes, not too big mistakes so you cause a lot of damage, but you know, learning from them mistakes and using that knowledge and trying to pass it on to other people. (Evan)

> My role in maintenance was a technical group leader, so I was the next level up from the operator, if he couldn't solve the problem, because I was a bit more technically-minded, so you'd quite often have to re-programme robot paths to avoid collisions, or for any improvement work on the glue paths, because sometimes they vary because of parts, or the actual viscosity of the glue can vary, so we'd be always tweaking and improving to get the better quality parts, and to reduce the downtime for maintenance. (Evan)

> In the body and white, we'd do certain checks to, make the equipment safe to work with, you'd have to switch the robot to manual, take control of the pendant which also had a deadman switch on it, so if for any reason something went wrong or the robot was moving too quickly you could just let go and the robot would stop everything and from that you'd have control of the robot using a joystick and a variety of different actions on the pendant, you could manipulate the robot and get it to do whatever you wanted to do. (Evan)

In these quotes, the worker describes using the robot in creative ways, to solve situated and unpredictable problems. This is similar to the ways in which an artisan might use any convivial tool.

Blackboxing and Its Limitations

In a cybernetic system a 'blackbox' has inputs and outputs and process is not important. Contrary to this, workers touched on the idea that some people rely more on tacit-styles of knowledge such as feeling and emotion, whilst other workers were more prone to rational and systematic forms of work and learning:

> To some people, the machine doesn't speak back, and doesn't have any feelings, doesn't have any emotions, doesn't need a drink, doesn't need feeding. But to other people that understand the machine, it does speak back, and the machine talks to you in its own way if that makes sense, through the sound of it running, the feel of it running, even the smell. (Jacob)

> I don't have pet names for them … for me, the process for each model is very very similar, what you do do, you get to the stage whereas if you went to the booth now and observed the robots painting the car, they would all be doing so in a very similar way. From being involved in the programming and writing the programmes, without a car in the booth I could probably tell you what model the robot was painting without the car being in there, because you do watch it quite a lot. (Riley)

'Blackboxing' also refers to 'the way scientific and technical work is made invisible by its own success. When a machine runs efficiently, when a matter of fact is settled, one need focus only on its inputs and outputs and not on its internal complexity. Thus, paradoxically, the more science and technology succeed, the more opaque and obscure they become' (Latour 1999: 304). This idea that it is only when the technology breaks down that one needs to learn about the internal complexity was echoed by one worker:

> I think you only understand a system when it breaks down. When it breaks down, or it's not working, that's when you truly understand how a system works, through the process of fixing and maintaining it. (Jacob)

At the micro-level of a specific machine, blackboxing refers to not seeing the microprocesses inside the tool as something under control. In contrast to blackboxing, 'transparency' refers to the extent to which the inner workings and processes of machines and technology can be understood by users. Some of the workers expressed a high degree of understanding of the robots (transparency) and seemed to think that a high degree of understanding is an important value rather than seeing them as black-boxed entities. Robots were seen to be a tool, and the better you understand them the better you can operate them:

> No, I've always found with a robot that they're only as good as the person on the end of the controller, so if you understand how a robot works, then you're alright, but if you … if a robot has a collision it's because it's been programmed by a human incorrectly. (Evan)

> They're just a tool. But you have to know it well. (Adam)

> I know how every step of the process works. I might not be able to be an expert within the electronic or the software side of the press or from a system point of view but I have a very good understanding of how a press functions, how a press works, a very good understanding of the materials, the dyes, manufacturing processes in general, from the training I received in my previous company. (Jacob)

Blackboxing can be problematic because it can embed certain imperatives or prejudices of which users may not be aware, therefore shifting moral culpability or removing humans from the decision-making process. Conversely, in complex machines, blackboxing can increase accessibility and usability by creating, for example, a more user-friendly interface. Workers expressed that there was a balance to be struck:

> It's important for maintenance to be able to [programme the robots] and to be able to modify things, but you wouldn't want it so that anyone would be able to walk up to it and do things without a full understanding of what

> they're changing, so I think it's at a good level at the moment where you have to have a key to go in to change it. (Evan)

The idea that a particular interface could disempower some users was sometimes portrayed as a matter of choice rather than power:

> I think it's about the specific understanding and capability of the person. For example, if you have a skilled associate and a non-skilled associate, the skilled associate will have an understanding or a desire and understanding to understand the machine itself. Some unskilled associates might not be too interested in the technicalities of the machine, they'll just be pleased that the parts are coming out on target. But you might have an unskilled associate who would like to learn about that machine. So there is a mix of understanding and ambition within the team. (Jacob)

The idea of the robot as a mere tool suggests it can be utilised rationally with complete control by the human; however, some workers did not seem completely resistant to the idea that one might learn from the robot/tool in an embodied sense:

> If a robot could detect that the action you were about to carry out could be potentially dangerous or have some kind of lasting effect, and give some kind of prompt on the screen or some kind of haptic feedback on the pendant, a vibration before it would allow you to do it or something. (Evan)

Furthermore, some workers did not seem resistant to the idea that the robot could learn through AI to take over some of the tacit knowledge of the workers mentioned above:

> I know about the potential of AI and how it teaches itself to improve or sometimes make things worse. I think it would be a good technology to have, it would remove a lot of the times where you have to go and tweak something based on the conditions, for example weather conditions can vary the glue viscosity. If it had that knowledge from previous years or previous conditions then it could take away a lot of the little jobs and then we could focus on the bigger things, I think it would be a good thing to have. (Evan)

For some workers, the particular way in which the Human-Robot Interface was blackboxed, into a series of screens, was frustrating and problematic:

> Some of them are really easy to use, some of them are really hard. The ones we've got now, I think they're particularly difficult, because they've got multiple layers behind them, and if you want to find something, you've got to go through 3, maybe 4 pages to get to where you want to be, and then you've got to come back, it affects, you know, someone in the middle of the night, 3 o'clock in the morning, it's not the best time to be thinking, difficult breakdowns, you don't respond as well at that time in the morning and when you're having to jump about pages on an HMI [Human-Machine Interface] trying to find something, it doesn't help at all, that's how mistakes are made. (Adam)

Blackboxing can also refer at a macro-level to working with little or no knowledge of the process or machine beyond your immediate process. For example, a worker may see the machine they work with as a tool and have an excellent knowledge of the complex constituent parts of that tool, but they might not understand the factory itself as a larger-scale technology.

Anthropomorphism

One aspect of blackboxing that is quite common, and perhaps linked to tacit or instinctual knowledge, is the practice of giving robots personalities and to consider that entities were on the same conceptual and intellectual plane as humans. Some of the workers scoffed at the idea that one might form an emotional or personal bond with a robot:

> Interviewer: Do you ever give any of the robots personalities or names?
>
> Worker: No I've never done that and I don't know anyone who has. (Evan)
>
> Going back a long time, maybe 18, 20 years, a senior manager made me paint smiley faces on the back of the robot. I remember that. I thought he was joking at the time, but he wasn't! Obviously he had a different perspective on robots to me. (Adam)

However, other workers did seem to hint towards a more personal or intimate relationship of some sort. The machine that they worked with was seen to have some kind of emotional or affective relation. While the following worker did express a good knowledge of the technology he worked with as a tool, there was, however, also some implication that not only did he control the tool but also that the machine controlled him too, in the sense that a 'bad day' would impact on him physically and emotionally. This perhaps suggests forming an assemblage with the tool, or perhaps it signifies that both worker and tool are subordinated to the larger machine/assemblage of the factory line:

> We always refer to the machine we use as a 'she', now you mention it, and I rarely reflect on that, we're there every single day of our working lives, we spend more time with that machine than we do with our families. The machine almost becomes a part of the family to be honest with you. Like most families, you'll fall out every now and then. You'll have some fantastic experiences together and some fantastic memories together, so for me, when the press performs, and I achieve my targets, we've had a really good day. But when we have a bad day, it's the equivalent of a family falling out I suppose. But what's really key is that we maintain focused on the situation at hand to be able to get the press back up and running. (Jacob)

Some examples of anthropomorphism were more extreme:

> They put faces on the vehicles that were driving around [city] so that people felt more interacted with them. (Lewis)

> Relationship with the machines: Dare I say? Quite intimate. Because if you're not, that's when you're going to struggle. You need to know the systems, that's the basis of a good engineer. You need to know the sequence, if you don't know the sequence of the machine then you're going to struggle to get it back up and running if it breaks. (Adam)

Some of these quotations seem to signify some kind of mystical or affective relation with the machine beyond its use as a tool. The technology is 'blackboxed', but the worker has a relationship with the 'sequence' of the machine.

The Possibilities of Industry 4.0 and Cybernetics

Some interviewees did consider that there was the possibility of the types of integrated systems that were broadly cybernetic or of the type which would be similar to Industry 4.0. For example, interviewees considered that humans might take the tasks of attendant workers who either have a role only in starting and stopping a system:

> Robots are in a production line and also in their own cells ... no one can get in their cell but they are on a production line ... the only time you would go into a cell would be to maintain them. (Jamie)

> We can simulate it, we have a complete simulation programme but then we have to validate it with a teach pendent and a dead man's switch … you will be the one controlling it. (Jamie)

Although closing a system was always problematic, there was a role for robotics and technology in taking over that role from a human operator:

> Whilst the cells are loaded manually by operators, the robot then does the rest of it, there's quite a lot of technology in there. (Evan)

Many workers saw the potential for further automation:

> I suppose a robot can be anything that removes the need for a human interface … I don't know how to describe really, but where the part is placed by the operator and the robot just takes care of it, picks it, places it, does the rest. (Evan)
>
> In the short term [we deal with problems and issues – variation in quality] through better training, but myself, I'm always looking for opportunities to automate or to introduce more robust processes. (Evan)
>
> Jobs which are quite labour intensive which could be quite easily automated, and there are systems out there which could quite easily automate, for example changing tips on weld guns, we were paying for a quite highly skilled maintenance person to go in the cells just to remove a tip and put a new one on twice per day, it's something which could quite easily be automated with the right investment. (Evan)
>
> Asked about enhancement / greater collaboration – 'That's not really something I've looked at or seen much of at the moment. I know for the foreseeable future in my area there's nothing planned from that side, it would be less human interaction from what I understand, more automation, more AGVs delivering parts and more sort of modular parts in cassette form where it wouldn't take an operator to load the part, it would come in a cassette and the robot would do the rest. (Evan)
>
> It's not feasible to the scale that we do, but there are always processes that you can look to improve through automation, but ultimately you still need to have somebody who is driving the machine … to be there, should the system fail. (Jacob)
>
> At the moment the machine isn't able to detect that it has a defect in it or producing a part that's got a defect in. So we're heavily reliant on people to

> do that detection for us. But as I mentioned, we're looking to automate that now. (Jacob)
>
> If it was more intelligent – 'it would make things easier for us. We have to move forward and move with the times. In the situation we find ourselves in at the moment, there will always be mechanical interaction. As the time comes when robots became more intelligent, they can read the panels of the vehicle and so on and so forth, then I suppose I'll look for a new job'. (Lewis)
>
> The track, as far as communication and intelligence perspective, doesn't communicate with the robots in any way. The robots understand where the vehicle is in relation to the track and the world that is the booth, but with the track starting and stopping, there's no real relationship between the two. (Evan)

There were a number of emotional responses to the idea of further automation:

> [How do you feel about more robots and fewer humans]: A mixture of emotions. It would be a good thing from a quality point-of-view. Consistency, probably make my job easier. But then the downside to that is loss of jobs, and how do we replace the jobs and how to you redeploy people? (Evan)
>
> It's important from a wellbeing and mental health point of view to have that interaction with people on a daily basis, have a bit of a joke and a laugh with people. I always try to have a good relationship with the operators, try to be personable to them, and try to make them feel like I'm interested in their problems, well I am interested in their problems, but I always try to make them feel like I care and try to improve things, and then obviously if you need some kind of help in the future you get that help back from them. It would be a strange place if you just walked into the body shop and it was just all equipment and moving around and you didn't have any interaction with anyone, I don't think I'd like that. (Evan)
>
> [Could robots replace managers or management roles?] (extremely enthusiastic!) ooh that's a good question! I like that question! Ultimately yes. I feel if the system runs and the system has key clear escalation points in it, for example like a siren or a light to alert a particular individual. But there's only so many of the managerial responsibilities that a system can take … For example in a process, if you have 4 managers, you could remove a number of those through system improvements. But it ultimately still falls into that category where you will still need someone to monitor and to make those decisions and lead the team to make those decisions. (Jacob)

> [Is it a good thing to replace managers?] If the system works and it's proven to work, then I think it's a good thing, because it's all about cost at the end of the day. (Jacob)

Workers gave a number of instrumental reasons for the adoption of automation:

> The reason the technology is there is to make more products faster with a better quality, to increase profits at the end of the day, make them as quick as possible and as quickly as possible, improve the quality, as long as it's all done in a safe manner. (Evan)

> We've got one system on the cladding line [...] where it goes into a robotic cell and it measures the gap and flush all around the car. This used to be manual, we used to have two operators which used to do that, but it's how that data would then be used and if an operator could be trusted because it could measure the car in a different position every time and it would give you a different result, but with a robot its more consistent it measures the car in the same place every time, it's more trustworthy. (Evan)

> The way business is going you have a certain escalation depending on a certain condition, like in logic programming – if this happens, what's the reaction to that? So if that's how managers are currently thinking, now that's happening, now what should I do, then there's no reason you couldn't programme something to do that. And with the improvement or less people to manage and more machinery then maybe it would remove the need for so many managers. (Evan)

There was also evidence that workers were changing their routines and procedures in order to fit in with the demands of 'Industry 4.0':

> We measure ourselves within a few key areas, which is safety, quality, delivery, cost, people and environment. On each of these indicators I have key targets that I must achieve by the end of the day. [During the working day] I am constantly thinking about opportunities for improvement, and how I can improve the process to be a lot leaner. I am thinking about the challenges that we face in the next 24 hours, I think about how I need to guide the team and what direction I need to give my team in order to achieve any challenges we might face in that specific day, and I am also thinking about quality and performance and safety constantly. So every time the press is stopped for maybe 20 minutes, that plays on my mind, that I know that's 20 minutes I need to try to catch back during the day, and if I can't catch it

> back during the day, then I will need to run overtime in the weekend, which is cost and waste, so every time the machine stops, in my mind the clock is ticking, I need to get the machine back and running as quickly as possible. (Jacob)

> The press is extremely complex, but very capable as well. When it's not playing ball and it has a bit of a hissy fit every now and then, it can get very frustrating to try and fault find. When the team are getting stuck into the breakdown, you do start to see that control turn, when the control starts to turn. And it's all about that leadership and direction for me, when we're in the midst of a major breakdown, it's about ensuring the team are all around, we're all present, it's about ensuring we're all aware of our roles in the breakdown, who needs to go and do what. (Jacob)

As these quotations show, whilst positive about the possibilities of automation, workers were ambivalent concerning whether it could replace human workers. Humans were always necessary as mediators of technology, to effect repairs and to form meaning from what automation was doing. It was also necessary from a mental health and wellbeing perspective that workers had contact with other workers. Humans were the final arbiter of automated output, ready to terminate the process if it did not meet standards.

Embodiment and Enhancement

We found that some respondents were positive about the idea that robots and automation could enhance human capabilities. One respondent in particular, a manager (Lydia) gave several examples of this. When humans are asked to do things that physically they can't do or would find physically difficult due to repeated actions, then enhancements may be required. Workers were positive about the enhancement of human capabilities through data integration into processes:

> Measurement was with every car, a daily occurrence, as for the manufacturing robots that made the car from the parts although I relied on them every day I did not have any software interaction with them ... they measure every single car at 49 points ... we use the robots to give us an indicator of when we might have a problem. (Thomas)

> At present we decide (tolerances) ... we literally look at the trends that are graphed on the software by the robots and we scan if they are going off or

> up away from that nominal … It was a difficult process at first to get people to believe in it but know it is second nature. (Thomas)

> Now, it is integrated, you know exactly what to do and when to do it. (Thomas)

> 99% of the time we are in control because we know which factors are causing which issues … we have the team and knowledge to make these decisions. Without the data it gives us we would be blind. (Thomas)

> I appreciate how fundamental they are to my targets … I would not be able to achieve this without the robot element. (Thomas)

There was some speculative discussion of how future projects may enhance human capabilities beyond what was currently possible. In outlining these, concerns were raised regarding how they might impact on health and safety and occupational health if these systems were allowed to operate without human feedback. There were also a variety of responses regarding future technologies, with some employees actively seeking out future opportunities and others regarding these technologies as an admission of their 'weakness'.

Conclusion

The interviews present a picture of production whereby tacit knowledge and what we refer to as 'hobbying' are part of the production system that would not be easily incorporated into Industry 4.0 or cybernetic systems. These seem to be human capabilities that cannot be extracted from human bodies and minds and, we would argue, cannot be reduced to cybernetics. Workers were also generally sceptical concerning 'blackboxing'. On the other hand, we also considered that workers were somewhat accepting of Industry 4.0 systems, sometimes giving them human characteristics (or altering their own behaviour to become more 'mechanical') and considering both instrumental and emotional benefits of using these techniques. There was also some evidence that CYBER4.0 was using Industry 4.0 technologies ahead of many companies in this sector.

This investigation shows that there is a possible limit not only to the application of Industry 4.0 techniques but that Industry 4.0 (in its desire to subsume all aspects of knowledge and cybernetically code production) as a paradigm and as a cybernetic system is, in itself, limited not because there is an intrinsic human essence, but that tacit knowledge and the human as an entity without a 'cybernetic' component, and with a history and a body, has creative and innovative possibilities that can never be captured by such a system. We would advance as a hypothesis that the drive towards Industry 4.0 may be a limit, within capitalism itself, to the productive and innovative capacity of 'factories of the future' and encourage a scaling of production towards human uniqueness and collaboration. This was alluded to strongly by one of our interviewees.

> We have tried central databases, we have tried process areas … we have a lot of data, we do store data, we are looking at how we can take that data up into cloud systems. We have people taking data off machines to create spreadsheets … but if that person leaves no one knows how to use them … we are never getting to industry 4 or industry 5 using AI [unless we can gather data] … we have tried training courses and trying to get them to input data into different systems but there is nothing to compare with somebody telling you something … it is great having lots of writing but you have to find the knowledge you are looking for … asking a question to all of our data we are not going to get an answer … it's possible [with a new facility that you have built] to get to that [Industry 4 or 5] … a plant like this is so massive, 20K people working on it … we don't have money to throw at making everything digital. It is really hard to move yourself to Industry 4.0. (Lydia)

Finally, there were areas of Industry 4.0 and cybernetics that could not fully be explored in our interviews and qualitative work. One of the requirements for access to the company was that the topics we discussed in interviews were negotiated and approved by the organisation, which limited discussion related to collective worker views on safety and union views on these systems although these were alluded to in some of our interviews:

> We are very cautious about what we do, not just because people might get issues but also because we might have to stop the line. If we stop the line because a process is inadequate it is not simple … it is hard to use collaborative robots … here you have large parts that collaborative robots would not be able to lift … industrial robots are really not that safe that is why we are looking at smart space … as soon as you put up safety cells and fences that restricts you. (Lydia)

> Our plants are heavily unionised … so far we have positive feedback on our machines but when it comes to data and tracking this will become more controversial. (Lydia)

In conclusion, the promise of 'Industry 4.0', as a paradigm and as a cybernetic system in an advanced manufacturing company, has its own theoretical and practical limits. We would argue that these are limitations of cybernetic thinking more generally. The potential benefits of areas such as 'tacit knowledge' and 'hobbying' cannot be contained in cybernetic systems, even in advanced capitalist manufacturing systems of 'Industry 4.0'. This hints towards that even in what are supposed to be 'contained' cybernetic systems, there are forms of knowledge and skill that are outside the cybernetic model.

References

Collins, H., 2010. *Tacit and Explicit Knowledge*. University of Chicago Press.

Dreyfus, H.L., 1992. *What Computers Still Can't Do: A Critique of Artificial Reason*. Massachusetts: MIT Press.

Latour, B., 1999. *Pandora's Hope: Essays on the Reality of Science Studies*. Cambridge, MA: Harvard University Press.

Leng, J., Sha, W., Wang, B., Zheng, P., Zhuang, C., Liu, Q., … & Wang, L. (2022). Industry 5.0: Prospect and retrospect. Journal of Manufacturing Systems, 65, 279–295.

Loizides, G.P., 2004. *Deconstructing Fordism: Legacies of the Ford Sociological Department* [PhD thesis] submitted to Western Michigan University, June 2004.

Moore, P.V., 2017. *The Quantified Self in Precarity: Work, Technology and What Counts*. Routledge.

Moore, P. and Robinson, A., 2016. 'The quantified self: What counts in the neoliberal workplace'. *New Media & Society*, 18(11), pp. 2774–2792.

Polanyi, M., 2021. *The Tacit Dimension*. University of Chicago Press.

Preston, J., 2017. *Competence Based Education and Training (CBET) and the End of Human Learning: The Existential Threat of Competency*. London: Palgrave.

CHAPTER 5

Co-operative Utopias in Automation

Description of the Interviews

Of the six interviewees, four were owner-workers, and one was an employee, who was in the process of seeking to become a worker-owner. The respondents included two controls/electrical engineers, a mechanical designer, a machinist, a purchaser and a mechanical engineer who also had a project manager role. Pseudonyms are used throughout. (Table 5.1).

Table 5.1 Details of interviews

Interviewee alias	*Interviewed by*	*Date*	*Job/department*
Alexander	Rhiannon Firth	18 February 2019	Mechanical engineer (mechanical designer)
Henry	Rhiannon Firth	18 February 2019	Manufactured parts purchaser (mechanical engineering)
Owen	Rhiannon Firth	18 February 2019	Machinist
Jack	Rhiannon Firth	18 February 2019	Controls engineer (electrical engineering)
Cameron	Rhiannon Firth	18 February 2019	Controls engineer (electrical engineering)
Charlie	Rhiannon Firth	18 February 2019	Project manager (mechanical engineering)

R. Firth, J. Preston, *Utopia in the Factory*,
https://doi.org/10.1007/978-3-031-87132-0_5

Introduction: The Utopianism of Co-operatives

In the previous chapter we considered the case of an advanced manufacturing company using Industry 4.0 techniques which was run following a model primarily for the maximisation of profit and shareholder revenue. Counter-intuitively we found the objective of developing a full cybernetic system to capture the inputs and outputs of workers and machines failed due to tacit knowledge, hobbying and the limitations of 'blackboxing'. Even within the peak of advanced industrial capitalism, neoliberal forms of cybernetics were not fully successful in their own terms. Aside from its alienating and political consequences, cybernetics is epistemologically unable to account for the kinds of activities real-world workers engage in as part of their labouring. We now turn to consider a form of organisation which might seem to be more amenable to the forms of prefiguration desired by anarchists and autonomist Marxists, being a worker co-operative. In this analysis we show how similar issues of tacit knowledge, hobbying and distrust of blackboxing emerge, which again present a challenge to cybernetics. However, we also consider how co-operatives may prefigure alternative forms of worker organisation, without necessarily adopting cybernetic tendencies. We will start by outlining some of the history and goals of the co-operative movement.

The co-operative movement began in Europe in the nineteenth century, primarily Britain and France. Co-operative organisation and ethical principles predate this by many centuries; however, during the industrial revolution, a strong movement coalesced around applying these to business organisation to address the mechanisation of the economy which threatened the livelihood of many workers. In 1844 the Rochdale Pioneers established the Rochdale Principles on which they ran their own co-operative, which became the basis for the modern co-operative movement. An international association was formed in 1895 (Williams 2016). One of the largest and most successful examples of co-operation has been the industrial Mondragón Co-operative Corporation in the Basque country of Spain, founded under (and against) the oppressive conditions of the fascist military dictator Franco. Mondragón continues to thrive and inspire co-operatives worldwide, including members of Isthmus Engineering and Manufacturing (IEM), in Madison, Wisconsin, the United States, the case study that forms the basis of this chapter. Several interviewees cited Mondragón as an inspiration, illustrating the international nature and federated solidarities of the co-operative movement.

Although the co-operative movement began in Europe, there is also a long history in the United States, in which the case study for this chapter is based. Historically the United States has a particularly strong tradition of Credit Unions run on co-operative principles. There is also a long tradition of agricultural co-operatives, but these tend to be socially conservative rather than progressive and are founded in situations where farmers cannot obtain essential services from investor-owned firms because the co-operative model had benefits allowing farmers to pool production and/or resources (Cobia 1989). Electrical co-operatives also became an important economic strategy in the 1930s for bringing electricity to rural areas, although this too was largely for pragmatic rather than principled or progressive social and environmental reasons. It is worth noting that the co-operative model in the United States is frequently adopted for pragmatic rather than ideological reasons (also often both).

There is a varied and diverse culture of worker co-operatives around the United States, which is socially and environmentally progressive and has its roots in Labour movement organising. However, this is highly variable by state, and some states such as Wisconsin and California are particular hotspots. There has been a surge in the number of co-operatives in the United States since the 2008 financial crisis, and the number has nearly doubled (Harvey 2018).

The co-operative movement is international and is based upon a version of the principles put in place by the Rochdale Pioneers in 1844. These are now known as The Seven Co-operative Principles. Since it is a co-operative, IEM abides by these principles and proudly lists them on its website, as well as adorning its walls:

1. Open membership
2. Equitable economic participation
3. Democratic control
4. Autonomy and independence
5. Co-operation among co-operatives
6. Education and training
7. Concern for community

(IEM 2024)

The ways in which these principles are adopted in practice at IEM will be elaborated in the following sections, although the emphasis of this chapter is on human knowledge and the ways in which it is embedded within and exceeds cybernetic organisational systems.

Co-operatives are of particular interest in this context because they organise in a way that aims to empower workers, so one might expect that the forms of knowledge outlined in the previous chapter are articulated differently. IEM can be understood as a worker co-operative that uses and manufactures automation technology developed within the cybernetic paradigm (although the co-operative and its members do not themselves use the language of cybernetics). As we have argued earlier, cybernetics is a pervasive sociotechnical framework, so is unavoidable. Co-operatives have frequently been interpreted under the auspices of utopian studies as examples of grassroots or prefigurative utopias; however, this has generally been limited to housing co-operatives and intentional communities, where people choose to both live and work together in order to enhance their shared values and act as living examples that another lifeworld is possible (Firth 2012, 2019). There is a burgeoning literature on the utopianism of intentional communities, which are also often housing co-operatives with ecological values based on ideas of degrowth (e.g. Pepper 1991; Sargisson 2000). There is very little work on the utopianism of worker co-operatives, let alone workers co-operatives that work with or, as in this case, produce automation. Worker co-operatives are organisations in which the members are the working staff. Management decisions concerning the organisation are made democratically by members, on the basis of one member, one vote. Each member shares in the responsibility of managing the business, and each member also takes a share in ownership of the business. Therefore, if the business is profitable, members take their share of the profit, and they also take financial responsibility for losses. Worker owned co operatives do organise very differently to capital-owned corporations; however, they still (by necessity) produce and trade within a capitalist economy and growth paradigm, so exhibit less autonomy as communities than intentional communities, many of which aim to be as self-sufficient as possible, for example through producing their own food and energy. Nevertheless, the core argument of this book is that utopian forms of grassroots knowledge—which cannot be automated or systematised, and which prefigure something outside and beyond cybernetic capitalism—can be found even in the most profit-oriented businesses. One might therefore expect at least similar findings in a worker co-op, and indeed this chapter argues that the co-operative structure creates more space for such forms of knowledge to flourish.

Background: The Co-operative Ethos and Governance

IEM is based in Madison, the state-capital of Wisconsin with a city population of over two million. The city itself is situated on an isthmus between two lakes: Monona and Mendota. The city is renowned for its University, the University of Madison Wisconsin (UW-Madison), which is one of America's 'Public Ivy' (Greene and Greene 2001) universities. Madison is known for its liberal and progressive culture and democratic politics, and has historically been a hotbed of political activity, protests and demonstrations. This history and culture provided fertile ground for the growth of the co-operative movement. Wisconsin boasts around 844 co-ops representing 2.7 million members, contributing $5.6 billion in gross sales to the state economy (Ginsberg 2012). Madison is based in Midwest America, which historically had a strong manufacturing and automotive sector, which saw a steep decline after the 1980s. The area has seen a revival in manufacturing recently, with an emphasis on new technologies (Still 2018). Madison's economy today is evolving from a government-based economy to a consumer services and high-tech base, particularly in health, biotech, manufacturing and advertising sectors (Forbes 2018). This economic base is partially reflected in the business of co-operatives such as IEM, which is high-tech, with many of the other co-operatives hailing from consumer services, such as Common Good Bookkeeping Co-operative, Interpreters' Co-operative of Madison, Wisconsin Citizens' Media Co-operative, Union Cab and Union Technology Co-operative (MadWorC 2015).

IEM started in 1980—when industry in the wider area was in steep decline and employment was plummeting (Billeaux et al. 2011: 3). The organisation began as a partnership, meaning the four founders—three mechanical engineers and a bookkeeper—were jointly responsible for financing the business. In 1982 the group became a co-operative (Billeaux et al. 2011: 6). Before long, despite challenges in the surrounding economy, the business was sufficiently successful that it could fund much of its growth internally and attract bank financing for large investments such as a new building in the late 1980s (Ginsberg 2012). This was built at substantial risk to members who were required to personally co-sign the loan; however, the building allowed the co-operative to grow significantly, and IEM grew from the initial 8 partners to 50 people in 12 years. IEM moved to their current four-million-dollar building in 2004, this time financed solely by the co-operative (Ginsberg 2012: 6).

IEM follows the co-operative principles set out in the introduction to this chapter. It adapts these principles to an engineering-specific context. The organisational structure is divided into six disciplines: sales, controls/electrical engineering, mechanical engineering, controls/electrical assembly, mechanical assembly, machining. There is an administrative staff including an HR manager, sales staff, a purchasing agent, a scheduling manager and a general manager. In a worker co-op the workers themselves invest in, own and control the business. This is not to be confused with 'employee-owned', in which your payoff is determined by how many stock shares you can afford to purchase. In a worker co-op the principle is 'one worker, one vote', and all decisions are made democratically.

IEM is composed of approximately 76 workers in total, including 36 worker-owners who share company ownership and approximately 40 employees, who are not co-operative members so do not have a share in ownership. One member said that in recent years they had kept the ratio of employees to members at 'about half'. Employees are eligible to apply for membership after two years working at IEM, whether they are a mechanical engineer or receptionist, but the sales manager and general manager are not eligible. The reason for this is to limit how much total power and control one position might have, since both these management positions are responsible for large amounts of information. Non-members receive employment benefits that members do not. For members, the money that would have gone towards benefits stays in their profit share. Members only receive their wages if the company is profitable. Non-members are not eligible to participate in decision-making on the Board of Directors (BoD). In daily work, however, there is a socially enforced rule that there is no division or hierarchy between members and non-members. The cost of membership has been described as 'the price of a small car' or 'under $20,000' (Billeaux et al. 2011: 6, 15). The process for becoming a member is straightforward but needs to be approved by the Board of Directors at a rate of 90%. IEM also uses contract workers to fill gaps, to take on larger jobs than the workforce could handle alone, and to handle peaks and troughs. Contract workers are generally much more expensive than a stable workforce, but prevent over-hiring and then having to lay people off (Billeaux et al. 2011: 24).

All workers have a large degree of temporal autonomy; ability to arrange their own schedules and explicit monitoring by owners is actively discouraged. There is a long and convoluted selection and membership joining process for this reason (Billeaux et al. 2011: 18–19). Annual evaluation by peers continues after membership, and whilst it is very difficult to remove a member—this requires a 90% vote—this has happened in the past.

Governance of the co-operative is by the Board of Directors (BoD), comprised all 36 worker owners, which meets once every fortnight on a Monday. Decision-making is based on one person, one vote, no matter how long a member has worked at the company. All decisions are made by all members—from the colour of paint, to employing new staff, purchasing new machinery, inviting guests and researchers (like myself, Rhiannon) on a tour. Profits are shared between members based on a formula that includes hours worked and a 'value ladder' that also helps determine salary. Members did not disclose the financial value of the profit shares. Interviewees frequently spoke of absence of hierarchy, and the feeling of autonomy that was bestowed by having a say in decision-making. Whilst there is no overall authority, free-riders are not tolerated, and interviewees spoke of diffuse social pressure and mutual peer-monitoring as sources of authority and discipline, rather than any individuals or bosses.

IEM designs and builds custom, innovative machines and automation systems for other companies. The co-operative oversees the whole process, from customer consultation, engineering research, concept, design, build, installation and staff training. Their products vary from assembly machines to large system integration. They have the capability to do everything they need from start to finish from design and engineering to the build. The sales and design teams liaise with engineering teams from large manufacturers and collaborate with them from the beginning to the end. Once the machine or system has been built, the project team goes to the customer site, installs, supports, starts up the equipment, trains the staff and carries on the service for the life of that machine. Since the machines are custom-made, many of the parts are also custom-made, so IEM keeps a database of every part that goes into every machine in case something goes wrong, and the customer needs the part to be replaced.

Activity is organised around project teams. Projects are initiated when the sales team and management liaise with the customer to discuss their needs, assess feasibility, undertake research funded by the customer if required and provide a quotation. If this is accepted, a project manager and controls manager are assigned by the general manager, and after further scoping work, a design team is also assigned. A 'kick-off' meeting is held including everyone on the project. Project phases are broken down and a plan put in place. This is followed by the design phase, after which work begins. During this phase, there are weekly design review meetings, and updates are provided to everyone in the firm. A project manager takes primary responsibility for communications with the customer, sales team and general manager, and receives final approval from the customer and design team to release the design to fabrication and assembly. The product now enters the building phase, and requirements are sent to the scheduling manager and purchaser who then decide whether components will be manufactured in the in-house machine shop or outsourced elsewhere. The project manager maintains weekly meetings and communications with all parties throughout. Before the machine is installed, a 'factory acceptance test' is undertaken with the customer to ensure the machine meets their needs; if this is satisfactory, the machine is shipped and the project and controls manager provide a manual and training. The product enters the closing phase which involves follow-ups and a closing meeting (Billeaux et al. 2011: 9).

When IEM was founded, 90% of its work was local, and 75% in the automotive industry, drawing on the strong industrial base in the area which meant a skilled labour force and competitive regional supply chain (Billeaux et al. 2011: 9); however, this came at a cost since the industry was volatile and in decline in the area. In order to survive, IEM had to expand their customer base. This led to the present situation, where IEM's customer basis comprises US coast-to-coast and international US-based large companies, including many Fortune 500 companies. Core industries include consumer products, medical and life sciences, automotive and heavy-duty industrial, and emerging markets such as sustainable technology and renewable energy production. IEM competes at the very highest end of the market in automation manufacturing, and many of their customers return time and again due to their reputation and proven quality of their work, which is also known for being more expensive than competitors, but worth the extra layout. IEM regularly accrues more than $20 million in annual revenue (MadWorC 2015).

Tacit Knowledge

In the previous chapter, we defined tacit knowledge as practices involving creative and artisanal relationships to work and technology that could not be systematised and captured by organisations and defy models of automation and training. It might also refer to informal, fluid and changing relationships between workers that are not instrumental to the organisation (resembling the kind described in Chap. 2 in terms of Bird-David's anthropological works) and/or are impossible to map or code. In general, tacit knowledge refers to forms of knowledge that defy systematisation.

Even though IEM was working with automation (in the sense of producing it), the variety of work means the work is not easily automated. In comparison to other engineering companies, IEM exhibits a great fluidity of roles: 'Team-based project management is an increasingly common organizational feature in manufacturing industries, but the IEM structure is distinct because managerial and administrative roles blend into production roles' (Billeaux et al. 2011: 17). The variety of work is an effect of the variety of markets that IEM works with:

> We build automation for the consumer industry to make consumer products, so things you'd buy instore: batteries, toothbrushes, home goods. Also, industrial, so things that you as a consumer may not be aware of, but are very much needed, like, water filtration, air filtration, things that are larger industrial products that go into plants or factories, that a normal layperson not in business would not know about. Medical: so it could be a medical device, implantables, like a pacemaker, or a dispenser, insulin that would be implanted in you, medical could also be things like dispensing of fluids into containers, reagents for DNA testing, things like that. Packaging: that's not really an industry. Automotive: parts that go into cars, boats. Then we'll dabble some in things we consider emergent technologies, things like solar, other areas. (Alexander)

> Working with lots of different industries means working with lots of different types of technology. This prevents us from getting pigeonholed into narrow types of business, which as they dramatically fluctuate with need, so does our business have to be adrift on the same waves. So for example, medical at the moment, it's very competitive, there's not a lot of work, so we can look at some other areas, we can be nimble that way, so our sales work hard, to sell whatever they can for the most amount of profit in the industries that need it the most. (Alexander)

IEM has moved into emerging markets over time, e.g. solar and medical, but these changes have been conservative and gradual. At the same time, they emphasise flexibility as they maintain capacity to make custom automation for a range of industries (Billeaux et al. 2011: 17).

The work is demand-driven, which means that the co-operative does not have to come up with innovative new products to then try to sell. Whilst they make 'crazy machines' which are different each time, they do have a fairly fixed formula for doing so that works, and within this formula the work is highly technical, rather than innovative; partly due to not needing to worry about, or predict, market take-up (Billeaux et al. 2011: 17).

Workers expressed enjoyment of the variety and variability of the work:

> It is exciting, the challenge is always new, you don't have to continue to polish and refine something that's known, you get to reset your brain process and dig into something new. The frustration that comes with that is sometimes you're learning things that if you had more experience you could have avoided certain problems and pitfalls...sometimes if you don't do your research thoroughly you end up reinventing the wheel. (Alexander)

> Our jobs vary so much, in most jobs I'd either be at my desk all the time, or at a machine all the time, I wouldn't get part of both … Not very many people want to sit behind a desk all the time. As an engineer you want to see both things, you want to design something and then see it work. (Cameron)

> It's extremely exciting. Most people who work in a factory they will just sit in front of a machine and hit a button and make parts all day. I make different parts every day. Everything I do is completely different every day. I honestly don't know what I'm working on. Maybe every two days. It's very very fresh, and that's exciting to me. (Owen)

Workers also expressed a high degree of autonomy and flexibility to find their own place in the company and refine their talents.

> I really enjoy the design aspects of the project, the blue-skying, when you have a blank sheet of paper … how to at a high-level address these challenges… do we want to use a robot to do this or get our own set of servomotors and our own custom fabrication to address the same thing, I like being involved in these discussions and coming up with those things, the project management aspect is something I have a natural ability for. I did [agile systems project management training] because I saw that I had a natural talent for it even untrained, compared to most of the people here, it is also not one of my favourite aspects of the work, but I saw it as a way I could be very effective for this company, and being a member-owner of the co-operative, I just thought this is somewhere I can really contribute to making this business better. I saw it as an opportunity that I could fill, I pursued

> more what I saw the company could get out of it than my own interests in my career. I like the design and de-bug, I find those more pleasurable, but I find the project management aspect something I have more talent for. (Alexander)

Another worker related feelings of autonomy and control to more fluid division of labour:

> Because we have control of our work environment, we try to capitalize on that. How can we make the best machine by having the same team work on it, from design, to build, to debug, to installation. We keep the same project team with it through the whole process and it allows everyone to work on completely different equipment. That's what's different about us, we really have a huge variety in the kinds of machines that we build, and most of our competitors either build medical, or automotive, or consumer products, whereas we do all of those. And that's because each one of us can work on any one of those machines. (Cameron)

This worker also expressed enjoyment of the variability in terms of the different locations in which he worked. Whilst he said that at a more traditional engineering firm, a worker would be almost entirely based on one of these locations only, he argued that his own job was split: '30% of the job is sitting behind a desk, 30% is out on the floor, debugging the machine, 30% is out on the field at the customers' (Cameron).

Many workers (including all of the engineers) cited the importance of ongoing learning due to the variability of the work and the nature of the technological field, which is continually developing. This was often seen as a form of hobby knowledge or instinctual problem-solving knowledge, rather than taught, and also something that couldn't be instilled through education or training:

> As controls engineers, most universities don't teach us directly how to do what we do. So we get the basic fundamentals in engineering school, but then we have to learn by doing it. Some of the vendors have training classes for their particular equipment, but every day we learn something new, we have to figure something out, more than 50% of it is on the job. (Cameron)

> Anyone who starts here isn't quite prepared for all that's required. (Cameron)

> Technological change has a more real-time effect, it moves really quickly, that's where technology is constantly changing at a much more rapid pace.

> As a result, a fair amount of our day-to-day existence is dedicated to constantly learning and adapting to new technologies. (Jack)

> Everything's on the job, because guys like me ... have been around for a long time, longer than we'd care to admit, but in the process of that, the automation field, industrial automation field in particular was relatively young, pretty much non-existent, and if you rewind back to the 80s, and you can see that manifested in the types of machines that we've made over the years. We didn't actually start out in automation, that grew out of an expanding need in our end-users, to employ it. A lot of what happened here, there were custom machines, that did things automatically, but, they were things that were happening more on for example, metal moving machines ... that really wasn't automation, that was providing a process that needed to happen for a given part or a given project as a secondary operation to a die casting for example, but it wasn't automation in today's definition of it, where it's either labour reduction, or higher accuracy or higher throughput, all the reasons that you use to automate. Over the years, as we grew, a lot of the training for the automation we do was really through the job through these baptisms of fire. That is organically how we did it. (Jack)

> Of course we're constantly learning. Even though I've been here a long time, I love change. (Henry)

> Continually learning. Technology is changing daily in the CNC world. Cutting metal you would think is easy, but they're always coming up with new ways of doing things. (Owen)

One interviewee expanded on the role of learning as both a privilege and a challenge of working at IEM in particular, rather than more rule-bound engineering firms. Indeed, the interviewee expressed a particular view of learning as a creative process anathema to rules that is nurtured by an organisation such as IEM:

> We don't have a lot of written processes and procedures that dictate how we carry out our day-to-day job. The people who are successful here are the people who are interested in learning, people who don't necessarily like to follow rules, regulations, procedures, job aids, those kinds of things ... To feel successful here, it's more about that open-ended, what does it take to get the job done, and the people that gravitate toward that and are the most successful are the ones that are always learning, and are willing to pay that investment on the eventual return, and that's learning new things, applying new technologies, I do believe it takes an environment that fosters that, and its best situation which I believe we have here, it takes individuals that

> embrace that ... There have been individuals that could not work in that environment – they struggled without rules, and they struggled with the constant challenge of learning, and chasing new technology. (Jack)

The same interviewee also expressed, however, that learning could be overdone or could get reified as a more academic form of knowledge that is not always useful:

> In the midst of learning all this new stuff, you can overdo the educational part of it, and the term I use is when we take something that's new and innovative, and turning it into a science project, because we're an engineering firm, so one of the things that can happen occasionally, and I am sometimes guilty of the same thing, is when you start to think too academically about what you're doing, the aspect of the technology that you're using, and trying to keep in mind that the end game here is a return on that investment, so trying to keep that in mind and balance getting stuff done, and then getting too much stuff done and getting stuck in the past, because you're not learning new things. And I think everyone is afforded that balance here ... which results in a lot of really smart people, who are also getting a lot of stuff done. (Jack)

Several interviewees cited interest in technology since childhood, an innate or 'natural' interest in technology, or an interest passed down through generations in the context of an area of the Midwest heavily influenced by the automotive industry:

> This is how I felt when I was a kid, I liked technology a lot, and I liked figuring out how things worked, and I liked playing video games a lot. (Owen)

> I've been here 30 years ... I've grown with the business. I just naturally had computer skills which was a good fit. (Henry)

> I think it started as a kid, my father taught at a local technical college, he taught automotive body repair, but he also had a side-business restoring antique cars, so I grew up working with him when I was a kid, learning how to weld, how to fabricate, then I went to University of Wisconsin-Madison and got a degree in mechanical engineering, and the first job was a company that imported a German robot that they didn't know how to run, so they asked me if I could at least figure out how to make it move, and then it all just started snowballing from there. (Charlie)

What does tacit knowledge, as revealed at IEM, prefigure? In the previous chapter, tacit knowledge in a mainstream industrial factory was largely sensory and aesthetic and was based in experience rather than education or training, yet still tended to be articulated in terms of ability to meet the instrumental needs of the factory. Rarely was it articulated in terms of internal drives or desires, enjoyment or excitement, which appeared to be more the case at IEM. Aspects of work in the co-operative which might be seen to prefigure something beyond Industry 4.0 included fluidity of roles and variety of products produced, which prevented workers or the organisation as a whole being pigeonholed into particular roles and markets, and an artisanal relationship to the product was expressed as the idea of creating 'crazy machines'. The term 'autonomy' was used frequently to describe the ability of workers to find their own place rather than being trapped in set roles, and there was a fluid division of labour. Similarly to workers in CYBER4.0, workers in IEM felt that the knowledge they developed was through experience and was instinctive and driven by internal or 'natural' desires rather than something that could be imposed extrinsically through training, and indeed one worker explicitly opposed this kind of knowledge to any kind of reified academic knowledge or rule-bound processes, emphasising that the kind of worker who struggled without rules would find it difficult to get along at IEM.

What does the way tacit knowledge works at IEM tell us about cybernetics? While there are elements of work at IEM that prefigure something against and beyond cybernetic capitalism, there are also ways in which they are captured within it, and/or ways in which cybernetic elements of the organisation itself operate to recuperate and reify the prefigurative elements. It is notable that IEM operates within (as well as against and beyond) a capitalist economy, producing automation that enables other factories to produce very conventional commodities such as batteries, toothbrushes and home goods. The work of the co-operative as a whole is demand-driven, so they are still working according to external imperatives rather than autonomously decided desires. One wonders if they were operating as a self-sufficient intentional community, what kinds of technologies and crazy machines they might make. While workers used terms like 'flexibility' in a positive sense, it was noted in earlier chapters that there are exploitative aspects to ideas of flexibility within neoliberal ideology, and in cybernetics it is often used interchangeably with terms like resilience and adaptability to 'feedback'—which in a neoliberal context mean resilience and flexibility to the shocks and crises of capital.

'Autonomy' was mainly internal to the organisation rather than external—the co-operative structure created a buffer of security and autonomy for workers, but the organisation as a whole is still subject to the whims of capital (although it did currently appear to be doing exceedingly well at this).

While tacit knowledge was *opposed* to rules on the factory floor, it is worth noting that the co-operative structure itself, particularly in terms of decision-making, tends to be replete with rules and defined processes that *can* be mapped in ways similar to those that radical cyberneticians (e.g. Swann 2020) propose (and indeed are within the co-operative movement's principles). This will be discussed in more detail below.

Hobbying

In the previous chapter, we found that hobby knowledge, involving tinkering and experimenting with technologies outside of their mandated usage, was prevalent even in a mainstream factory. This was even more evident at the co-operative, and the lines between personal and profit-oriented forms of creation were even more blurred. This was even visible in the usage of space in the building: a portion of floorspace was allocated for a member's personal project of building his own car.

Some of the motivations for their work expressed by workers included money/profit; feelings of belonging in the company; satisfaction at seeing the final product; social values such as knowing that the co-operative was contributing to social justice, and not just economic goods. Interviewees rarely mentioned emotional or affective aspects of labour and tended to focus on more practical and technical aspects of their work. However, another motivational force came up at least twice, which might be described as an 'engineering impulse', or a consuming desire to problem-solve and fix things, as well as enjoyment and excitement at watching the technology in operation:

> As an engineer you're trained to break things down into the simplest elements, and make each piece work like you would expect. Even a huge job, you still have to break it down to the same small elements and build it back up. Unfortunately as engineers, even if something runs or works, we're still going to tear it down and figure out how it works, why it works, and how we can make it better. (Cameron)

> There's so many details and so many specifications a customer gives. You have to immerse yourself in the project and almost live it 24/7, I know that sounds corny, but I spend a fair amount of time at home thinking about work, or on the weekends if I'm somewhere, it's just in the nature of the job. So yeah we're generally thinking about the job. (Charlie)

> Six-axis robot mimics a human arm, it has all 6 axes of movement, there's a SCARA robot, we've used those in the past, those are quite interesting, then there's a spider robot which is real thin carbon-fiber legs, it holds a tooling head that's very light and it just flies around the top like a spider. We use vision-guided robots from time to time, I find them really interesting to use, just because they're so cool, we bring kids in here on a local STEM robot and that makes a big impact when they see it. (Charlie)

> I love things that are very hard to do because they're engaging, and the Wire EDM is really exciting. (Owen)

The most commonly expressed relationship between workers and machinery at IEM seemed to be a relation of creativity or artisanship. The products are unique and custom-made, rather than mass-produced, which requires the worker to form a creative rather than merely instrumental relationship with the technology:

> We're tinkerers, right? Almost everyone here is in their spare time not watching the TV or going to the movies, we're tinkering on something, there's guys with motorcycles, there's guys into cars, bicycles, snow mobiles, mechanical things. (Charlie)

> I've always regarded education, whether it's yourself or others, it's an investment based on a return, obviously individually a lot of people, myself included, although we're from an engineering ilk, there's a lot of creativity that happens in this building. A lot of that is because the latitude exists here for that, we don't have a lot of written processes and procedures that dictate how we carry on our daily jobs. (Jack)

What does hobbying prefigure? This creative or artisanal relation to technology is interesting if one considers the role of co-operatives as a prefigurative alternative to capitalism. In pre-capitalist and early capitalist economies, most production was structured in artisanal or craft terms. Skilled specialists with high levels of autonomy and knowledge produced goods and services. This is the case even as the commodity form begins to take hold. However, capitalism tends to de-skill particular jobs, to break them up into components in processes that have a history in Taylorism and have been theorised in terms of 'McDonaldisation' (Ritzer 1992). Taylorism involves repetitive labour where tasks are divided up into increasingly small components and one person is working on the same small part every day and is increasingly alienated from the finished product of their labour. A worker at IEM expressed quite the opposite:

> You can see that our hard work paid off, and that's something … it makes a huge difference to see the end product, the end result and the team-work it took to do it. (Owen)

The idea that playing with technology can be creative and fun was already emergent within CYBER4.0 and again appeared even more starkly at IEM. Artisans and professionals typically seek relatively high levels of relative autonomy from the state and capital, and will often have the power (based on their qualitative knowledge monopolies) to achieve this (Boltanski and Chiapello 2007). Proletarianisation and de-skilling historically undermined this relative autonomy; however, co-operatives such as IEM seem to have created a space of relative autonomy. The idea of a consuming impulse to use their skills to problem-solve came through in many of the interviews, and blurring of work with personal identity and pride seemed commonplace, reflected in blurring of boundaries between work and leisure/play. Since each machine was unique and custom-made rather than mass-produced, workers would form a creative and dis-alienated relationship with the product.

Nevertheless, workers still expressed their personal salaries and earning profit for the co-operative as a whole as strongly motivating factors in their work. The fact that they enjoyed tinkering with other products during their spare time, such as motorcycles, cars, bicycles, snowmobiles, still illustrates an enduring division between consumer and producer technologies, and the fact that 'leisure' time is used as a space of learning for profit-oriented work, with 'education' equated with 'investment' in capitalistic terms.

Blackboxing and Anthropomorphism

The introductory chapters considered how technologies themselves can enhance or reduce autonomy, as well as the organisational features in which human-technology relationships are embedded. While cybernetic discourse views 'blackboxing' as a positive feature of systems as it shows that they are running smoothly, in Chap. 3 we considered how blackboxing can tend to treat humans and machines as interchangeable or merely reduces humans to their function within a system—this normative ideological stance masquerading as empiricism/ontology can act as justification for replacing humans with machines, and it is true that within capitalism humans and machines are simply replaceable units for the generation of profit. 'Blackboxing' refers to 'the way scientific and technical work is made invisible by its own success. When a machine runs efficiently, when a matter of fact is settled, one need focus only on its inputs and outputs and not on its internal complexity. Thus, paradoxically, the more science and technology succeed, the more opaque and obscure they become' (Latour 1999). In contrast to blackboxing, 'transparency' refers to the extent to which the inner workings and processes of machines and technology can be easily accessed and understood by users. These terms tend to be used in cybernetics in a 'generic' sense—which assumes a universal/transcendental (in first-order cybernetics) or alternatively a communicatively shared perspective (in second-order cybernetics). When applied to humans within organisations, blackboxing serves to bracket out conflicts and complexity—if a black box is behaving as expected, then the internal stressors, repressed desires or psychic conflicts that it may be experiencing are to be bracketed out ('resilience' in cybernetics is resilience for a system—it may well be a stressor for a black box). If one brackets out the problems with blackboxing humans, on the technological level, Blackboxing can be problematic, because machines are created by humans and therefore can embed imperatives or prejudices of which users may not be aware, therefore shifting moral culpability, or removing humans from the decision-making process (e.g. debates around racist AI) (DeLanda 1991). Blackboxing removes transparency but can also have advantages; for example, in complex machines such as computers it can increase accessibility and usability by creating, for example a more user-friendly, accessible interface (Black 2022).

In interviews with IEM staff, there was very little evidence of technology being 'blackboxed', and engineers expressed a transparent understanding of technology contrary to cybernetics which tends to blackbox some entities and levels of analysis:

> When we look at what we are going to build and what we put into things, it's very much down at the component level, not at the higher level of hav-

> ing this already built unit. Most of the stuff that we're designing and putting into things would be the base-building components for automation, servo-motors, pneumatic cylinders, hydraulic cylinders, things that create motion...and then coordinating those motions to do different tasks, for example, grippers that grab things, motors that turn sprockets and belts. (Alexander)

This may be in part due to the nature of the work and the dispositions of the workers; i.e. they are all engineering professionals, trained and adept in taking things apart to predict and solve problems, and also in part due to the nature of the organisation, and the fluidity and informal boundaries between roles, and the good communication between different roles and parts of the organisation. For example, it was mentioned previously that the machinists are able to communicate with the designers on the parts they are asked to cut rather than simply being sent orders.

One interviewee also expressed how important it is that transparency is passed on to the end user:

> Automation in its fundamental form and engineering in general is all about employing tools ... we are paid to understand what each one of these building blocks does and how to put them together to make them work. That's really important for [IEM] because that's what we do. But it's equally important for the end user, because they need to understand that these are the individual pieces and this is how they work together, and this is how they accomplish what you're trying to get done. (Jack)

While the co-operative members tended to suggest that their own relationship with technology was transparent, there was certainly a sense that the customers were sometimes prone to blackboxing the technology through anthropomorphism. This was particularly evident in the way in which interviewees reported that customers were prone to humanising or personalising robots and technology, endowing it with a personality or other holistic characteristics that do not relate to the way its component parts operate:

> What's interesting being on the provider side of it, a lot of the time you'll get an offhanded comment about how someone wants to name a robot, give it a recognizable name... customers will do that, "I'm going to name this one so-and-so", I think that's a reflection of their general interest in it and excitement about, "hey, I get to work with a robot", and so long as they're

not threatened by, this is gonna replace them, or supplant them, they usually get a charge out of it, and a lot of times when we're actually at a end-user site, and we're installing the system, we'll have a parade of people coming by, saying "hey look at this". (Jack)

There's one other aspect of that when you talk about humanizing, or the relationship they have with automation, and that's out on the floor, like when you see us developing a system, from a humanizing standpoint, we've seen it internally and at customers, this platform will take on its own personality, they actually get to that point, even though it's not a humanized robot or artificial intelligence by any stretch of the imagination, you will have one machine that's good at doing *X* and the one next to it is better at something different, even though they're the same machine. (Jack)

When I tell people I work with robots, they think I do humanoid-type stuff, and that I'm like competing or collaborating with them. (Jack)

Our customers do that, we have a customer across town and every robot that goes in that facility, the lead woman on the programme gives them a name and they're referred to by that name from the last 15 years. I don't know if we do it that much here ... nobody looks at a robot anymore and thinks "wow, that's so cool", we used to but now we've seen so many, we've done so many, it's not amazing anymore. (Charlie)

We generally don't have them long enough here to develop that sort of attachment to them, because as soon as they're producing well enough we've got to get them off and get them on the customer's floor because they want to start making their money back or investment. But they do develop personalities for sure, and our customers will reference that when we visit, like how it's 'behaving' and things. (Alexander)

Whilst none of the interviewees reported giving names to machines or humanising their characteristics, some reported discourse and terminology moved towards humanising or anthropocentric discourse; for example, a worker reported that a previous project manager's phrase would be 'is the machine behaving today?' (Jack) and sometimes the language was anthropocentric/humanising; e.g. a controls engineer described his job as working with 'the intelligence, or the decision-making parts of the machine' (Cameron). There was also some evidence of blackboxing when workers bought technology straight from a catalogue:

Stuff that we go out and purchase from catalogues, like robots, we don't invent our own robot we go to [inaudible company name] and we buy a

> robot from then, we bolt it down, we custom design our own end for that, we take the end and teach it a programme or whatever, but we did have to buy that piece, we didn't have to design our own robot, so at that level we will take commercially available things and integrate them into a much larger more complex system. (Alexander)

What does the relationship to blackboxing and anthropomorphism at IEM prefigure? The playful attitude to the automation products they produce, articulated as crazy machines, the excitement for the work and the pleasure at seeing customers' excitement, and anthropomorphism reminds one of the more utopian elements of cybernetics, articulated by Andrew Pickering as an ontology of performativity, play and hobbying (Pickering 2010: 112). The engineers' attitude to transparency and technicality is interesting. Although black boxes are central to cybernetics, the idea that this exists in a binary or tension with 'transparency' is also fundamental to cybernetics. 'Transparency' is a cybernetic concept that has been recuperated in the Third-Way ideology of the neoliberal era (an ethos of open-plan and glass-fronted offices, and constant bio-surveillance). It has roots in honesty and dis-alienation, and the utopian optimism for democratisation in the early internet days. Some aspects of this are still evident in the co-operative, although the alienation between engineers who view automation as a merely mechanical process and users who endow it with almost mystical abilities or 'intelligence' was evident at both CYBER4.0 and IEM. The fact that the producers of the technology and the users (not to mention the consumers of end-products, for whom the entire production process may be blackboxed) have such different relationships to the technology—from seeing it as a completely transparent piece of mechanical engineering, to seeing it as a form of magic or a living being—suggests the extent of alienation in knowledges caused by the division of labour in capitalism.

While the co-operative exhibits a more utopian and optimistic attitude towards working with technology, as an organisation and as individuals they still exist—and seek to thrive—within capitalism. Even though the machines themselves may not be 'black-boxed' for the engineers, they still embed the imperatives of capitalism. For example, a robot that makes snack boxes may not be blackboxed for the engineer who made it; however, it may be blackboxed for the end worker who uses it. As discussed in the previous chapter, the entire factory may be a black box with workers as its components—even though it is a co-operative and adopts co-operative principles, the workers and the collective may or may not understand the ways in which their own aims, principles and desires are shaped and limited by the wider context within which they operate.

Conclusion: The Possibilities of Co-operatives as an Alternative to Industry 4.0—What Does It Prefigure?

It is not uncommon to hear expressed in popular and media discourse as well as in academic debates the idea that robots and automation exist to replace humans. This idea was rejected by several of the interviewees who saw technology as a supplement or complement to human power. This echoes the previous chapter where we saw how workers at CYBER4.0 believed that robots and automation could be used to enhance human capabilities. Machines have very different strengths and advantages to humans and were seen to play a different role in the manufacturing process:

> Repetitive tasks lead to issues with ergonomics and joint problems and joints or back, workstations have to be designed so well to prevent repetitive motion injuries. Machines break down but when they do you just service them or replace them, but it's not a person's life it's a hunk of metal that you can melt down and turn into something else. So you have a person tending that machine, and it's much safer. (Alexander)

> What machines can do that humans can't: 'quality; processes, traceability; again with the automation if you're doing medical, you're tracing lots and batches so that's very necessary information; particularly if you live in the United States, we need to automate if we need to compete with other markets, because we don't have as cheap labour' (Henry)

> Normal humans can't keep their mind from wandering. It's impossible for them to think about doing the same thing over and over and over and over. The speed at which they do it, the accuracy at which they do it, the strength, the power it takes to do something can be limited. (Cameron)

> [Humans] are not accurate. They have bad days. They come in hung-over because they were out drinking too much the night before. (Charlie)

In summary, machines are seen to be more consistent, reliable, efficient, fast, better able to deal with dangerous tasks, better able to deal with very repetitive tasks. Humans were seen as better able to make choices and decisions, particularly in complex situations, better at tactile and variable tasks. Workers at IEM tend towards using discourses that are humanist (i.e. they view humans as essentially different and separate from technology), and are optimistic, ambivalent or strategic about the uses of technology and the role technology plays in human society; that is, the purpose of technology is to be used for human good, and in general, the workers believed the automation they produce does achieve this. There is a feeling that humans can master technology, rather than vice versa, and that the relationship between humans and technology should be that of an actor or master using a tool. Technology at IEM tended to be viewed and used in a transparent rather than a blackboxed way, and there was a feeling that this transparency of knowledge should be passed on to the customer.

Interviewees expressed that they often experienced the reception of the machines at their customers' premises as being empowering for other workers:

> Usually, the people in the plant are excited to get the machine, they are usually involved in the process, in our world, most manufacturers have realised that if the workers, the maintenance people, the technicians, the engineers are not on board with what's going on, that it's going to be a failure, so most places have learned that you need to involve those people in the whole process. (Alexander)

> I've seen [empowerment] first hand … in the process of doing that, collaborating with the operator, which would happen quite often, I'll end up with operators who are thanking me for the additional on-the-job training that they're getting, they'll be like "I run a robot now, I don't know a lot of people who do that!" so they do feel better about it, they enjoy it, I think, as most people would, as I do every day, enjoy the benefit of knowing that you're capable of providing more than just a human resource. A lot of these people find themselves working up their own corporate ranks. (Jack)

> Some of the people that I've come to know, at the places that we work for, have become very good acquaintances and in some cases friends. One of my friends is from Scotland. I met him when we built a machine here, 25 years ago, started interacting with him, since then, and then the company and everything else he's worked with, and a lot of that I think comes from the appreciation that we shared common values, and the people, the operators, everyone that interacts with automation, if they have an affinity for it, then it's definitely empowering. (Jack)

There was also a feeling that the machines were doing important and socially necessary work that humans would not be able to do at all or do safely:

> I'm staring out the window, looking at the machines we're building right now. One of the machines lifts a 75lb engine block. You would have all sorts of health issues if you had people lifting 75lb engine blocks all day long. Nobody wants to do that. Plus it's reaching in and out of a live machine that's cutting metal. So it would be very dangerous for a human to do. Sitting right next to that is a medical machine that does medical testing and it's testing faecal matter. How many people want to have their hands in that testing? So there's a good reason to have automation on a lot of those operations, because you don't want people to be in there doing that. (Cameron)

In some ways this resonates with accelerationist and FALC utopias articulated in Chap. 1, as workers seek to speed production and technological development to the extent that humans are relieved of dangerous, undesirable toil and/or blend seamlessly with machines without friction. One might even imagine a human-machine relation that exceeds the possibilities of capitalist management practices or cybernetic encoding/systematisation by developing a 'we' perspective of the kind outlined by Bird-David's (1994) oil-in-water sociology. The idea of forming friendships as a utopian aspect of the work should not be underplayed, and there was a definite feeling of worker solidarity and wishing to see other (possibly unknown) workers thrive. This is a dream of human liberation from toil, but without displacement. On the other hand, there were more conservative or nationalistic utopias of wishing the United States to remain competitive in the world economy in a context where cheap labour comparable with China is not available.

There was a strong feeling amongst several of the staff that the co-operative structure was particularly suited to working with high technology and with undertaking specifically custom, rather than mass-produced machines. One worker described the difference between the type of business that IEM does, in comparison to other companies:

> What we do in terms of automation is very different from other businesses. If you were going to go to a show on packaging automation you'd see a bunch of people trying to sell the machines. The largest group of automation developers in the world have developed their own products to go out and sell to people who have needs for that kind of thing, like a bottling

> machine or a case packing machine, where they can say, your part, the size is a little different but we can massage the machine to fit your product. But they have essentially already invented the machine and they're going out to sell it. We don't do any of that here. What we do is we have no standard platform, catalogue, or products. We start with a blank sheet of paper every time. Which means our customers come to us. They've invented their product. We don't get involved in product design. They say "we have this product, but now we need to build so many of these parts per year at some level of quality and we need a machine to do that but there is nothing out there we can buy that does that, so we need you to come up with something. (Alexander)

The non-hierarchical aspects of the organisation mean that it is flexible and nimble and involves non-hierarchical communication between autonomous members, which is better suited to custom project-based work:

> I do believe that is a very good reason why we are a co-op – you have mechanical engineers, electrical engineers, you have us, the machine shop, then you have assembly out there, it's a very cohesive team, we rely on each-other constantly, and we're very aware, and it happens all the time where I'm really glad we have this person. (Owen)

> We all have our niche talents … it takes all those people to make one machine, you can't just have mechanical engineers and that's it, by doing it that way I feel like ours works … I think if you had all just mechanical engineers, and we had a co-op, it might be kind of boring, with this, we're going from design that they thought up 6 months ago, to fully functioning and it's in your hand. (Owen)

> Because we're *developing* automation, because we're project-based, because we have very definable things that we're doing, because we're all of an engineering ilk to begin with, having a co-operative structure that allows these empowered teams to make these decisions on technical merits than organizational limits, obviously there are commercial limitations to whatever we do, we can't do whatever we want, what we do has to make us money, that's why this particular co-operative, this particular corporate structure, the team-based structure, the reason that has meshed so well here. (Jack)

Another aspect of co-operative organisation which suited working with highly developed technology and at the cutting edge of custom work was the fact that co-operatives were more willing to invest in both technology and people and also give workers autonomy of choice over which technology they would like to work with:

> Our machine shop is a very, very, nice machine shop overall compared to what you would find in a similar-sized place… they've definitely invested very well in that … does that empower me? Yes, I like working with very nice equipment and very clean equipment. (Owen)

> We definitely do [have a lot of autonomy in how we use technology], and that applies to virtually everyone in the place, and that has a lot to do with our structure as a co-operative and our form of governance, and the way we've set this one up, where the teams, the project teams themselves, are afforded an immense, and I say immense based on traditional engineering technology firms, where a lot of these things are subscribed to by management, and these are the tools you're going to use, and if you get new ones, [management] will mandate those new tools or revisions. Here, virtually every project team, down to the individual, including myself, can discover those new things as needed, but that's only because the latitude has been provided by the co-operative structure, and the fact that if you look at it in governance terms you could almost regard each of our project teams as an ad-hoc committee trying to accomplish an incremental goal for the business. Because committees are empowered with the ability to make certain pre-agreed upon decisions autonomously and then bring those back to the larger group, for example, 'I found something that works really well and I think everyone should learn that'. (Jack)

> I used to work for a company that was privately owned, with a very corporate structure, and one of the downfalls of working in a machine shop, that was similar to what we're doing, but privately owned, you couldn't spend as much money on training. Your education – they weren't really interested, it was more like, what can you do right now, not 'hey I want to go and do this CNC class because I think it would better us', it was like 'we don't want to spend the money', they never invested it back. Here it's the opposite, we're very in tune with the need to progress and evolve and invest in the technology to better ourselves. (Owen)

In more hierarchical organisations, one might expect that there is differential access to technology amongst workers, for example a more qualified, better-paid worker may have access to better technology, or more power to choose what technology they use, or input into decisions over technology, than a minimum-wage worker. At IEM, which does not have these kinds of hierarchies, there did not seem to be any hierarchies or restrictions on access to technology. At IEM, the only formal hierarchy was between members and non-members, but this was backed up by a socially enforced norm that employees were not treated differently from members on the factory floor, and this was also the case in terms of access to technology and technology education:

> I can say, this is something to look into, but I don't have a vote…but I've never been turned away, I've continued my education here, taken classes, 100% support behind me, but there are things that as an employee that you cannot do versus a member … but it's not rigid. (Owen)

> The cool thing about the co-op environment is that if you want to learn something, you just want to ask, we are inclusive. (Henry)

There is a definite feeling that there's affinity between the organisation and the type of work, but also that the co-op model is generalisable to all types of work and that the co-operative structure in itself is transgressive of hierarchies and rigidity in other realms, such as access to technology and education. There was apparent consensus amongst interviewees (and other co-operative members at the MadWorC meeting) that the co-operative model could, and should, be used universally, regardless of type of business, exemplified in this quote:

> Within 5 miles of this business, there's 10 or 15 other worker co-ops. One of the other co-ops, which has very similar by-laws, the same structure, their board meetings are facilitated almost identically to how we facilitate our meetings, they're a cab company, it's a completely different type service and industry. There's a pharmacy that sells pharmaceutical goods. There's a martial arts studio, a video store, a fairtrade coffee roaster, a bakery, all structured very similarly to how we're structured, even though they're completely different markets, industries and products. (Cameron)

Working in a co-operative can have a 'levelling effect', so if a business that was very hierarchically organised, with a rigid division of labour, was transformed into a co-operative, the work would tend to become more variable (i.e. less rigid hierarchy and division of labour). During the observed MadWorC meeting, I was given an example of the 'levelling effect' of the co-operative structure. A coffee roaster co-operative, prior to having a co-operative structure, had a hierarchy between public-facing service staff (who spoke English and were paid more) and production/coffee roasting staff (who spoke Spanish and were paid a minimum wage). When the company became a co-operative, the non-native speakers had an equal say in the decision-making process, and they campaigned for English lessons. The other co-operative members were on board with this because the co-operative structure meant that they all had an equal wage and equal interest in developing the company (and profit), so diversifying the skills of a section of staff seemed a 'no-brainer'. This is because, during decisions at board meetings, members of a co-operative would be likely to demand and vote for education and access.

What is the relationship between co-operativism and growth/degrowth? In the first two theoretical chapters, we considered accelerationism as an articulation of the idea that technological development may have its own a- or in-human agenda, for example an agenda completely complicit in the agenda of capitalism, regardless (and potentially in conflict with) of human needs (technological determinism). The degrowth critique of accelerationism also suggests that the pace of technological development is getting faster, and as it does so, humans become more dependent on technology. Some interviewees expressed views that fit with this perspective:

> The cost point has gone down, the requirement and demand for automation has gone up. What we see is ourselves getting busier and busier all the time, and finding we're getting more and more reliant on technology, not just using it, you *have* to use it, not only to stay competitive, but to also field projects that are cost effective and just overall effective enough to the end user. (Jack)

> I've been doing this my entire career, which is going on over 35 years, and I can feel myself ageing out of technology. We just interviewed a kid who's got 5 years experience, and he's got more experience with IT than I do, because of the way that technology is aging, and I'm not learning that stuff as quick as I used to, I'm not afraid of it, but I can see that it's happening. (Cameron)

> It's just going to continue being the same thing, it's probably reasonable to expect there will be an exponential level to it, the benefits realised by end-users, people who work with automation, those things are just going to continue to evolve, improve, increase all of the benefits, drive down the cost of manufacturing in particular, it's the reason it's being done, it's the motivation for the existence and furtherance of technology to begin with. (Jack)

Interviewees mentioned lack of hierarchies or rigidity in all spheres of working at IEM, particularly in allocation of tasks and performance management. Nonetheless, there was a feeling that there were informal pressures in these spheres which contributed to keeping the co-operative running.

> I do mechanical [engineering] we don't have titles here or tiers of any sort, just based on experience, aptitude and whatnot you tend to gravitate towards more, er, certain types of work than others, so I do a lot of project management of large projects, I also do everything down to menial tasks on other people's project when I am between jobs. (Alexander)

> We are very different here as a co-operative in that people of all levels, experience levels, will do a wide range of work, we don't have a designed system of efficiency where there are tiers of engineers and giving the difficult high-end level of work to this level of engineer and they are going to trickle-down to supporting engineers at lower tiers underneath them, we don't do that here at all, we do obviously, if we just brought a multi-million dollar project in here and handed it to someone with two weeks of experience, it would be a complete failure, so clearly there is more to it than that, but that is mostly handled through a natural system of knowing each-other, we have a, operations manager, he doles out the work, he sees where people's talents are, we talk about things as a business, when I get a project and I get kicked off on it, I look at the project requirements and I go to [operations manager] and say 'these are the kinds of people I need, these are the skills I need onboard to pull this project off, and he says 'here's who I have available', and I say 'well I know this person, they have the skills to do this' … 'all those conversations happen, but it's not through a system that defines it, it's just done through normal conversations, trust with each other and our jobs'. (Alexander)

The co-operative structure transgressed traditional hierarchies between forms of work that one might find in a traditional factory. For example, I was informed that mechanical engineers upload their designs to the cloud, and the machinists download them and programme their own machine, which is an unusual step in manufacturing where machinists usually do not programme themselves. The unique structure of IEM also means that the machinists can immediately ask the engineers if they have any questions. One of my interviewees verified this 'our machinists have access to our engineering files', which was essential in a business where 'everything we make is unique' (Henry).

The BoD as a collective entity of all worker-owners does not play role of motivating, disciplining or formally performance managing workers; however, there is a diffuse social pressure from the expectations that workers place on one another. This has only rarely been a basis for conflict:

> We're a flat organization, everyone you have spoken to today is my boss ... If I don't do my job well, everyone will know it soon and that'll become a problem, but if you do your job well and carry your load as the way it should be, then everything works out. (Charlie)

> It's happened once before, we had to take disciplinary measures, and that person is not here anymore. It does happen from time to time, someone will take things for granted and think 'oh, now that I'm a member I can put my feet above the desk and not do my job', that's not how it works, you're expected to do your original job *and* continue to help run the company by serving on various committees and doing your part in those committees and we look pretty gloomily on people who take advantage of it. (Charlie)

I was informed that the membership process was designed to vet whether workers seemed likely to pull their weight, and while the process is relatively simple, it is not necessarily easy. The lack of formality and rigidity also led workers to express that they felt they had a large degree of autonomy. However, this autonomy was often seen as complimentary with, rather than in conflict or resistance to, the autonomy of the organisation.

Workers have a greater degree of autonomy than they would in a traditional, capital-owned factory. For example, workers have a much greater than usual amount of control over their time, and how they organise and control their tasks. Workers also feel they have a great degree of autonomy to make executive decisions; for example, a project manager can make a decision on meeting a customer requirement with very little 'red-tape', whilst a machinist can make decisions about how they produce a part so long as it meets design requirements. Workers also have a lot of opportunity to switch between roles, to take on multiple roles, or to choose to specialise. However, whilst there is some overlap in division of labour, clear occupational categories are still in place (Billeaux et al. 2011: 28).

Interviewees tended to agree that their decision-making structures constituted an effective form of management and yielded good-quality decisions, but many noted that the process can be very time-consuming. The quality of decisions is often better because the long process and necessity for negotiation often yields creative outcomes. Group decision-making tends not to yield 'high-risk, high reward' (Billeaux et al. 2011: 16) decisions.

> There's issues that we'll discuss as a group that really are right-brain questions, what colour to paint the mailbox, it's an old joke from a meeting a long time ago, there was a very long protracted decision about what colour to paint the mailbox ... the inordinate amount of time that was used in the discussion, and the fact that there was a result, and then someone asked "wait, how long have we been discussing this"... when everyone looked at that, the second thing, was people went "yeah, why did it take that long?" realising it was a whole bunch of engineers that were using a whole bunch of kooky reasons for their perspective on it, the entire democratic process had gone down the rails like you wouldn't believe it, and everyone just ended up laughing, and it ended up being an inside joke that we have here, about what colour to paint the mailbox. Because you've got a bunch of engineers discussing something that has nothing to do with engineering but they're looking at it in such an engineering way that you barely, if ever, reach a decision. (Jack)

Such lengthy decisions have obvious disadvantages, in particular using large amounts of time can be costly and detract from other tasks. However, there are also advantages. People are more likely to trust and abide by decisions if they played a role in making them and are less likely to feel alienated and excluded, and to feel that they have autonomy as an individual who is part of a group:

> We have autonomy here, we have a say, and because we're part of the board, I'm a member so we have a say in the direction of the company, what decisions are made. (Charlie)

As the company grew larger, there had been conversation as to whether all owner-members should sit on BoD or whether it should be elected representatives. The committees evolved to prevent introducing layer of representation. There is a strategy of staying small or not expanding too much: 'IEM has had 50 workers for 15 years, which means that 2/3 of our interviewees have always worked with this number' (Billeaux et al. 2011: 26). At the time of my visit, the number was slightly higher, at 76 workers, but the number of members was only 36. Interviewees in the Billeaux et al.'s (2011: 26–27) study expressed a strong preference for staying small or not growing too large whilst some of my own interviewees also expressed similar views.

References

Billeaux, M., Reynolds, A., Young-Hyman, T. and Zayim, A. 2011. *Worker Cooperative Case Study: Isthmus Engineering & Manufacturing*. Staff Paper, 9.

Bird-David, N. 1994. Sociality and Immediacy: Or, Past and Present Conversations on Bands. Man. *New Series, 29*(3), pp. 583–603.

Black, M.L. 2022. *Transparent designs: Personal computing and the politics of user-friendliness*. Baltimore: JHU Press.

Boltanski, L. and Chiapello, È. 2007. *The new spirit of capitalism*. London: Verso.

Cobia, D. (ed.) 1989. *Co-operatives in Agriculture*. Englewood Cliffs, NJ: Prentice-Hall.

DeLanda, M. 1991. *War in the Age of Intelligent Machines*. New York: Swerve.

Firth, R. 2012. *Utopian Politics: Citizenship and Practice*. London: Routledge.

Firth, R. 2019. "Utopianism and intentional communities." In *The Palgrave Handbook of Anarchism*, pp. 491–510.

Forbes 2018. "The best places for Business and Careers #48: Madison Wisconsin" *Forbes*. Available at: https://www.forbes.com/places/wi/madison/ [Accessed 5 March 2019].

Ginsberg, M. 2012. "Madison co-operatives offer an alternative to a system of haves and have-nots" *Isthmus* [Madison local news]. Available at: https://isthmus.com/news/news/madison-cooperatives-offer-an-alternative-to-a-system-of-haves-and-have-nots/ [Accessed 4 March 2019].

Greene, H.R. and Greene, M.W. 2001. *The Public Ivies: America's Flagship Public Universities* (1st ed.). New York: Cliff Street Books.

Harvey, R. 2018. "What has caused the number of US worker co-operatives to nearly double?" *Co-op news*. Available at: https://www.thenews.coop/130862/sector/worker-coops/caused-number-us-worker-co-ops-nearly-double/ [Accessed 12 March 2019].

IEM 2024. "Our Company" *Isthmus Engineering and Manufacturing Website*. Available at: https://isthmuseng.com/our-company/ [Accessed 8 August 2024].

Latour, B. 1999. *Pandora's hope: essays on the reality of science studies*. Cambridge, Massachusetts: Harvard University Press.

Madison Worker Co-operatives (MadWorC) 2019. Available at: https://madworc.org/ [Accessed 14 March 2019].

MadWorC 2015. "Pathbreaker: Isthmus Engineering and Manufacturing" *MadWorC blog*. 10 June. Available at: https://madworc.org/news/ [Accessed 14 March 2019].

Pepper, D. 1991. *Communes and the Green Vision: Counterculture, Lifestyle and the New Age*. London: Green Print.

Pickering, A. 2010. *The cybernetic brain: Sketches of another future*. Chicago: University of Chicago Press.

Ritzer, G. 1992. *The McDonaldization of society*. New York: Pine Forge Press.

Sargisson, L. 2000. *Utopian Bodies and the Politics of Transgression*. London: Routledge.

Still, T. 2018. "Signs of 'Rust Belt renaissance' evident in Wisconsin, Upper Midwest" *Madison State Journal*. June 2. Available at: https://madison.com/wsj/business/tom-still-signs-of-rust-belt-renaissance-evident-in-wisconsin/article_de56e080-9f86-5f79-9199-dff3e55111fb.html [Accessed 5 March 2019].

Swann, T. 2020. *Anarchist Cybernetics: Control and Communication in Radical Politics*. Bristol: Bristol University Press.

Williams, R.C. 2016. *The co-operative movement: Globalization from below*. London: Routledge.

CHAPTER 6

Hackspaces and Automation as Hobbying

Description of the Interviews

Interviewees were accessed by sending an email to the London Hackspace mailing list, described as 'a very widely-read list with thousands of subscribers'.[1] Despite being a large and busy list, a small number of interviewees came forward as being involved in automation specifically, although those who did seemed to have incredibly well-thought-out definitions of the boundary between technology which is non-automotive and that which is (though notably, their definitions differed). The interviewees were all currently undertaking personal projects using automation, while one also used it in his professional life, and all three had a broader interest and knowledge in the technological development and social purposes of automation, and were keen to talk about automation more broadly than their own projects. Pseudonyms are used throughout. (Table 6.1).

Introduction: The Utopianism of Hackspaces

In the previous chapter, we considered the case of a co-operative that designed and produced automation technologies in ways that we argued were reminiscent of artisanal labour. We identified a tension between hobbying and tacit forms of knowledge in the co-operative and capitalist

[1] London Hackspace Mailing List: https://groups.google.com/g/london-hack-space accessed 15 November 2024.

R. Firth, J. Preston, *Utopia in the Factory*,
https://doi.org/10.1007/978-3-031-87132-0_6

Table 6.1 Details of interviews

Interviewee alias	*Interviewed by*	*Date*	*Job/department*
Andy	Rhiannon Firth	15 May 2019	Has built some remote-controlled robotic pieces
Harry	Rhiannon Firth	17 May 2019	Building a simple fully automatic model railway using Arduino
Carl	Rhiannon Firth	15 May 2019	Software engineer and maker who uses elements of machine learning to automate tedious parts of his own processes as well as a hobbyist

imperatives towards growth and profit. In this chapter, we seek to further develop our critique of cybernetics and our understanding of alternative, prefigurative forms of knowledge such as hobbying and tacit knowledge. Due to the small number of interviews, this chapter is briefer than the foregoing chapter, yet it offers a valuable contribution especially to our key concept of 'hobbying' as a transgressive and difficult-to-systematise form of knowledge that exists within, yet also against and beyond cybernetic capitalism.

Hackspaces, also referred to as hackerspaces, makerspaces, makespaces or hacklabs, arose as a movement in the early 2010s, with the first one often traced to Paul Böhm who started Metalab in Vienna in 2006 and was a founder member of the website Hackerspaces.org (2006–2022), which offers information and resources on how to start new Hackerspaces. Hackerspaces.org defines Hackspaces as 'community-operated physical places, where people share their interest in tinkering with technology, meet and work on their projects, and learn from each other' (Hackerspaces.org). In Chaps. 2 and 3, we historicised the rise of technocratic information society, as well as utopian and resistant alternatives. It is in the context of the networked, information-based society that hackers started as a counterculture to form online and offline communities, sharing knowledge, tools and ideas (Kostakis et al. 2015: 557).

Hackspaces can be defined as 'physical, community-led places where individuals, immersed in a hacker ethic, are to be met with on a regular basis engaging with meaningful, creative projects' (Kostakis et al. 2015: 557). This idea of a 'hacker ethic' is essential to understanding the movement. The mainstream tends to associate 'hacking' as 'bad', for example tabloids frequently propagate (somewhat justified) moral panics about fraudsters who seek to compromise the computers of civilians to steal their bank details or about 'Russian' hackers who seek to undermine national security (e.g. Winder 2024). Yet there is also an emancipatory discourse of hacking, particularly in terms of the 'hacker ethic' that arises from radical political theory and social movements. Within this discourse, 'hacking' refers to reappropriation: rearranging or mis-using elements of the system to make something subversive or radically utopian.

According to Kostakis et al., drawing on Wark (2004) and others: 'fundamental aspects of the hacker ethic include freedom, in the sense of autonomy as well as of free access and circulation of information; distrust of authority, that is, opposing the traditional, industrial top-down style of organisation; embracing the concept of learning by doing and peer-to-peer learning processes as opposed to formal modes of learning; sharing, solidarity and cooperation' (Kostakis et al. 2015: 556–557). Theoretically, hacker culture has a basis in poststructural, posthuman, anarchist and decolonial theory, and autonomous Marxisms. As an offshoot and development of the Situationist movement of the 1970s (Wark 2008; Dery 2017; O'Neill 2009) hackers seek to seize, hack, repurpose, détourn, select or develop technology so as to empower weaker social groups and create experiences of freedom, joy and empowerment. The important questions about new technologies are how they alter the balance of power among elements in assemblages and whether they can be reappropriated. Hacker culture also has resonances with anarchism and decolonial theory and has been portrayed as a subversive counterculture involving gift economy and an ethos of sharing, non-instrumentality and information freedom (Levy 1984; Stallman 2015; Coleman 2003; Reimens 2002; Raymond 1999; Dasgupta 2003: 335–336), and as creating 'a sense of belonging and mutual generosity' beyond traditional communities (Albert 2003: 338). Other works point towards a specific hacker assemblage, 'closer to the creative artist and the ivory-tower professor than to the risk-taker or the possessive individualist' (Boutang 2011: 90). Qualitative research on Hackspaces has revealed they have meaning to participants beyond simple access to tools and/or social spaces centred on shared interest in technology; rather, they articulate alternative imaginaries and prefigurative visions insofar as they are 'configured through situated practices of care and affective experiences of intimacy, solidarity, and repair' (Mora-Gámez and Davies 2023: 4190).

Hacker culture has been enthusiastically adopted as a subject in post-structural, posthuamanist and new materialist literatures, and especially in those radical strands that seek to differentiate themselves from the more technocratic milieu. While technocratic cyberneticians value technological development *per se* as empowering or augmenting humans, hackers do not eschew technology yet value processes of becoming-other and decentring binaries, over development/growth/progress. The ability to transgress and decentre binaries or fixed process in ways that enable expression of suppressed desires, queerness and otherness is understood to be immanent in technological/cybernetic assemblages and therefore amenable to hacking (Haraway 2016; Kaloski 1997). This can involve a critique or rejection of humanism, yet not in a sense that valorises technological development or existing sociotechnical frames. Deleuze critiques both cybernetics and humanism: 'there is no need to uphold man in order to resist' (Deleuze 1988: 92). The basis of Deleuzian philosophy in ontology assumes that everything is part of assemblages, but resistance is possible based on desires, lines of flight or forces of life entrapped within assemblages. While there are many empowering posthuman assemblages (man-horse-bow, wasp-orchid), cybernetics is treated as disempowering. It is an economic machine to fragment and recompose labour (Deleuze 1988: 131) or for channelling flows (Deleuze and Guattari 1987: 510–512). Hacking is therefore a way to disrupt the cybernetic machine and create empowering affects.

Autonomous Marxists have similarly weighed into the debate and play a significant role in the discourse. For Mackenzie Wark, the current situation (information society) is a further abstraction above capitalism, which establishes a temporary primacy of information (Wark 2017: 189). Information society does not replace human labour, but rather displaces it to the field of cognitive production (Dyer-Witheford 1999: 94). Alongside workers and peasants, there is also now a 'hacker class', composed of creative workers such as programmers, artists and scientists (Wark 2004: s013)[2]—here, the 'hacker' is portrayed as already recuperated in capitalism. This class operates through constantly creating newness, bringing the virtual into the actual (s074), which Wark terms 'the hack'. Capitalism has been partially succeeded by vectoralism, which extracts rents on hacks/creativity through control of the vectors of information (s29, s118, s336). The hack potentially leads to abundance (s010) but is contained by vectoralism, mainly through intellectual property systems (s079). Like other post-autonomists, Griziotti believes in a reciprocal, assemblage-like

[2] *Hacker Manifesto* lacks page numbers and is denoted by numbered sections, instead.

human-machine exchange (Griziotti 2019: 13, 144) but sees socioeconomic forces as primary (Griziotti 2019: 15). New technologies, including automation, aim to wear down the machine-life boundary to a point of indistinguishability (Griziotti 2019: 107, 148). It is technically possible to self-organise the digital common, but in practice the internet is dominated by corporations (Griziotti 2019: 180). Cybernetic automatisms—such as Hackspaces—emerge as ways to contain the increased creative power of labour (Griziotti 2019: 147). Cybernetic control operates through manipulation of entrance points into networks for purposes of behaviour modification (Griziotti 2019: 147), and spaces like Hackspaces offer an alternative means of organisation and creative production.

Politically, proponents of hacker culture tend to be tactical rather than strategic, on the basis of de Certeau's (1984) distinction, which associates strategy with rigid hierarchies and tactics with cumulatively powerful micropolitical everyday resistance. Tactical media—a milieu associated with hacker culture—is based on de Certeau's theory and involves *bricolage* and *détournement* of technologies outside their usual assemblages. It refers to bottom-up, flexible, hybrid and provisional approaches (Garcia and Lovink 2008). Assemblages provide different levels of power to actors within them. They can be assessed in terms of how far they provide joyous experiences, empower individuals or collectives, equalise power, produce cooperation and so on. Technology is not neutral, but its impact depends on the assemblage it is part of. This means that some (not necessarily all) technologies can be reclaimed, hacked and repurposed into more emancipatory assemblages. The important questions about new technologies are how they alter the balance of power among elements in assemblages and whether they can be reappropriated. The Hacker is therefore cast as a creative role—producing something from within, and for, the commons (Wark 2004). We shall see below in the interviews that this radical framing fits well with some of the ideas participants articulated in interviews. Nevertheless, some works hailing from a radical/Leftist perspective also suggest that Hacker culture in general (Wark 2008; Turner 2006), or Hackspaces in particular (Braybrooke and Smith 2018; Taylor 2005), are partially or wholly recuperated in neoliberal cyberculture. There is indeed a neoliberal discursive strand within the movement and academic works on it, which will be discussed now.

Hackspaces have also been taken up by non-radical, social democratic and/or managerialist academic literatures. These often take an associationalist approach to theorising a role for Hackspaces in bolstering neoliberal governance or contributing to incremental democratic reform. For example, Allen (2017) takes an institutionalist approach to theorising Hackspaces as spaces for entrepreneurial innovation which can bolster capitalist markets. There are established academic and populist literatures on network theory that draw on rational choice concepts to laud the benefits of seemingly anarchic organisational structures for fostering innovation within capitalist modes of production (Benkler 2006; Shirky 2008). Anderson (2012) theorises Hackspaces as presaging a recomposition of capital in a 'new industrial revolution'. Cuntz and Peuckert (2023) draw on county-level data in Germany to articulate a symbiotic relationship between Hackerspaces and new digital start-up formation in local economies. Lindtner et al. (2014) argue that by facilitating access to new technologies and participation in DiY making, Hackerspaces are 'experimenting with new models of manufacturing and entrepreneurship', which extends beyond 'hobbying and leisure practice … as a professionalizing field functioning in parallel to research and industry labs' (Lindtner et al. 2014: 439).

Researchers have also put forward a role for Hackspaces in fostering social justice and inclusion within existing educational institutions and as useful spaces for informal skills and learning (Archer et al. 2022). Academics have also advocated for the institutional recuperation of Hackspaces by systematising and bringing their practices into the academic space for more formalised experiential learning (Bilandzic and Foth 2016). This ethos has found commercial and even military sponsors, such that *Make* magazine partnered with the Defense Advanced Research Projects Agency (DARPA) to fund 1000 makerlabs in US High Schools (Finley 2012).

The extent to which Hackspaces are radical, recuperated or essentially non-radical is therefore contestable from an academic perspective, but what are the views of those involved, of active participants in Hackspaces? Despite the basis in, and ongoing affinity with, radical movements, theories and discourses, it is also the case that Hackerspaces are incredibly diverse; many of the spaces are autonomous and adopt 'hybrid governance' (Kostakis et al. 2015: 555), with models that vary between spaces and within spaces over time. Some adopt more hierarchical and rule-bound policies than others. Austin Toombs draws on a discourse analysis of mailing lists and discussion boards popular with Hackspace users to show how the international movement shares common discursive threads, with identities and community values propagated through these electronic spaces. Discussions on such lists reveal ongoing tensions in the movement between those who argue for and against formal rules versus informal social policing within the spaces (Toombs 2017). Adrian Smith draws on an extensive literature review to argue that makerspaces are pulled in different directions: a global innovation agenda which seeks to integrate their creativity into 'business as usual' versus those who see their practices as 'an inchoate infrastructure for a commons-based, sustainable and redistributed manufacturing economy' (Smith 2017: 1). Activists themselves internalise and reproduce these contradictions in their own understandings, whilst tending to view their actions as playing a role in democratising access to technology and prefiguring post-consumerist sustainable production and consumption (Smith 2017: 10). This is similar to our findings from the very small number of interviews. In the context of our broader project we would like to place the emphasis on non-systematisable, non-recuperable forms of knowledge and experience articulated through hobbying and tacit knowledge. Although it is of course *possible* to understand the practices of Hackspaces as socially and economically useful for capital, we argue that this is missing something important in that they also prefigure relations and forms of knowledge against and beyond capital, and that any attempt to understand or replicate their practices cybernetically in the terms of usefulness for a larger system (e.g. as social capital) will lose what is most radical and transformative.

Background: London Hackspace Ethos and Organisation

London Hackspace was first created as an idea and a mailing list in 2009, and subsequently formed as a Limited Company. It was initially based in various locations in East London, ultimately Hackney, and between 2009 and 2014 it grew in size to 1000 members. One member recounts:

> I first heard about Hackspace I think through another group called Dorkbot. It's an international thing very connected with the London set. Can't remember how I learnt about those – 5 or 6 years ago, went to a few meetings, heard about the Hackspace at one of those, in the first location it used – an archery club Islington. This was very brief and where they started up – a series of pub meetings before that, then it moved to a small industrial unit in Shoreditch. It was there for 2 or 3 years, and then moved to Hackney road. (Carl)

Due to rising rents and gentrification, it moved further out the city to Ujima House in Wembley, West London, where it was based at the time of this research, which took place in 2019. In December 2022 the lease ended at Ujima House, and the Hackspace equipment was put in storage awaiting a new home, and at the time of writing it has been announced that the Hackspace has relocated to a new, temporary space in Park Royal, West London (London Hackspace Wiki 2024). At the time of my visit (2019), a member informed me:

> The present position it's only been there about a year, but it used to be in Hackney, I've been a member about 4 years. It's not a problem for me to get to because I've got a car. Hackney road was much easier for some people, but it wasn't such a nice space. First of all, it was smaller, secondly, it didn't feel as good. You go to Wembley and it's a nice place to be. (Harry)

The research for this chapter was undertaken in May 2019. Rhiannon visited the Hackspace premises and was given a tour on 7 May 2019, which was an advertised regular Open Day (but my presence as a researcher was agreed in advance). At the time, the space was very quiet, only my tour guide was present and around three other members who came and went during my visit. I was informed that this was due to the move and people who had joined the group in the space in East London were struggling to travel to the new premises in West London. However, I was informed they were hoping to recruit more people locally as well as for ongoing members to find ways to fit it in their schedule once the relocation had settled. I recruited interviewees via the mailing list, asking specifically for people who worked with automation. Only three came forward (initially four, but one deselected himself after a discussion and deciding he did not work with automation). I interviewed one of these in a café, and the other two via Skype videoconferencing.

It is worth taking a minute to describe the interviewees and their relationship to automation since these were incredibly unique, issuing as hobbies from personal interests, desires and identified problems, rather than from the imperatives of an external organisation or system. The interviewee with the pseudonym Andy had held an interest in automation and robotics for a long time. He claimed to have initially picked up robotics from the Hackspace forums, and this had led to the development of two specific interests. The first was focused on developing prosthetic limbs, including one that was sponsored by a computer game company to emphasise connections to a computer game, as well as a robotic hand. The second was a project for an artist who sought help via the mailing list. It was a small robot to wheel itself around a gallery, 'trying to look as though it's intelligent, but it certainly isn't' (Andy). This echoed themes from interviews in the other two organisations that many forms of so-called automation and artificial intelligence are in fact simulacra, designed to appear as such: 'they're not intelligent, they're basically puppets' (Andy). The interviewee pseudonymised as Harry was building 'a fully automatic model railway', which he described as:

> an end-to-end piece of track with a station at either end, with a loop. The train will go from one station to the other and at the far end, the loco will uncouple, go round the loop, come back onto the carriage, and go back to where it came from, and it will do exactly the same at the other end, so it will just go backwards and forwards, but the loco will be at the front of the carriage every time. (Harry)

Prompted to define what he understood by automation in this hobby context (which one might imagine may disturb assumptions around aiding efficiency in cybernetic systems), Harry responded: 'Turn it on and leave it, and it'll go by itself' (Harry). The electronic components that Harry was working with included an Arduino, a type of micro-controller popular with hobbyists: 'it's basically a very small computer with input and output pins which you can control switch on and off. You give the Arduino a programme and it runs through. The input pins can be used to detect things using sensors, so that way I'm using a detector to tell where the train is at a given time' (Harry). The interviewee with the pseudonym Carl used the Hackspace for access to tools that would be infeasible to keep at home due to space or cost or maintenance. He used these tools to make scale models, and the relation to automation is that parts of this process are automated: 'I could sit down with a scalpel and a saw and cut out all the parts for a building … or I can draw it all up in CAD and shunt it into the laser and the laser will do it a hundred times without breaking a sweat, and it will do it perfectly every time' (Carl). The scale models included 'buildings, people, vehicles, quite often either science fiction or fantasy-related stuff' (Carl). The purpose of summarising the ways in which these three interviewees related to, understood and used automation is to illustrate how diverse these articulations are—just three interviewees were using automation in wildly different ways and also in ways that were perhaps more individualised (geared to individual goals and desires) than in the previous organisations, although the interviewee working with prosthesis was doing so as part of various communities and groups for social purposes. This obviously has something to do with the relationship to community and technology that is nurtured in Hackspaces, and while just three interviews cannot represent this, they do open up this field of thought and it is worth considering them in terms of the themes covered in the previous chapters.

Tacit Knowledge

In previous chapters we have developed the theme of 'tacit knowledge' as creative, artisanal knowledge ensuing from human workers and human-technology relationships within organisations, yet which transgresses the instrumental goals of organisations and which cannot be captured, modelled or systematised. As a form of organisation that valorises, and indeed exists for, the expression of novel and original creative knowledges, one might expect Hackspaces to be hothouses for tacit knowledge. Indeed, insofar as 'tacit' connotes 'implicit' one might expect a Hackspace to nurture such knowledge that it become no longer tacit, hidden, implied but rather explicit and freely articulated! Nevertheless, as outlined above, Hackspaces have also been viewed as 'innovation factories' where novel technologies created by humans at leisure can be captured and capitalised upon for profit. Instrumentalised knowledge is anathema to what we are trying to articulate with the concept. It is worth thinking through how Hackspace members themselves understood the nature and definition of knowledge and learning.

The interviewee Harry echoed ideas articulated under the theme of tacit knowledge in previous chapters, of learning as essential to life, and not (just) instrumental for capitalism 'You can always learn. If you stop learning, you stop living' (Harry). He emphasised that learning does not require an expert to impart universal knowledge but rather arises situationally: 'The way I write the programme for it is to have a guess at the beginning and then amend it until it works properly, like trial and error' (Harry). The interviewee Andy resisted the idea that human knowledge could be systematised in any way in order to be replicated by machines. As someone who had built robotic pieces, he argued that although they were not 'primarily mechanical they were extremely stupid: they're about as intelligent as an automatic washing machine' (Andy). This was not only true of the automatons that Andy built, but also of others built in the Hackspace and 'generally true of most of the marketing-led commercial projects too. Even when they're only processing data (rather than operating limbs etc.) they're really only "expert systems" - machines which operate in accordance with a large number of stored rules which encapsulate a desired behaviour'. Sometimes those rules are partially created by the machines themselves ('machine learning'), but this is done by providing an example of desired operation and allowing the system to accumulate the rules. The 'desired behaviours' are ultimately decided by the humans making the machines, meaning they are expressions of human desires and human creativity, rather than autonomously intelligent. Andy continued that 'a system that copies its teacher isn't intelligent in my view' (Andy). This interviewee articulates an incredibly interesting point here that is highly congruent with our own argument. Pushing further this conceptualisation, knowledge that arises autonomously—tacit knowledge—is the only true intelligence. Systematised and technocratic knowledge within an organisation or cybernetic system is not truly intelligence at all, since it is designed technocratically, and therefore replicates the desires of its designer.

The interviewee raised a further interesting point that more and more knowledge is recorded and stored, increasing the potential for automation. He used the example of the 1960s F-1 rocket engine involved in programmes that took people to the moon. He enthusiastically told the story:

> We don't know how to build them anymore. And it seems weird, because they must've written it all down, but because they were made by people in an era before computer design, every rocket engine was built by hand and the people building them were tuning them as they went, so half knowledge about how to make an F1 rocket engine lived in the engineer's heads, and no-one ever wrote it down. (Carl)

As a continuation of the story, he told how a group of graduate students tried to tackle the problem of building one when half of the information was missing or was not systematisable using modern instrumentation. They reconstructed the plans using a combination of modern techniques and the blueprints left behind (a version of this story which partially verifies the interviewee's tale is available via Hutchinson 2013). This is an example of how conceptions of hobbying and tacit knowledge intersect. A 'puzzle' with missing pieces of knowledge, involving an engineering problem, is approached using a combination of collective, crowdsourced, knowledge and tacit knowledge. Although the experiment did not lead to a functioning rocket engine, it was a meaningful exercise insofar as it produced knowledge about historical changes in technology and design. Carl continued that modern rocket engines are entirely computer designed, and the human labour only contributes to construction because they are cheaper than machines that could be built for the task. This idea of humans' knowledge as subordinate to systemic needs is theorised by Raunig (2010) as 'machinic enslavement'.

Hobbying

In previous chapters we found that even in companies oriented to making profit—either for capital or for workers themselves—not all production was capitalist production, and workers in both types of organisation went beyond the profit imperative by playing and experimenting with technologies in ways that brought joy or satisfaction. We termed this playful and transgressive production 'hobbying'. In a leisure space like Hackspaces, we might expect this of course. Harry stated that his model railway was 'of no social use'—it was purely a product of his own interests, 'I've been a model railway enthusiast for a long time, and interested in electronics for a long time, and interested in computers for a long time, and the idea amalgamated the three streams into one' (Harry). His interest arose when 'about 5 years ago, my son bought me an Arduino, knowing my interests, for my Birthday, and I got interested in it' (Harry). There was a social aspect to the Arduino hobbying, which had also integrated itself into the fabric of the building: 'There is an Arduino Group that meets fortnightly at Hackspace. You may have noticed that members use their cards to get in doors. That is controlled by an Arduino. It's called Door-Bots' (Harry).

Some interviewees articulated links between hobbying and work that echoed the ideas put forward earlier in this chapter about the recuperation and capitalisation of Hackspaces as both leisure spaces and innovation factories, creating conditions for the ideal post-Fordist entrepreneurial precarious subject. Although Hackspaces are informal spaces for producing hobby knowledge, one interviewee instrumentalised this by discursively commodifying the hobby as self-development: 'I've worked with various companies but always with this sort of thing in mind, so I've just accumulated the knowledge I'm accumulating. I'm keeping up with new technology. Formal education was useful, but vast majority is what I've learnt along the way. I don't really do things that are the same things over and over again, and I wouldn't really do that if it wasn't new all the time. I am freelance so I change jobs all the time, the Hackspace offers a continuation for self-development' (Carl). The discursive blurring of boundaries between labour and leisure continued: 'both of these ones have been semi-commercial. I was more interested in doing them than what I could earn from them, not high-paid … I'm nearly retired and just looking at keeping myself going; I've got a couple of art projects going, sometimes I do straightforward commercial contracts, sometimes it's just at home' (Carl). Projects Carl was currently involved with included taking data from a satellite called the Lunar Reconnaissance Orbiter that took a map of the moon and 3D printing of small sections for the 50th anniversary of the lunar landing, 'I will be putting a small portion of real rock from the moon into about 10 casts of the landing site of the Apollo 11 … My plan is to keep one, and the rest I am going to sell' (Carl).

In the Introduction, we linked 'hobbying' to what Ivan Illich (1973) terms the creation of 'convivial tools'—forms of technology that do not foster dependency but rather can be appropriated and adapted by non-specialists. The organisation of the Hackspace is well-suited to the use and development of convivial tools, but not to mass production: 'The Hackspace is great for doing ad-hoc stuff, like prototypes or R&D stuff, but because it's a shared workshop, it's not great for being able to reliably do stuff … I don't want to be the person monopolizing time or space or tools at the Hackspace, because it is supposed to be there for everyone' (Carl). Carl spoke of the value of convivial technologies as a form of art, citing the example of a company who 'proudly claim their robots are completely useless – one robot is called robo-thespian, it's an actor, it can't do anything useful, you can't rely on it for anything' (Carl). The idea of an unreliable robot offers an appropriate segue to ideas around anthropomorphism articulated in the Hackspace.

Blackboxing and Anthropomorphism

Blackboxing refers to the technological imaginary articulated within the cybernetic paradigm whereby systems are made more efficient through the systematisation of generic features, reducing a component to inputs and outputs without the need for understanding inner workings. The discourse of inputs and outputs was present at the Hackspace, in a hobby context:

'It's using an Arduino, which is a micro-controller, which is basically a very small computer with input and output pins which you can control switch on and off. You give the Arduino a programme and it runs through. The input pins can be used to detect things using sensors, so the way I'm doing it is I'm using a detector to tell where the train is at a given time, and when it's passed a certain point' (Harry). However, for this hobby user, it was possible to open the Black Box: '[Arduino] is an open-source technology, so you know all about its internals, how it was made. What it can be used for is whatever your imagination decides you want to do with it. There's so many different things that it can be used for. There's no pre-set purpose just, what do you want to do with it?' (Harry). The innovative and personalised nature of the technology was illustrated in an amusing interaction:

RF: What terminology do you use to refer to the system you're making? Is it a train set?

H: It's *not* a train-set! It's a fully automatic model railway. It's something I've had in mind for a long time, it's a proof of concept. That you can fully automate model railways.

RF: Has it not been done before?

H: It has, but using different methods. Not with an Arduino, as far as I know.

RF: Do you ever humanise the machines? Give them names, or anything?

H: No. I give the stations a name, but they're not human names, I've decided to call them 'hither' and 'thither'. (Harry)

Nevertheless, the interviewee articulated the centrality of human labour and social imagination in automation and in cybernetic systems (whilst the dominant discourse and capitalist production often disguise this):

> Most of the things that are automatic involve some human interaction. I mean, all of it does, because someone has to imagine and make the automatic part in the first place. An automatic car with an automatic gear box, someone still has to operate it, set it to drive, someone still has to drive the car, there's human interaction there, somewhere along the line someone has to feed the starting materials in, even at the end you have the finished product, but the starting materials have to come from somewhere. Even if it

> means you set up a factory to do this, you still need humans to drive the trucks to take the goods in and to drive the goods out. Although an automatic railway might help [laughs]. (Harry)

Similarly, Carl was cynical about anthropomorphism, and like Harry this seemed to be tied to a critique of blackboxing and machinic enslavement within a cybernetic system:

> Whilst yes, tools may have idiosyncrasies, I always shy away from saying a tool has got a personality, because that way leads to anthropomorphisation, and we're outside the realms of, this tool sticks a bit on the x axis, or this tool makes a funny noise when it warms up, or this tool overheats too quickly, to 'it's got a temperament, it's a bit unhappy', and that gets in the way of being rational about the capability and limitations of the tool. (Carl)

Andy summed this up in terms that linked a critique of blackboxing back to convivial use of tools: 'I think working in a hackspace, people are comfortable and more likely to see [a robot] as a tool than a competitor' (Andy).

Embodiment and Enhancement

In previous chapters we have looked at how the line between automation and embodiment becomes entangled and blurred. Some practices in the Hackspace, however, illustrated a possible prefigurative intersection of hobbyism in automation and anarchist mutual aid. Ernst Bloch (1986) wrote of the utopian potential of medicine as play and not labour; embedded in the human urge to be social and empathic, and to intervene in human problems and ameliorate suffering at a non- or less-abstracted level. A Hackspace member articulated a living example of this which, although involving appropriation of capitalist funds, offers a stark contrast to bodily enhancements for capital:

> One project involved a gamer guy who lost his leg in a rail accident. He had sponsorship from a computer games company to have a prosthesis made [with] electronics in it to emphasise connections to the game you could operate in novel ways with the limb [...] Hackspace was used for meetings, and some of the parts. (Carl)

In this context, the prosthetic limb was intended for pleasure and interactivity in a gaming context and not for capitalist production.

Conclusion: The Possibilities of Hackspaces as an Alternative to Industry 4.0—What Do They Prefigure?

A key theme throughout this book has been how prefigurative dis-alienated, even anarchist, relations to knowledge and technology exist at a human level even in the most alienated cybernetic systems. Conversely, convivial organisations like the Hackspace also exist within capitalism and activities cannot be isolated from being mobilised to capitalist means. Social learning and conviviality are of value to both humans and capital, but do they prefigure something beyond capital?:

> The [most important tool at the Hackspace] is the community. Going there and wanting to get some work done can be a lost cause, you start talking to someone and bloody hell, it's 7 o'clock and I've got to go home … but one of the best things I find about the Hackspace, it's a skills exchange, where if you don't know how to do something, there's usually someone there who can explain things to you and show you how to do it, and vice versa. (Harry)

The beliefs and values of members of the Hackspace community also speak to the possibilities that such an organisation could prefigure. While my interviewees should not be seen as representative of the organisation as a whole, they give insight into the diversity of views and some of the discussions and debates around the role of automation happening in activist spaces beyond academia. Carl spoke to a mixture of Fully Automated Luxury Communism (FALC) discourse alongside more anarchistic ideas around convivial tools and resisting machinic enslavement. He argued, 'I don't think that there is any kind of inherent value in work. There's value in doing stuff, there's value in labour, but there's no value in work. There's nothing inherently noble about toiling for someone else'. He believed that this put him 'at odds with everyone' or 'at least out government'. While he viewed automation in technological determinist terms as largely a positive force for good which would ultimately reduce toil, he did also touch on a critique of capitalism, hinting that automation would not mean an end to exploitation and also that states and governments are complicit in this exploitation rather than acting as a buffer through welfare:

> Part of me believes that as long as people need money, the cost of human labour will always remain lower in a large proportion of cases than automa-

> tion … companies already automate a huge amount, and companies also hire people for stuff they could automate, but only where people are cheaper than automation. (Carl)

He cited 'programmes where governments are paying companies to not automate things, to keep the cost to a business of hiring a person lower than the cost of automating it', which he claimed only affirmed his feeling 'that there is no inherent value in work, I would rather the government just gave that money to the people who are displaced, why have we suddenly decided that the business is more deserving of that money to hire a person to do a job sufficiently menial that a robot can do it' (Carl).

This brings us to the radical and prefigurative elements in this interviewee's deeply philosophical outlook, which he linked to the social purpose of the Hackspace, which was constantly under attack from capitalist appropriation in the form of gentrification: 'Maybe if everyone could afford their own tool. Or if tools became affordable enough that they could be shared more easily than having to have just one in a Hackspace, and if London wasn't so much of a hellpit where half of the city isn't locked off to everyone who isn't oligarchs, then the Hackspace wouldn't need so much space, which would mean you could have smaller organisations that could replicate the social aspects of the hackspace' (Carl). His thoughts resonated with anarchist and open Marxist ideals that technology, to be convivial, must be embedded in community and meaningful human relationships, rather than being something that can be systematised and mobile: 'the Hackspace used to be in Hackney … I worry that as the Hackspace moves further out it will become more tool-oriented … I'm not quite sure that the community survived the move to Wembley' (Carl). Ultimately, Carl cited failures of councils and governments to support such spaces as having a limiting effect on the role they might play in social justice: 'I don't think the Hackspace is going to be a massive institute for social change, because as a society we're not willing to provide a next step. And I get angry about that' (Carl). In the concluding chapter, we will think more about the relationship between prefigurative knowledges and utopian social change, which we have developed throughout the book drawing on theory and on worker and activist accounts.

References

Albert, S. 2003. 'Free as in Air: An Interview with Vortex', in Sarai Collective (eds.), *Sarai Reader 03: Shaping Technologies*, Delhi: CSDS/Sarai, pp. 337–345.

Allen, D.W.E. 2017. *Hackerspaces as Entrepreneurial Anarchy.* Available at SSRN: https://ssrn.com/abstract=2749016 or https://doi.org/10.2139/ssrn.2749016. Accessed 10 August 2024.

Anderson, C. 2012. *Makers: The New Industrial Revolution*, New York: Random House.

Archer, L., DeWitt, J., Freedman, E. and Thomas, K. 2022. *Developing Equitable Practice with Youth in Makerspaces: Ideas and Case Studies from the Making Spaces Project-Main Report.* Available at: https://discovery.ucl.ac.uk/id/eprint/10155189/1/Freedman_Making%20Spaces%20project%20report%202022%20-%20main%20report.pdf. Accessed 10 August 2024.

Benkler, Y. 2006. *The Wealth of Networks: How Social Production Transforms Markets and Freedom*, New Haven: Yale University Press.

Bilandzic, M. and Foth, M. 2016. 'Designing hubs for connected learning: Social, spatial, and technological insights from coworking spaces, hackerspaces, and meetup groups', in L. Carvalho, P. Goodyear & M. de Laat (eds), *Place-Based Spaces for Networked Learning*, New York: Routledge, pp. 191–206.

Bloch, E. 1986 [1959]. *The Principle of Hope* [Vols 1–3], trans. N. Plaice, S. Plaice & P. Knight, Cambridge, MA: MIT Press.

Boutang, Y.M. 2011. *Cognitive Capitalism*, Cambridge: Polity.

Braybrooke, K. & Smith, A. 2018. 'Editors' introduction: Liberatory technologies for whom? Exploring a new generation of makerspaces defined by institutional encounters', *Journal of Peer Production*, vol. 12. Available at https://ssrn.com/abstract=3210701. Accessed 10 August 2024.

Coleman, B. 2003. 'The (Copylefted) Source Code for the Ethical Production of Information Freedom', in Sarai Collective (eds.), *Sarai Reader 03: Shaping Technologies*, Delhi: CSDS/Sarai, pp. 297–302.

Cuntz, A. & Peuckert, J. 2023. 'From hackers to start-ups: Innovation commons and local entrepreneurial activity', *Research Policy*, vol. 52, no. 2, article 104675.

Dasgupta, R. 2003. 'Beyond the Apocalypse: An Unfinished Meditation on Ethics', in Sarai Collective (eds.), *Sarai Reader 03: Shaping Technologies*, Delhi: CSDS/Sarai, pp. 236–242.

de Certeau, M. 1984. *The Practice of Everyday Life*. Berkeley, CA, University of California Press.

Deleuze, G. 1988. *Foucault*, London: Continuum.

Deleuze, G. & Guattari, F. 1987. *A Thousand Plateaus*, London: Continuum.

Dery, M. 2017. 'Culture jamming: Hacking, slashing, and sniping in the empire of signs', in M. DeLaure & M. Fink (eds.), *Culture Jamming: Activism and the Art of Cultural Resistance*. New York: NYU Press, pp. 39–61.

Dyer-Witheford, N. 1999. *Cyber-Marx: Cycles and Circuits of Struggle in High-Technology*. Illinois: University of Illinois Press.

Finley, K. 2012. *The Military-Maker Complex: DARPA Infiltrates the Hackerspace Movement.* Available at: http://www.technoccult.net/2012/02/24/the-military-maker-complex-darpa-infiltrates-the-hackerspace-movement/. Accessed 10 August 2024.

Garcia, D. & Lovink, G. 2008. 'The ABC of Tactical Media'. Available at: http://www.tacticalmediafiles.net/articles/3160. Accessed 6 August 2019.

Griziotti, G. 2019. *Neurocapitalism*, New York: Minor Compositions.

Hackerspaces.org 2006–2022. Available at: https://hackerspaces.org/. Accessed 10 August 2024.

Haraway, D. 2016 [1985]. 'The Cyborg Manifesto: Science, Technology and Socialist Feminism in the Late Twentieth Century', in *Manifestly Haraway*, Minneapolis: University of Minnesota Press, pp. 3–90.

Hutchinson, L. 2013. 'Saturn V "moon rocket" engine firing again after 40 years, sort of', *Ars Technica*, 1 January 2013. Available at: https://arstechnica.com/science/2013/01/saturn-v-moon-rocket-engine-firing-again-after-40-years-sort-of/. Accessed 10 August 2024.

Illich, I. 1973. *Tools for Conviviality*, New York: Harper and Row.

Kaloski, A. 1997. 'Bisexuals Making Out with Cyborgs: Politics, Pleasure, Con/Fusion', *International Journal of Sexuality and Gender Studies*, vol. 2, no. 1, pp. 47–64.

Kostakis, V., Niaros, V. & Giotitsas, C. 2015. 'Production and Governance in Hackerspaces: A Manifestation of Commons-Based Peer Production in the Physical Realm?', *International Journal of Cultural Studies*, vol. 18, no. 5, pp. 555–573.

Levy, S. 1984. *Hackers: Heroes of the Computer Revolution*, New York: Doubleday.

Lindtner, S., Hertz, G.D. & Dourish, P. 2014. 'Emerging Sites of HCI Innovation: Hackerspaces, Hardware Startups & Incubators', in *Proceedings of the SIGCHI Conference on Human Factors in Computing Systems*, New York: ACM, pp. 439–448.

London Hackspace Wiki 2024. Available at: https://wiki.london.hackspace.org.uk/view/London_Hackspace. Accessed 10 August 2024.

Mora-Gámez, F. & Davies, S.R. 2023. 'Afterlives of the Californian Ideology: More-Than-Tech Communities: Alternative Imaginaries Within Hacking and Crafting', *International Journal of Communication*, vol. 17, pp. 4182–4195.

O'Neill, S. 2009. 'The interactive spectacle and the digital situationist', in P. Turner, S. Turner and E. Davenport (Eds.), *Exploration of Space, Technology, and Spatiality: Interdisciplinary Perspectives.* Hershey: Information Science Reference, pp. 155–167.

Raunig, G. 2010. *A Thousand Machines: A Concise Philosophy of the Machine as Social Movement.* Los Angeles: semiotext(e)

Raymond, E.S. 1999. *The Cathedral and the Bazaar: Musings on Linux and Open Source by an Accidental Revolutionary*, Sebastopol, CA: O'Reilly.

Reimens, P. 2002. 'Some Thoughts on the Idea of "Hacker Culture"'. Available at: http://cryptome.org/hacker-idea.htm. Accessed 6 August 2024.

Shirky, C. 2008. *Here Comes Everybody: The Power of Organizing Without Organizations*, London: Penguin.
Smith, A. 2017. 'Social Innovation, Democracy and Makerspaces', *SWPS 2017-10*. Available at SSRN: https://ssrn.com/abstract=2986245 or https://doi.org/10.2139/ssrn.2986245. Accessed 10 August 2024.
Stallman, R.M. 2015. *Free Software, Free Society: Selected Essays of Richard M. Stallman*, Boston, MA: GNU Press.
Taylor, P.A. 2005. 'From Hackers to Hacktivists: Speed Bumps on the Global Superhighway?', *New Media & Society*, vol. 7, no. 5, pp. 625–646.
Toombs, A.L. 2017. 'Hackerspace Tropes, Identities, and Community Values', in *Proceedings of the 2017 Conference on Designing Interactive Systems*, New York: ACM, pp. 1079–1091.
Turner, F. 2006. *From Counterculture to Cyberculture: Stewart Brand, the Whole Earth Network, and the Rise of Digital Utopianism*, Chicago: University of Chicago Press.
Wark, M. 2004. *A Hacker Manifesto*, Cambridge, MA: Harvard University Press.
Wark, M. 2008. *50 Years of Recuperation of the Situationist International* (Vol. 3), New York: Princeton Architectural Press.
Wark, M. 2017. *General Intellects: Twenty-Five Thinkers for the Twenty-First Century*. London, Verso.
Winder, D. 2024. 'Paris Olympics Security Warning – Russian Hackers Threaten 2024 Games', *Forbes*, 19 July 2024. Available at: https://www.forbes.com/sites/daveywinder/2024/07/19/paris-olympics-security-warning-russian-hackers-threaten-2024-games/. Accessed 10 August 2024.

CHAPTER 7

Conclusion: De-naturalising Cybernetics—Against a Dystopian Future

Introduction

In this book we have presented a critique of cybernetic and associated technological (particularly Industry 4.0) systems in terms of their epistemological and liberatory limitations. Epistemologically, cybernetics is unable to capture human knowledge and potential, and it cannot prefigure a liberatory model for future human societies. We followed this with a discussion of markedly different forms of production, which revealed their prefigurative and non-recuperable elements in terms of both tacit knowledge and what we have referred to as 'hobbying'. In this conclusion, we reflect more broadly on the prefigurative and liberatory limitations of cybernetic theorising and practice. Cybernetics has been naturalised in social theory, and societal modelling, as an encompassing, and natural, metaphor, for existing and future societies. To return to our research questions, through this discussion in previous chapters we have shown that cybernetics is not an appropriate and progressive model for future human societies and politics. In this concluding chapter we de-naturalise cybernetics and argue against the limited form of futurity that cyber-thinking leads towards.

Firstly, we take issue with 'cybernetic' theorisations of capitalism, techno-feudalism and distributed capitalism: as these framings can lead to assumptions that cybernetics is a natural form for a future utopian society, and that with a different form of cybernetic management capitalism can be overcome. At the same time, we disagree with the ideas that the 'factory'

R. Firth, J. Preston, *Utopia in the Factory*,
https://doi.org/10.1007/978-3-031-87132-0_7

and the associated working class are disappearing from class struggle to be replaced with some more organic, fluid, social formation of a cybernetic nature. As explained in the introduction, the idea of the factory, as an example (or for Marx, the exemplar) of how capitalist production exploits abstract labour to produce profit, with its authoritarian methods of control, is frighteningly and obviously apparent in all aspects of contemporary life. Secondly, we argue that tacit knowledge, and hobbying, means that there are limits to cybernetic control and that complex co-ordination problems are amenable to anarchist principles of de-scaling, federation and collective co-ordination. Thirdly, we explain that cybernetics is not a 'prefigurative' liberatory form of political or social organisation and that we need to look elsewhere for prefigurative alternatives. In this concluding section we draw on lessons from our case studies.

Capitalism, Cybernetics and Revolution

There are tendencies in contemporary Marxist, and revolutionary, theorising to assume capitalism is naturally cybernetic and, mistakenly, that this means any future society that has communist or otherwise liberatory elements could and should possess cybernetic features. Revolution involves seizing the cybernetic means of production to create a workers' state. At face value, there might seem to be some logic to this. As we have argued earlier in this book, contemporary corporations and states do, in actuality, manage their business affairs and populations through cybernetic principles and systems. Cybernetics is a technology and a form of management, labour discipline and social control. The ubiquity of cybernetic management, and cybernetic technologies in capitalism, has, in social thought, led to a misrecognition of both the nature of power and the operations of power, and a resurgence of arguments regarding a vanguardist seizure of the means of production, including cybernetic forms of management and control, as the principle means of working-class power. The widespread quotation, and circulation, of parts of Marx's famous 'Fragment on Machines' in the *Grundrisse* (1993) in social theory is partly responsible for this tendency. This 'Fragment' is extrapolated far beyond its original context. It is often interpreted as predicting that the productive powers of machines would grow to such an extent that labour power as the source of value would become irrelevant and that there would be no further need for humans to work. Therefore, all that is required for the working class to achieve Communism is to seize these machines from the capitalist class, leading to a society of permanent leisure and technological progress. The meme and joke of 'Fully Automated Luxury Communism' hence becomes a programme for human liberation (Bastani 2019). Preston (2022) points out three problems with this position. Firstly, Marx's work on this theme is based on notes and fragments, and the reading of this section is selective. Hence, it stands in opposition to Marx's more mature work (Capital), which provides an extensive theoretical elaboration of capital, drawing on empirical observation. Indeed, in other sections of the 'notebook', of which the fragment is a part, the depiction of what we could call 'the human within the machine' works in tandem with alienation and disassociation, portraying the human as an alienated node in the system. Secondly, in other works (particularly Capital) Marx explicitly describes the purpose of machines as dividing and controlling human labour for explicitly capitalist functions. There is no assumption that such a mechanised society would be positive for human development. Humanist Marxists consider that forms of 'State Capitalism', including the Chinese and former USSR Communist Party's surveillance-led, authoritarian state, were the antithesis of his intention. These are not 'cyberutopias'. Thirdly, that creation and production for individual, familial and social needs was, at least for the Young Marx, part of human, culture and a distinguishing feature of humanity (Marx 1992). Therefore, simply seizing the means of production, including cybernetics and cyber-systems, would still carry the (capitalist) mode of production even if that were in its state-capitalist form.

'Fragment thinking' carries with it a particular way of thinking about technology and meta-technologies like cybernetics. Metaphorically, the algorithmic nature of capitalism and the ways in which the abstract nature of social forms in Marx's theory are expressed, produce a misrecognition of the 'nature' of capital and the state. In particular, formalist and analytical Marxism builds on Marx's simple expressions of 'value in motion' and appears to be calculative, or even cybernetic. The circulation of money and commodities (M-C-C'-M' where money is thrown into commodity production, producing through the labour process a transformed commodity and a greater sum of money) and in expanded forms of capitalist reproduction, bringing in capital accumulation, appears itself to be a cybernetic, embedded, process. Frustratingly, the mechanics of circulation and value obscure the very process by which labour power is extracted from individuals and collectives in the labour process, which is violent, bloody and visceral. The means of production themselves are not only built upon human blood, sweat and tears but are in a dialectical relationship with them—you cannot have one without the other. Separating the mechanical from the visceral leads not just to 'Fragment thinking' but increasingly a disavowal of the specifically capitalist nature of capitalist production until it becomes not capitalism but feudalism (or techno-feudalism), or a socially reproductive form of distributed capitalism.

Cybernetic theorising of capitalism, and fetishising the role of technology and machines, can mislead us to the assumption that cybernetics is a natural system for post-capitalist governance, whereas these merely reproduce the extractive dynamics of capitalism. It could be, for example, that capitalism has changed into a feudalist or socially reproductive or distributed form, but these assumptions also tend to naturalise cybernetic forms of governance which consistently reappear in those arguments. Morozov (2022) argues that theories of monopolisation and a reinvention of capitalism as primarily extractive of intangible labour have been used to argue that capitalism is no longer cyber-capitalism but has regressed into a feudalist form of production. If the nature of the system is feudal (with monopolistic tech-firms taking the place of feudal lords), then changing governance could mean simply seizing the means of production and maintaining cybernetic systems. However, although capital may structure and restructure itself (almost by definition as self-valorising value), it has not mutated into a proto-communist or regressive feudalist form of 'techno-feudalism'. As we argued in our Introduction, commodity production and the factory (or factory-like systems, often enabled by digitisation and platform capitalism) mean that capitalist production is still ubiquitous. Morozov similarly argues that extractive processes and making use of islands of cheap resources have always been part of capitalism, but they have not supplanted the regular forms of capitalist exploitation and innovation. Feudalism has not supplanted capitalism, but forms of sovereign power (often through the state as an instrumental form of ruling class power) have always been part of capitalist production as the raw expression of the class struggle of the ruling class to maintain its existence.

Cybernetic forms of capitalism are also implicit in what has been referred to as 'bio-political production'. Negri (2018) considers that the primary site of capital and struggle has moved from the industrial worker and the factory to the multitude and the metropolis, a fluid, cyber-metaphorical relationship between component parts. This is part of 'bio-political production' (Hardt and Negri 2000: xiii). However, this does not mean that class struggle has come to an end. The position of the worker (if not the working class as a unified class) is evidently still relevant for

Negri (2018: 184), but the worker is part of the cyber-type multitude, which is an 'irreducible multiplicity' (Hardt and Negri 2006: 105). 'Multitude is a class concept' (Hardt and Negri 2006: 103) which arises through class struggle but the multitude work beneath the rule of a form of mutated capital (Hardt and Negri 2006: 106), rather than a single capitalist company, and have the potential to refuse it, rather than being in a direct, dialectical and symbiotic relation to it. Hardt and Negri arrive at this depiction of the multitude on the basis of a critique of reductive conceptions of the working class. They argue that a description of the working class as industrial labour does not take into account immaterial (service) labour, as waged labour ignores unwaged labour and all of these categories ignore the social reproduction work which is necessary, as well as non-working-class groups such as peasants, the owners of small capitals, such as agricultural small-holders and owners of food stalls, and the 'poor'. A new, hegemonic form of 'biopolitical labour' (Hardt and Negri 2006: 108) is a better depiction of the multitude than a traditional class conception. Rather than the relation between capital and labour, various strands of business (capital) and international and national institutions and militaries (Empire—Hardt and Negri 2000) structure the multitude 'into the global political body of capital, divided geographically by hierarchies of labor and wealth, and ruled by a multilevel structure of economic, legal and political powers' (Hardt and Negri 2006: 189). This is cybernetic in nature.

As an example of this, the transformation of the city has transformed life itself ('forms of life', Negri 2018: vii) and changed the nature of struggle in terms of contestation of what is a new articulation of the commons (Hardt and Negri 2000: 302) in 'midway terrains' (Negri 2018: 21) that exist between the 'old' capitalism (the factory, the industrial proletariat, the industrial capitalist) and the 'new' (the metropolis, the social beehive, the finance capitalist). The metropolis is, apparently, the factory (Negri 2018: 94) although this is a very different form of factory to that currently understood. Cities, not factories, are a struggle between rentier and finance capital and the 'cognitive proletariat' (Negri 2018: viii). These struggles are those of singularities (Negri 2018: 46), individuals or groups located along axis of difference. The nature of struggle has changed dramatically from industrially based class struggle (Hardt and Negri 2000: 52) to that of a communicative 'social flesh' (Hardt and Negri 2006: 196), a system of singularities. One example of the ways in which such struggles have manifested themselves is the struggle of the public sector workers in the areas of communication, transport and infrastructure against restructuring and marketisation. Negri argues that such struggles go beyond circulation as they represent 'the global form that structures production itself' (Negri 2018: 4). In this struggle the users of communication, transport and infrastructure are involved as 'coproducers' (Negri 2018: 5). The struggle is hence diffuse and involves immaterial work and coproduced consumption although it may initially be located in a worker's struggle but is more properly a biopolitical regime of labour (Negri 2018: 57) in which despotism and exploitation are integrated. This presents a 'challenge for revolutionary theory' (Negri 2018: 11) as it is respecified as a contest between immaterial labour (a manifestation, perhaps, of the General Intellect) and bios (appropriated intellectual labour which becomes capital). In addition, 'power becomes entirely biopolitical, the whole social body is comprised by power's machine and developed in its virtuality' (Hardt and Negri 2000: 24). It is uncertain how this might be realised in practice (Negri 2018: 49–50). One possibility is that these singularities might be collected in communication nets and linked through communication structures. Negri (2018: 47) states that this requires the development of a new area of study and praxis that could bring about a new form of democracy based on a shared ownership and control of the commons.

In respecifying struggle, Negri asks a question central to our own concern with whether cybernetics could be part of a future utopian society: 'What does it mean to revolutionise social cooperation by democratically reclaiming administration in order to manage the entirety of production and social reproduction?' (Negri 2018: 12). Relatedly, we are reaching the end of Post-Fordism where the old systems of population control are breaking down (Negri 2018: 45). Simultaneously, finance capital is divesting itself from the direct ownership of factories whilst still benefiting from the general social productivity of immaterial labour—the 'metropolitan beehive' (Negri 2018: 12–13) that captures 'social value' which is itself immaterial. This means that rather than via direct exploitation through the more obvious forms of subsumption, capital 'steals' social value (Negri 2018: 17) through capitalist power (Negri 2018: 18), as a contestation of the General Intellect. In the final analysis, there is no other recourse for capital than to invoke a 'state of exception' to steal this social value (Negri 2018: 47), and it could be plausibly claimed that this is indeed the case with the global 'state of exception' initiated under the COVID-19 pandemic. As immaterial labour is beyond measure, there is no measure of exploitation, and profit arises through the contest between capital and labour for the extraction of 'social value'. Although 'productive places' still exist in the metropolis, they are being replaced by 'beehive' of social and immaterial productivity (Negri 2018: 20).

There are several problems with arguments based on 'bio-political production', which we would argue to be cyber-type in nature and its alternatives. Firstly, the rejection of the factory as a site of struggle is indicative of social theory that is in line with capitalist modernisation. Indeed, Negri replaces the idea of the revolutionary class with the multitude that is focussed on (separate) socioeconomic and socio-political struggle with an emphasis on democratisation and representation (Negri 2018: 52–53) with the aim of a 'radical exodus' (Negri 2018: 54) from capital or a grand new vision of democratic politics (Hardt and Negri 2006). The metropolis creates the 'common', the realm of immaterial labour, mass intellectuality and the General Intellect (Hardt and Negri 2000: 29), the social value of which is stolen by capital (Negri 2018: 94). This emphasis on a 'new theory' of value based on immaterial labour (Hardt and Negri 2000: 29) is very different from the negative critique of value and capital developed in the New Reading of Marx (Pitts 2018).

Secondly, themes of the multitude inspire contemporary social movements that may be reactionary and recuperated, and ignore the persistence of factory production and struggle. For example, the liberal ecological movement, driven by the idea of protest and disruption only to the extent that it can reform capital, has used the motif of the factory as the primal site of pollution and climate change. The industrial proletariat (frequently depicted as racist, ignorant and politically naïve on the left) is replaced by the more politically acceptable multitude, spinning wind farms and workerless Fully Automated Luxury Communist (FALC) lights-off factories (Bastani 2019). Meanwhile capital creates new scales of factory from the algorithms that manage logistics and deliveries to the ubiquity of commodity production in all sectors, including universities and the arts. Factories may seem to disappear from the developed world (but they are still there in the suburbs, industrial estates and other 'non-places'), and they are still a major form of production in developing countries (as is industrialised agriculture). The metropolis actually comprises factories of many scales and shapes and labour power is produced in edu-factories—schools, colleges and universities. In terms of the struggles of communications, transport and infrastructure workers, for example, these activities don't necessarily structure production but are part of production in that they can be commodified, the work made commensurable and labour power used to create profit. That is, they are part of capitalist production and not a super-ordinate aspect of that production. Furthermore, the consumers of these services are not necessarily the people on the Metro but more properly the State as it is here that the valorisation of the commodity (transport services) for money occurs. It is also a stretch to see how buying a bus ticket or turning on a light could count as co-production. The nature of immaterial labour occludes exploitation and underplays the ways in which capital makes forms of labour commensurable through primitive accumulation.

Thirdly, there is a tendency to assume that it is possible to 'reclaim administration' (Negri 2018: 12) resulting from the organic force ('social beehive') of a multitude that develops alongside capital, rather than being antagonistic to it. Similarly, the metropolis becomes, and is, the common, suggesting that all that is required is capture of the metropolis itself rather than a radical, anarchist, non-hierarchical restructuring of relations. In opposition to this, the metropolis can be seen as a variety of capitalist and statist enterprises, or capitals, many of which are homogenous to factories. For example, London can be seen as a metropolis, comprising singularities, that produces a social value that is stolen by capitalists and rentiers. This characterisation of the city flattens more than it reveals as it is as if a single social entity (the bios) is producing an incomprehensible thing that is siphoned off by finance and rentier capital. This in turn lends itself to organic, cybernetic metaphors of the metropolis as a body, having a single constitution. Indeed, Hardt and Negri (2000: 30) refer to a 'collective biopolitical body'. At every level, factory-type relations structure the Uber driver using an algorithm, the school producing labour power as a commodity as a paid service to the State, the McDonalds worker making burgers, the artist painting a sign, the estate agent making commission from rental flats and the sewing machinist in a back street sweatshop. Commodity production, exploitation, wage labour and profit are existent and evident relations. Rather than the metropolis being the primary site in itself of capitalist production, it is actually emptied of meaning other than 'the space where valorisation takes place' (Kurz 2016: 89), a non-place (Augé 1995) (and one could say the same of peripheries, towns or rural locations). Although immaterial labour may appear to be qualitatively hegemonic (Hardt and Negri 2006: 109), capitalism imposes a quantitative (value) hegemony on all forms of labour. It may appear that the 'working class has all but disappeared from view' (Hardt and Negri 2000: 53), but this does not mean that we need a rearticulated understanding of 'the new composition of the proletariat as a class' (Hardt and Negri 2000: 53). In particular, immaterial labour (Hardt and Negri 2000: 290) is still part of commodity production (Caffentzis 2013) and even what were thought to be the immaterial aspects of labour (emotions and affects) have been shown to be quantifiable (Moore 2017; De Angelis and Harvie 2009). However, even this conception of labour falls short of the nature of labour in capitalism. Pitts (2018) critiques both Caffentzis (2013) and Hardt and Negri (2000, 2006) as the nature of abstract labour is such that 'value's measurability lies elsewhere than in production. It arises through social validation' (Pitts 2018: 217). In other words, implying a measure, or the impossibility of measure but a transmission nevertheless, in the production process itself implies that labour is of a form that directly transmits value (measurable or not) to a commodity (or a collective 'commons') rather than labour that only becomes measurable and commensurable in exchange in any case as abstract labour.

To conclude, capitalism's naturalisation of cybernetics as a technology does not imply that capitalism itself has become cybernetic (despite analogies which are suggestive of this). Similarly, the antithesis of capitalism (Communism or post-capitalism) is not naturally cybernetic. Although we might redefine capitalism as 'neo-feudalism' or 'bio-political production', the 'essential' elements of capitalism, in terms of production relations and the capitalist factory, remain. Cybernetic management or some technological vanguardist state or party does not represent a progressive future for humanity. Here our views align with those of Dinerstein and Pitts (2018: 139–142), who argue that abstract utopias, based on conceptions of radical democracy whilst retaining money, the law of value and commodity production, and in this case cybernetic logics, simply reshape current social relations maintaining hierarchy and a form of state-capitalism where power is held by a 'post-capitalist' state. We note that this post-capitalist state may use cybernetic or other programmatic methods to achieve its aims. In opposition, Dinerstein and Pitts (2018: 142) argue for 'prefigurative translation' in learning from the emergence of prefigurative forms to create relations beyond capitalism and hierarchy. These prefigurative alternatives should arise beyond traditional forms of 'folk politics' and problematise normativity and Eurocentrism to give 'materiality to the not-yet through practice' (Dinerstein and Pitts 2018: 146, drawing on the work of Bloch 1986). This is an anticipatory form of utopianism, in terms of learning and discovery though material practice that is generalised through prefigurative translation rather than a programmatic form.

Prefigurative translation will still require people to make decisions about the realm of necessity rather than for a fully automated communist factory (Bastani 2019) to take care of them as a paternalistic, state-capitalist and cybernetic entity.

Tacit Knowledge and Hobbying Limit Cybernetics

Our concepts of tacit knowledge and hobbying mean that not all knowledge can be integrated into a cybernetic system. There are theoretical and empirical limits to this. This means that there must be a human element in any system of (meaningful) making. We would also dismiss arguments that some kind of central control or cybernetic system is needed to run infrastructure on a large scale. For example, David Harvey (2017) states that 'I certainly would not welcome a pilot landing at JFK proclaiming that as a good anarchist she does not accept the legitimacy of the air traffic controllers' authority and that she proposes to disregard all aviation rules in the landing process' (Harvey 2017: 239). Even on a common-sense level this would not make sense as an anarchist would be more likely, in that instance, to want to preserve human life by landing the plane safely than people of other political philosophies (such as a militant fascist-libertarian or an anti-imperialist Marxist), since the principle of mutual aid is central to anarchist ideology. In any case, if the anarchist is so anti-authoritarian why did they sit through all of those corporate flying lessons and comply with the take-off instructions? A more believable, fictional, example (and where it is hard to think of a moral objection) would be a 'good anarchist' refusing to follow state instructions that involve the inhibition of freedom (such as the compulsory attendance, in a future dystopian society, of a Maoist re-education class), hence enhancing her own freedom and the liberation of others. In our work we have shown how the conception of a 'hobby' guided by collective interest and tacit knowledge can allow large-scale infrastructural arrangements to take place without a centralising, cybernetic system.

In previous chapters we have shown how human, spontaneous, collaborative activity cannot necessarily be codified or systematised in cybernetic forms. The concept of tacit knowledge (Polanyi 2009) was a rejection not of science but of scientism and systemisation and of the mechanical conception of humans (and perhaps by extension also of animals and other living forms). We can 'attend to things that may not be able to tell' (Polanyi 2009: 10). This means that formalism and the sorts of nested systems beloved of cybernetics are reductive and, furthermore, that the possibility of different forms of tacit knowledge across social levels (individuals as compared to groups, for example) means that 'it is impossible to represent the organising principle of a higher level by the laws governing its isolated particulars' (36). Collins (2010) builds on this distinction between levels of tacit knowledge distinguishing between somatic knowledge (that which arises from embeddedness of knowledge within a body or brain) and relational knowledge (that which arises through relations between people and entities). In principle he considers that these forms of knowledge could eventually be mimicked by an artificial intelligence. However, a third form of tacit knowledge (Collective Tacit Knowledge) operates at the level of society and can never be disembodied from its context (society) or formalised. Tacit knowledge and 'hobbying' are concepts we use to demonstrate how—even in capitalist or 'capital-adjacent' workers' co-operatives—collective human improvisation and knowledge that is impossible to formalise is central to making things. Future organisational forms, beyond capital and the state, are prefigured in the present by these and other alternatives. For example, skillshares are collective collaborative spaces where non-commodified production can take place as explained in the previous chapter.

Conclusion: Non-cybernetic Prefiguration and Potential Futures

To return to our research questions, we previously asked to what extent do prefigurative forms of learning arise within different organisations? And to what extent can we observe prefigurative knowledges within or despite cybernetics? We also enquired whether prefigurative forms of learning can be fully captured by cybernetic systems, do they disrupt cybernetics, and/ or prefigure something else? In this section, we address these questions through summarising the previous arguments in the book and address what we see as non-cybernetic forms of prefiguration.

Swann (2016) describes prefiguration as a future society as activated in the present, rejecting consequentialism (where the ends justify the means but prefiguration is also a process of setting goals in organisations), and Swann defines prefigurative strategy as 'a way of understanding how (this) goal forming function can be realised in anarchist organisations' (Swann 2016: 72). Swann further defines this in terms of a functionalist imperative in that such a prefigurative strategy would involve people stepping out of their Systems One and Two roles to undertake Systems Three and Four (decision-making) functions (Swann 2016: 136). This 'stepping back' still maintains the integrity of the cybernetic organisation and the individuals who occupied the System One and Two nodal positions, following promotion to System Three and Four nodes, again return to those nodal areas. This is not a prefiguration, as it does not prefigure anything other than the replication of itself. The cybernetic structure is equivalent to a 'state', determining actions and positions, through a democratic governance mechanism. Cybernetics cannot be prefigurative in a truly emancipatory sense, as it privileges a mode of governance and a technical tool (in the traditional sense of the word). We have argued throughout the book, and above, that cybernetics does not prefigure a society that is free of statist, capitalist and anti-liberatory tendencies. Epistemologically, the forms of knowledge that we have identified (tacit and hobbying) are not compatible with the systematising we see in cybernetics. In simple terms, as we have shown not everything in life is systematised or can be placed into a hierarchy or nesting. Any future utopia, at least a non-authoritarian one, must be arrived at collectively and people (and collectives) are whimsical, idiosyncratic and open to change whereas cybernetics is not. Cybernetics is the antithesis of the sort of Communism that Marx describes in *The German Ideology* that 'makes it possible for me to do one thing today and another tomorrow, to hunt in the morning, fish in the afternoon, rear cattle in the evening, criticise after dinner, just as I have a mind, without ever becoming hunter, fisherman, herdsman or critic' (Marx 2021: 78). Another reference point might be the more utopian and prefigurative emphases within degrowth anarchist perspectives, for example Ivan Illich who imagines more convivial relationships with tools, eschewing the manipulative technologies of the industrial mode of production in favour of voluntary, creative and artisanal small-scale production (Illich 1973). These visions do not foreclose a multitude of prefigurative utopias including organisational forms of anarchist mutualism and federalism, mutualism, grassroots Communism and primitivism. None of these require cybernetics to imagine a different society—in fact, a cybernetic system forecloses future possibilities. As we have shown in this book, there are human knowledges and practices that are nascent, yet supressed, in capitalism and statism that prefigure utopia.

From our case studies, we can draw some points that might be of value to activists, workers' organisations and social movements interested in prefiguration and alternative forms of social organisation. Firstly, the notion of *excess* in organisations, in terms of hobbying and tacit knowledge, in all of our case studies. Naturally, organisations will try to recoup this excess for purposes of control or profit, but this (alongside conflict and disruption) can provide a space to build alternatives both with and aside from the organisation. Secondly, that 'blackboxing' often runs in line with anthropomorphism, which has become a method through which capital exerts control through creating mechanic, human or animal-like, competitors. Rather than sit in awe of capitalist technologies, as if they were magic, our case studies show how removing the black box, and demasking the mechanic anthropomorph, are ***necessary demystifications*** for social movements. Thirdly, that organisational form and ***logistical distance from capitalism and the state*** are powerful contributors to prefiguration. In CYBER4.0, a fully capitalist organisation, the spaces for radical alternatives were minimal and even in IEM the space that organisation occupied in the capitalist supply chain meant that they were not fully able to develop a radical autonomous form of co-operative organisation (not that this was necessarily desired). Even in the Hackspace, despite a more leisure-oriented ethos and function, production was often seen in terms of future capitalisation and entrepreneurship.

In making the above points we recognise the limitations of our study. In terms of our unit of analysis, we started with organisations rather than with workers' movements, trade unions or social movements. This means that we may have accepted processes and responses at face value, without considering the underlying power dynamics. For example, whether workers or co-operative members in CYBER4.0 or IEM could talk with authenticity in the interviews. We also did not focus on conscious forms of anti-capitalist political organisation or the emergence of forms of class consciousness. This was partly a consequence of the modality of our research funding, which was focussed on the interdisciplinary pragmatics of the 'factory of the future'. This research was also focussed in England and the United States, and perhaps different results would have been obtained in factories in China or the Global South. Paradoxically, without this funding or approach we would not have gained access to the organisations concerned. This leads us to suggest that there may be an epistemological gap between worker/activist studies and more technicist studies of workplace knowledge and its prefigurative possibilities which may be an area for further research or exploration. One reference point for this may be for future research looking at less corporatist versions such as 'The

Lucas Plan', where industrial workers at Lucas Aerospace devised new technological and environmental solutions for society as a whole as an alternative to redundancies (Mc Loughlin 2017).

Of course, we are cautious optimists concerning our research and its possibilities. The wasteland of capitalist industrialisation, the spaces within and between the dead factories, means (of course) that there is a lack of hope and possibility, where the current British Prime Minister (Sir Keir Starmer) can say, with political pride, that 'things are going to get *worse*', but there are also spaces where ingenuity, conviviality and comradeship can emerge.

References

Augé, M. 1995. *Non-Places: Introduction to an Anthropology of Supermodernity.* New York: Verso.

Bastani, A. 2019. *Fully Automated Luxury Communism.* London: Verso Books.

Bloch, E. 1986. *The Principle of Hope* [Vols 1–3], trans. Neville Plaice, Stephen Plaice & Paul Knight. Cambridge, MA: MIT Press [1959].

Caffentzis, G. 2013. *In Letters of Blood and Fire: Work, Machines, and Value.* Oakland: PM Press.

Collins, H. 2010. *Tacit and Explicit Knowledge.* Chicago: University of Chicago Press.

De Angelis, M. & Harvie, D. 2009. 'Cognitive capitalism and the rat-race: how capital measures immaterial labour in British universities.' *Historical Materialism* 17(3) pp.3–30.

Dinerstein, A.C. & Pitts, F.H. 2018. *A World Beyond Work? Labour, Money and the Capitalist State between Crisis and Utopia.* Bingley: Emerald Publishing Limited.

Hardt, M. & Negri, A. 2000. *Empire.* Cambridge, MA: Harvard University Press.

Hardt, M. & Negri, A. 2006. *Multitude.* London: Penguin.

Harvey, D. 2017. 'Listen, Anarchist!' A personal response to Simon Springer's "Why a radical geography must be anarchist." *Dialogues in Human Geography* 7(3) 233–250.

Illich, I. 1973. *Tools for Conviviality.* New York: Harper and Row.

Kurz, R. 2016. *The Substance of Capital.* London: Chronis Publications

Marx, K. 1992. *Early Writings.* London: Penguin.

Marx, K. 1993. *Grundrisse: Foundations of the Critique of Political Economy.* London: Penguin UK.

Marx, K. 2021. *The German Ideology, Elecbook Classics* (online).

Mc Loughlin, K. 2017. Socially useful production in the defence industry: the Lucas Aerospace combine committee and the Labour government, 1974–1979. *Contemporary British History*, 31(4), 524–545.

Moore, P. 2017. *The Quantified Self in Precarity: Work, Technology and What Counts*. London: Routledge.

Morozov, E. 2022. 'Critique of Techno-Feudal Reason.' *New Left Review* 133 Available at: https://newleftreview.org/issues/ii133/articles/evgeny-morozov-critique-of-techno-feudal-reason accessed 11 August 2024.

Negri, A. 2018. *From the Factory to the Metropolis: Essays, Volume 2*. Hoboken, NJ: John Wiley & Sons.

Pitts, F.H. 2018. *Critiquing Capitalism Today: New Ways to Read Marx*. London: Palgrave.

Polanyi, M. 2009. *The Tacit Dimension*. Chicago: University of Chicago Press.

Preston, J. 2022. *Artificial Intelligence in the Capitalist University: Academic Labour, Commodification and Value*. Taylor and Francis: London.

Swann, T. 2016. *Anarchist Cybernetics: Control and Communication in Radical Left Social Movements* (Doctoral Dissertation, University of Leicester).

Appendix 1: Semi-structured Interview Schedule

1. **Tell me about your work.**

Especially prompt areas where the respondent considers that they are in a state of 'flow', fuse with the machine/work or feel separate. For example, what do you think about when you are working? Do you feel like you have control of the technology, or does the technology control you? Do you humanise your machines in any way (through names, personalities, gender)?

2. **Ask them to clarify their terminology about the tools/machines/robots/systems, etc., that they use—and ask them to explain that terminology.**

Subsidiary questions: Make comparisons between different tools/machines/robots/systems and use real-life examples (e.g. hammer(tool)/computer/robot/human/algorithm), e.g. in what ways is it similar and different working with A as compared with B? Explore not only process but feelings (affect), autonomy and repurposing.

R. Firth, J. Preston, *Utopia in the Factory*,
https://doi.org/10.1007/978-3-031-87132-0

3. **How did you learn to use the tool/technology/etc.?**

Are you continuously learning or have you learnt all you need to know? Have you had any need/issues that have led you to amend the technology/tool or the way in which it is used? Have you amended the tools/technology in any way?

4. **What is the purpose of the technology you work with (and produce)?**

Possible prompts:

- Do [tools/machines/automation/etc.] empower, enable or inspire people? If so, how?
- What are the limitations of humans/people for what you need to do in your factory?
- What can't humans do that machines/tools/automation, etc., can?
- What will this technology lead to, and how does it effect other workers/society as a whole?

5. **Does working with machines affect the way you work/organise collectively with other workers?**

Possible prompts:
Who does it give power to?
Is anyone excluded, does it disempower/displace?
Could robots/algorithms replace managers/owners—would this be a good or bad thing? Could you have AIs/robots as entities in a workers' co-operative?

Index[1]

[1] Note: Page numbers followed by 'n' refer to notes.

R. Firth, J. Preston, *Utopia in the Factory*,
https://doi.org/10.1007/978-3-031-87132-0

T

U

V

W

The manufacturer's authorised representative in the EU is Springer Nature Customer Service Centre GmbH, Europaplatz 3, 69115 Heidelberg, Germany. If you have any concerns regarding our products, please contact ProductSafety@springernature.com

Printed and bound by CPI Group (UK) Ltd, Croydon, CR0 4YY
01/10/2026
02225967-0003